AF323752

IMPOSSIBLE TO SAY

Recent Titles in
Contributions to the Study of American Literature

Solitude and Society in the Works of Herman Melville and Edith Wharton
Linda Costanzo Cahir

The Immigrant Experience in North American Literature: Carving Out a Niche
Katherine B. Payant and Toby Rose, editors

American Literary Humor During the Great Depression
Robert A. Gates

The Marriage of Heaven and Earth: Alchemical Regeneration in the Works of Taylor, Poe, Hawthorne, and Fuller
Randall A. Clack

The Divine and Human Comedy of Andrew M. Greeley
Allienne R. Becker

Teaching Faulkner: Approaches and Methods
Stephen Hahn and Robert W. Hamblin, editors

Songs of the New South: Writing Contemporary Louisiana
Suzanne Disheroon Green and Lisa Abney, editors

American Carnival: Seeing and Reading American Culture
Philip McGowan

The Post-Utopian Imagination: American Culture in the Long 1950s
M. Keith Booker

Songs of the Reconstructing South: Building Literary Louisiana, 1865–1945
Suzanne Disheroon-Green and Lisa Abney, editors

Word, Birth, and Culture in the Poetry of Poe, Whitman, and Dickinson
Daneen Wardrop

IMPOSSIBLE TO SAY

Representing Religious Mystery in Fiction by Malamud, Percy, Ozick, and O'Connor

L. Lamar Nisly

Contributions to the Study of American Literature, Number 12

GREENWOOD PRESS
Westport, Connecticut • London

Library of Congress Cataloging-in-Publication Data

Nisly, L. Lamar, 1968–
Impossible to say : representing religious mystery in fiction by Malamud, Percy, Ozick, and O'Connor / by L. Lamar Nisly.
p. cm.—(Contributions to the study of American literature, ISSN 1092–6356 ; no. 12)
Includes bibliographical references (p.) and index.
ISBN 0–313–32060–8 (alk. paper)
1. American fiction—20th century—History and criticism. 2. Religion in literature. 3. Percy, Walker, 1916—Criticism and interpretation. 4. Christian fiction, American—History and criticism. 5. O'Connor, Flannery—Criticism and interpretation. 6. Malamud, Bernard—Criticism and interpretation. 7. Ozick, Cynthia—Criticism and interpretation. 8. Jewish fiction—History and criticism. 9. Mysticism in literature.
I. Title. II. Series.
PS374.R47N57 2002
813′.509382—dc21 2001040594

British Library Cataloguing in Publication Data is available.

Library of Congress Catalog Card Number: 2001040594
ISBN: 0–313–32060–8
ISSN: 1092–6356

First published in 2002

Greenwood Press, 88 Post Road West, Westport, CT 06881
An imprint of Greenwood Publishing Group, Inc.
www.greenwood.com

Printed in the United States of America

The paper used in this book complies with the Permanent Paper Standard issued by the National Information Standards Organization (Z39.48–1984).

10 9 8 7 6 5 4 3 2 1

Copyright Acknowledgments

The author and publisher gratefully acknowledge permission for use of the following material:

Excerpts from the Bernard Malamud papers and letters. Reprinted by permission of Russell & Volkening, Inc., as agents for the Estate of Bernard Malamud. Copyright © 1963, 1973, 1979, 1980 by Bernard Malamud, copyright © renewed 1992 by Ann Malamud.

Excerpts from Henry Bettenson, *The Later Christian Fathers,* edited and translated by Henry Bettenson, copyright © 1970 by Oxford University Press. Reprinted by permission of Oxford University Press.

Excerpts from "A Good Man Is Hard to Find" in *A Good Man Is Hard to Find and Other Stories*, copyright 1953 by Flannery O'Connor and renewed 1981 by Regina O'Connor, reprinted by permission of Harcourt, Inc.

Excerpts from *The Complete Stories* by Flannery O'Connor. Copyright © 1971 by the Estate of Mary Flannery O'Connor. Reprinted by permission of Farrar, Straus and Giroux, LLC. Copyright © 1955, 1954, 1953, 1948 by Flannery O'Connor, renewed 1976 by Mrs. Edward F. O'Connor, Copyright renewed 1981, 1982, 1983 by Regina O'Connor. Reprinted by permission of the Harold Matson Co., Inc.

Excerpts from "A Good Man Is Hard to Find" in *The Complete Stories* by Flannery O'Connor. Copyright © 1955, 1954, 1953, 1948 by Flannery O'Connor, renewed 1976 by Mrs. Edward F. O'Connor, Copyright renewed 1981, 1982, 1983 by Regina O'Connor. Reprinted by permission of the Harold Matson Co., Inc.

Excerpts from *The Habit of Being* by Flannery O'Connor. Copyright © 1979 by Regina O'Connor. Reprinted by permission of Farrar, Straus and Giroux, LLC. Copyright © 1959, 1957, 1958, 1960, 1961, 1962, 1964, 1965. Renewed 1993 by Mary Flannery O'Connor. Reprinted by permission of the Harold Matson Co., Inc.

Excerpts from *Mystery and Manners* by Flannery O'Connor. Copyright © 1969 by the Estate of Mary Flannery O'Connor. Reprinted by permission of Farrar, Straus and Giroux, LLC. Copyright © 1957, 1961, 1963, 1964, 1966, 1967, 1969 by the Estate of Mary Flannery O'Connor. Reprinted by permission of the Harold Matson Co., Inc.

Excerpts from *The Assistant* by Bernard Malamud. Copyright © 1957, renewed 1985 by Bernard Malamud. Reprinted by permission of Farrar, Straus and Giroux, LLC.

Excerpts from *The Assistant* by Bernard Malamud. Reprinted by permission of Russell & Volkening as agents for the author. Copyright © 1957 by Bernard Malamud, renewed 1985 by Bernard Malamud.

For Deborah,
Jonathan, and Elizabeth

Contents

Preface

Dealing with literary presentations of religious mystery has been both a joy and a challenge. Because religious beliefs are important to me personally and since my academic discipline is literature, I am very interested in intersections between these two domains. Further, because religion does play a role in much of literature, it seems useful to study how one facet of belief is represented in fiction. But studying religious mystery also brings with it natural difficulties: because the notion itself goes beyond the rational, one is at times hard-pressed to find words to express the concept. Additionally, just as mystery is difficult to pin down, so religious beliefs more generally are very personal and open to varying interpretations. And my pairing of the four authors in this study invites an intriguing—but also potentially overwhelming—range of possible areas of inquiry. Thus, I have made a particular effort throughout the study to delineate both what is included in my work as well as what is outside its scope.

Before I proceed, I should say a word about the perspective that I bring to this study. Since I come from a Protestant religious background, I have obviously not experienced either Judaism or Catholicism on a firsthand basis. While my own perspective naturally colors my understanding of Judaism and Catholicism, I have attempted accurately to represent each religion. Besides the reading I have done and the useful suggestions I have received from various readers, I have especially been helped by conversations with Margaret Mahoney, a Catholic nun, and Ethan Seidel, a Conservative rabbi, both of whom generously read portions of my manuscript and assisted me toward a better understanding of their respective religions. I have been struck, though, in my various readings and conversations, by the differences of perception among believers in each religion. My presentation of Judaism and Catholicism may thus not resonate exactly with every Jew or Catholic, but I have, to the best of my ability, tried to remain faithful to important patterns of belief in each religion.

I should also explain my decision to pair authors from two distinctive religious backgrounds, Judaism and Catholicism. At a most basic level, it seems helpful to examine religious mystery from more than one tradition, to show that it is not the sole property of one religion: the nonrational is a central element of religious belief. More specifically, I have chosen Jewish and Catholic writers because even though there are significant differences, their faiths have sufficient similarities to make such a study illuminating. The two religions share the Hebrew Bible as holy writing, and that Scripture serves as a basis for each religion's monotheistic doctrine. Further, a central component in the practice of each religion involves the making physical of mystery. And on a literary level, in contemporary American literature, writers from these two traditions are the primary ones who deal with explicitly spiritual issues, making it seem appropriate to draw together these two religions.[1] Thus, although I have tried to acknowledge differences between the presentations of mystery in the two religions, my effort has been to emphasize the similarities in these religious writers' use of the nonrational. Certainly one could accentuate the divergences between the religions, but my central focus concerns what draws these religions and this fiction together instead of what pushes them apart.

Other religious fiction, besides that of the four authors I am studying, would likely lead to a productive examination of the portrayal of religious mystery. I have chosen Bernard Malamud, Walker Percy, Cynthia Ozick, and Flannery O'Connor both because their fiction rather clearly contains an anagogical level and because their narrative forms complement each other to highlight several different representations of religious mystery, namely the quest, the fantastic, and the grotesque. I should also mention that not all the works in each author's oeuvre fit the formal characterization I am outlining; I have selected the novels and stories I do examine both for their narrative form and because they seem to suggest a religious interpretation. My study thus is not a comprehensive analysis of each author's works but rather examines selected fiction from Malamud, Percy, Ozick, and O'Connor.

NOTE

1. There have been disproportionately few prominent Protestant novelists whose writings have a specifically anagogical level, but a few do have such concerns. For example, John Updike and Peter De Vries at times show a spiritual dimension, but even in their writing, the religious themes are generally muted.

Acknowledgments

I am indebted to many people and institutions for their assistance in the course of writing this book. Various people from the English Department at the University of Delaware were important to this work. I am grateful to the University of Delaware English Department for providing a year of funding, which greatly aided my writing. Barry Seidel, Ethan Seidel, and Margaret Mahoney each were kind enough to read portions of the first two chapters. Dr. Richard Davison offered helpful comments and support at various stages of this project. Dr. Sara Horowitz, Dr. Philip Flynn, and Dr. Gloria Cronin did careful readings of my work and offered useful suggestions. To each of them I offer my thanks. I am especially grateful to Dr. Elaine Safer, both for her continual encouragement and confidence that this project would be completed as well as her helpful guidance throughout my research and writing.

I am appreciative for a Bluffton College Study Center summer grant that supported my study of the Bernard Malamud Papers at the Library of Congress. In less tangible—but undoubtedly more important—ways, I have felt the support of my colleagues at Bluffton College as I have pursued this project. For their encouragement, suggestions, and friendship I am most thankful. Special thanks are particularly due to Sherri Wilson, now a graduate of Bluffton College, for her careful work with formatting and indexing this book, as well as to Bluffton College student Karen Bontrager for her help in finalizing the manuscript.

My work has also been greatly aided by the strong backing of my family. My parents, Paul and Laura Nisly, and my brother, Randal Nisly, have been extremely kind and supportive of me throughout my writing and revising. Additionally, I am especially grateful to my father, who is a Flannery O'Connor scholar, for generously reading through an entire late draft of my work and making valuable suggestions. Finally and most importantly, I thank my wife Deborah for her unwavering love and support of me throughout this process, even when my academic responsibilities cut into family time. And for their own contributions, I am grateful to my son Jonathan and daughter Elizabeth for reminding me through their energy and affection that there are more important parts of life than academic writing. Without my wife and children to help draw me into the "real world" of lived experience, my years of intensive work on this project would have been much more draining indeed. It is thus with love that I dedicate this study to Deborah, Jonathan, and Elizabeth.

1

Introduction

Trust in the Lord with all your heart, and do not rely on your own understanding.
— Proverbs 3.5

Now faith is the assurance of things hoped for, the conviction of things not seen.
—Hebrews 11.1

In Chaim Potok's provocative novel *The Promise*, a central tension concerns how the protagonist, Reuven Malter, will study Scripture: will he embrace the more traditional, orthodox approach, which accepts on faith that the Scriptures are accurate; or will he use his father's scholarly, critical method, which seeks to correct perceived errors in the text? Late in the novel, Reuven and his father attend an Hasidic wedding where Mr. Malter respectfully discusses Torah with the Hasidic rebbe, even though they have very different approaches to Scripture. Indeed, it is Reuven who is most disturbed by the Hasidic reluctance to accept scholarly methods for understanding Torah, as he tells his father on their walk home from the wedding:

> "I wish they weren't so afraid of new ideas."
>
> "You want a great deal, Reuven. The Messiah has not yet come. Will new ideas enable them to go on singing and dancing?"
>
> "We can't ignore the truth, abba."
>
> "No," he said. "We cannot ignore the truth. At the same time, we cannot quite sing and dance as they do." He was silent a moment. "That is the dilemma of our time, Reuven. I do not know what the answer is." (235–36)

This dilemma—between reason and faith, head and heart—that Mr. Malter articulates is one that has long tormented religious believers, and the strain against accepting beliefs that cannot be scientifically proven has become particularly pressing since the Enlightenment's emphasis on rationality.[1] Yet both the rabbinic Jewish and traditional Catholic (along with many other religions') understandings of belief contain a central emphasis that a believer should "not rely on your own understanding" and have "the conviction of things not seen." Religious faith includes a nonrational element, so that "[g]enuinely religious persons, whatever their beliefs, are always thoroughly impressed by the mystery of faith" (MacGregor 430).

The specific form that the nonrational facet of belief takes can vary significantly. For instance, one kind of movement beyond the rational involves an acceptance of beliefs that cannot be scientifically proven. At a basic level, a person may make a decision to act toward someone else in a manner that cannot be explained as mere self-interest, simply because he or she knows—from the teachings of a religious system—that the action is morally right. Such a decision in itself is a kind of nonrational religious commitment since it signifies a recognition and adherence to moral values established separately from that individual. On a somewhat more overtly religious level, accepting beliefs, such as the divine revelation of the Torah or Jesus Christ's atonement for sinners, requires a movement beyond rationality. Miraculous or even magical occurrences also are an aspect of religious mystery, since the events reported to have happened are attributed to divine power yet cannot be independently verified. At the center of religious mystery, and what belief in nonrational doctrines is ultimately designed to bring about, is a sense of—in Rudolf Otto's now-familiar term—the numinous. By the numinous, Otto refers to the "clear overplus of meaning" in the concept of holiness, the aspect of sacredness that cannot be rationally understood (5). While Otto argues that the numinous cannot be taught but only evoked, he nevertheless suggests that an encounter with the numinous brings a sense of "creature-consciousness" (10), awe (13), "absolute unapproachability" (19), even stupor before the wholly other (26). So even though Otto says that a concept of God begins in what is "clearly to be grasped by our power of conceiving," "beneath this sphere of clarity and lucidity lies a hidden depth, inaccessible to our conceptual thought, which we in so far call the 'non-rational'" (58). Thus, whether believers follow a religiously established moral code, accept nonrational doctrines, believe in miracles, or feel a sense of the numinous, they are in their own way embracing religious mystery.

This religious mystery, which may present a challenge for potential believers in forcing them to move beyond the strictly rational, introduces a different kind of difficulty for authors who seek to portray religious commitment: how can they find words to represent coherently what cannot finally be rationally understood? This task of portraying the nonrational, though, is not unique to religious belief. Narrative depictions of madness, frenzy, and the sublime, as well as novels of the absurd, also attempt to go beyond the rational. A somewhat similar experience of transcending rationality, as Erich Auerbach points out in *Mimesis* (1953), takes place in Virginia Woolf's *To the Lighthouse*, where the stress is on "what the occasion releases, things which are not seen directly but by reflection" (541). A primary way that Woolf is able to depict this nonrational element is through her stream-of-consciousness form. In a passage that Auerbach analyzes, the external events are separated by long sections of Mrs. Ramsay's scattered ruminations; this technique causes the narration of the external events to take much longer than the scene could actually have lasted (529). Woolf is able to stretch out her telling of the story to allow room for Mrs. Ramsay's unorganized thoughts. As Woolf did, an author can use the form of a novel to portray experiences that cannot be rationally explained. Since religious belief is in part nonrational, it seems plausible that authors might use their narrative form to embody this religious mystery.

Examining the linkage between literary form and religious mystery, however, is not a common theme among published studies of literature and theology. Instead, much of this criticism falls into one of three other categories. Some critics apply principles of literary study to Scripture in an effort to enhance or redefine their understanding of biblical material. Such a reevaluation is especially prominent among critics using contemporary literary theory as an avenue into the Scriptures, replacing an historical or spiritual study with a literary approach. Three titles of such studies—from a Bakhtinian, a Derridean, and a feminist perspective—can serve as examples of the kinds of poststructural methodologies undertaken: Walter L. Reed's *Dialogues of the Word: The Bible as Literature According to Bakhtin* (1993); *Reading Between Texts: Intertextuality and the Hebrew Bible* (1992) edited by Danna Nolan Fewell; and Alicia Suskin Ostriker's *The Nakedness of the Fathers: Biblical Visions and Revisions* (1994). And as noted later, understanding Jewish midrash through postmodern theory is an increasingly popular approach.

A second group of critics, departing from a concern about specifically religious issues, focus on American Jewish fiction to examine the position of the Jew in the United States. Allen Guttmann, in *The Jewish Writer in America: Assimilation and the Crisis of Identity* (1971), uses Jewish fiction to argue that as Jews are becoming more assimilated into American culture, they increasingly move away from a strong sense of Jewishness. Louis Harap's analysis of acculturation, *In the Mainstream: The Jewish Presence in Twentieth-Century Literature, 1950s–1980s* (1987), is similar to Guttmann's. In the years since Guttmann's study, however, Harap sees a return among some Jewish writers, such as Potok, Cynthia Ozick, and Arthur Cohen, to a stronger emphasis on belief in their fiction. Guttmann's and Harap's studies, and others like theirs, tend to be sociological inquiries rather than probes into the relationship of theology and literature.

A third category of writing does engage issues of belief and literature. Usually writing from a liberal Christian stance, these critics tend to universalize their religious stance so that they can find it in almost any fiction. Nathan Scott, a prominent critic in this camp, argues that Christians should not have a specific "Christian system" in mind when they come to literature; instead, they should determine "what in fact the function of art truly is and how it may co-operate with the kind of imagination of reality that is authentically Christian" (6). What Scott finds is that both art and religious faith "share a common intention to summon us into the presence of what is other than and transcendent to the human mind" (11). Similarly, Giles Gunn in *The Interpretation of Otherness: Literature, Religion, and the American Imagination* (1979) argues for a broadening of the concept of religion: we should see it as the "hermeneutical rather than the apologetic, the anthropological rather than the theological, the broadly humanistic rather than the narrowly doctrinal" (5). Thus, all of literature is in some sense religious since both literature and religion force us back before creed to the "felt possibility and the imagination of desire" (222). Although writers such as Scott and Gunn do link religion and literature, their approach seems so inclusive that it provides little insight into the role traditional theological understandings may play in literature.

If one is interested in discovering how belief can be presented in literature, it seems more profitable to examine fiction in which characters explicitly struggle with their faith rather than to assume, as Scott and Gunn do, that all fiction will offer instances of belief. Although many individual studies of such fiction have been done, some critics have also productively linked together several authors, based on a theme or theological similarity among them. One of the most successful of such studies is Ralph Wood's examination of Karl Barth's theory of divine comedy as represented in the works of Flannery O'Connor, Walker Percy, John Updike, and Peter De Vries. But even among these critics, very little has been done with linking narrative form with religious perspective. Indeed, the sense that the spiritual element in literature has not adequately entered the discourse of the academy led Dennis Taylor, editor of the journal *Religion and the Arts*, to argue in 1998, "A great critical need of our time is for ways of discussing religious or spiritual dimensions in works of literature" (3). Taylor goes on to ask, "Do we have a language to talk about the delicacy of spiritual conversation, its perils, its success, its implications?" (14). Clearly, we need to continue to press for new and provocative ways to understand the intersection between religion and literature.

One approach to draw together narrative and religious mystery would be to examine important narratives from the Jewish and Catholic literary traditions that involve some element of the nonrational. In Judaism, such an inquiry would certainly be profitable because "[s]torytelling has always been a prime vehicle for communicating spirituality. . . . Judaism is largely based on and communicated through stories" (Buxbaum xv). Any study connecting present Jewish narratives to their roots would have to begin with the biblical text; as Geoffrey Hartman explains, "the Jewish imagination has been dominated by a turn to the written word and has developed within the orbit of the Hebrew Bible. The Jews are a people of the Book, and their mind is text dependent, even when it rebels against the text" ("Imagination" 459). Thus, stories such as God's miraculous rescue of the Israelites in Exodus thematically show the mysterious power of

God as well as God's special care for the Jews. On the other hand, the Exile from the Promised Land and the dispersion of the Jewish people to other lands is shown in the biblical account to be a punishment for sins. Certainly in the United States, with the ever-present pressures of assimilation to the dominant culture, critics have harkened back to the Exile, wondering, in Irving Howe's memorable formulation, if the current Jewish literature shows "[t]radition as discontinuity" (qtd. in Wirth-Nesher 218). Even using terminology that suggests a link between biblical narratives and contemporary writing, Lawrence Willis argues that biblical texts such as Esther and Daniel, which show the protagonists' unwavering commitment to God and the Jewish people, were initially read as Jewish novels (2). While these early novels obviously vary significantly from twentieth-century writing, Willis' connection underlines the plausibility of seeing narrative linkages.

Besides the biblical texts, other parts of the Jewish tradition of stories also could be connected to representations of mystery. A significant portion of the rabbinic writings is made up of stories designed to make a moral point or to elucidate a biblical text. Often these *aggadah* (the generic term for rabbinic literature outside the legal teachings) or *midrash* (the more specific term for stories that seek to explain perceived gaps or problems in the text) involve elements that go beyond the rational. For instance, since in the account of the plagues in Egypt, the biblical text literally says, "And the frog came up and covered the land of Egypt," Rabbi Akiva suggests, "There was only one frog, and it covered the whole land of Egypt" (qtd. in Stern "Aggadah" 9)—a solution that certainly goes beyond our usual logical categories. Throughout the centuries of storytelling, Jewish legends outside the rabbinic tradition often involve magical occurrences, so they, too, could offer narrative patterns for portraying the nonrational. And in the twentieth century, the horrors of the Holocaust have been of central thematic concern, as writers have attempted to find ways to depict the inexpressible. One study exploring this unspeakable nature of the Holocaust is Sara R. Horowitz's *Voicing the Void: Muteness and Memory in Holocaust Fiction* (1997), in which she examines such occurrences as the muteness in characters, gaps in texts, and a concern with language and silence in narratives of the Holocaust. Horowitz argues, "Muteness expresses not only the difficulty in saying anything meaningful about the Holocaust; it also comes to represent something essential about the nature of the event itself. The radical negativity of the Holocaust ruptures the fabric of history and memory, emptying both narrative and life of meaning" (38). Encompassing a broad range of themes and emphases, these biblical, midrashic, or historical narratives within the Jewish tradition offer patterns for representing the nonrational in narrative form.

Catholicism, too, has narratives that stress mystery. Again, the biblical narrative is the most central of these stories, since Catholicism revolves around the mysterious conception that the crucifixion and resurrection of Christ bring about salvation for sinners. In the twentieth century, as Theodore Fraser suggests, such themes have been used by Catholic writers as they emphasize the key role of sinners in the life of the church—and of their novels—since "without sinners the drama of salvation cannot play itself out nor can Christ's redemptive mission be fulfilled" (xv). Because of the importance of this transformation, the conversion narrative, beginning with such early accounts as St. Paul's description of Christ's confronting him on the road to Damascus and St. Augustine's *Confessions*, has been an important Catholic narrative portrayal of the nonrational. Not uncommonly, such accounts—whether they are about saint's lives or fictional characters—show God as the "Hound of Heaven," pursuing the sinner who is resisting the power of grace (Fraser xv). Particularly in the Catholic renaissance of writing in the early part of this century, these narratives of conversion often show grace at work in the lives of seemingly unlikely—and unlikable—people (Wolfe 19). The New Testament theme of looking forward to an eternal home also ties into representations of the nonrational, since a commitment to Christ is often linked to a sense that one should not get too closely connected to worldly matters (Wolfe 22). Twentieth-century Catholic writers have used this conception to emphasize a sense of exile from elements of modern life and thought (O'Brien 213–15).

Although these various narrative patterns and themes in Judaism and Catholicism are touched on in my work, they are not my primary emphasis. Indeed, it would likely prove a valuable project to undertake a parallel study to the present one to examine how these tropes are employed by the writers I examine. In my work, though, I am focusing less on the historical narrative connections and more on the similar representations of mystery among the four authors I examine.

My study takes as its starting point individual concepts from two important readers of religious fiction, Robert Detweiler and Wesley Kort, even though their overall approach is not entirely congenial to my work. Detweiler, in *Breaking the Fall: Religious Readings of Contemporary Fiction* (1989), seeks to determine how a religious interpretation of literature should work. Using texts that "signal . . . an openness to a religious reading" (xiv), he finds that fictions of pain, pleasure, and worship show this possibility. It is within his discussion of texts of worship that Detweiler's comments bear most specifically on my work. Since our culture seeks to demystify existence through science and technology, a religious reading could entail exploring those texts that help to move us from the secular effort of explaining all mystery. Instead, these religious texts "demystify not existence but rather our most prominent demystifiers, science and technology, and guide us toward saving the sacred" (55). Detweiler believes that Christian and Jewish liturgy can serve, at least in a limited way, as a model for celebrating mystery instead of seeking to explain existence rationally:

> Liturgy offers a text that in the very thereness of its language provides no resolution—that is its mystery—but that leaves the celebrant not with a fear of chaos but rather with a sense of satisfaction and fulfillment. . . . The satisfaction generated by the confrontation with the intensity and inexpressibility of form in the liturgical text is based on the faith

> that discontinuity and the failure of representation are complicit with a mystery that encompasses chaos itself. (58)

Using Jean-François Lyotard's description of postmodernism as giving a "sense of the unpresentable," Detweiler suggests that religious narratives point the way to the "conceivable but unpresentable" (62).

Kort's primary aim in *Story, Text, and Scripture: Literary Interests in Biblical Narratives* (1988), as his title suggests, is to use literary methods to understand Scripture. But as he discusses biblical narrative, he reveals several important insights about the role of mystery in writing. Kort argues that because the four elements he finds in narrative—atmosphere, character, plot, tone—incorporate the writer's belief as the elements together create a "world," narrative can be described as "an articulated belief structure" (20). It is thus plausible for God to enter the biblical narrative through any of these four elements "because each of the elements leads to matters that are both crucial to human life and yet also beyond human understanding and control" (20). Moving from biblical stories to a discussion of all narratives, Kort says:

> the appearance of God in narrative form reveals not only something about God but also something about *the narrative form, namely, its liminal position, its relation to mystery and the sacred.* Human awareness is related to mysteries by means of narratives, whether the beliefs embedded in the narratives are conscious or not. (20–21, emphasis added)

While one might well argue with Kort's universalizing claim that "all narratives contend with mystery" (109)—or at least ask that he differentiate among some of the distinct kinds of mystery that varying stories evoke—Kort's analysis of the narrative form's connection with mystery is a helpful one. Narratives offer readers a chance to encounter truths beyond ordinary human experience as they enter into another's belief structure.

Drawing Detweiler's description of a religious text's mystery as a response to our culture's worship of rationality together with Kort's emphasis on the narrative form's role in presenting religious mystery, I am examining how four contemporary American writers, whose fiction shows a spiritual dimension, use their narrative forms to portray a mysterious step toward belief or moral focus that requires a movement beyond the rational. Bernard Malamud, Walker Percy, Cynthia Ozick, and Flannery O'Connor all show in their writing an acceptance of a truth that transcends rationality. This representation of the nonrational element of belief is the important commonality that draws together these Jewish and Catholic writers, even though they naturally explain the specifics of their beliefs quite differently. Jewish theologian Martin Buber, in discussing Judaism and Christianity, argues that belief can either involve trusting someone "without being able to offer sufficient reasons for my trust" or believing something to be true, again without adequate articulated reasons.

> In both cases my not being able to give a sufficient reason is not a matter of a defectiveness in my ability to think, but of a real particularity in my relationship to the one whom I trust or to that which I acknowledge to be true. It is a relationship which by its nature does not rest upon "reasons," just as it does not grow from such; reasons of course can be urged for it, but they are never sufficient to account for my faith. (7)

As shown in their fiction, Malamud, Percy, Ozick, and O'Connor all recognize this truth that Buber sets out and, I argue, use their narrative forms to portray this faith. They show "form being not simply an enabling means for handling the content, but in some essential sense *being* the content" (Fletcher and Bradbury 401).[2]

As I discuss in Chapter 2, Jewish and Catholic theologies contain elements of religious mystery, both by having beliefs that go beyond the rational as well as by cultivating a sense of the numinous. Even more significant, at the center of Judaism and Catholicism, each religion provides believers a concrete method for encountering the numinous: following the commandments in Judaism or partaking of the sacraments in Catholicism. In the fiction examined here, this giving form to mystery is mirrored by the use of narrative forms that lead to the nonrational as well as by the concrete images that evoke mystery.

In my study, I have linked Malamud with Percy and Ozick with O'Connor because the two pairs show a similarity in their narrative portrayal of religious mystery.[3] Malamud's and Percy's narrative form tends to be a quest for a deeper commitment, a movement toward that mystery. Through this narrative pattern, the novels of Malamud and Percy seem to follow the paradigms of these two religions as the narratives give structure to a portrayal of mystery. Further, in the course of these quests, physical actions or items seem freighted with religious significance, a parallel to each religion's use of the concrete to express mystery. As is made clear in Malamud's *The Natural* and Percy's *Lancelot*, these authors are engaged with the quest myth, so it is hardly surprising that they employ that pattern in other novels to represent mystery. Malamud's *The Fixer* and Percy's *The Second Coming* show characters on a journey as they wrestle with religious issues, which are for them—at least at some level—resolved by making a commitment to their community. In Malamud's *The Assistant* and Percy's *The Moviegoer*, the protagonists are dissatisfied with the "everydayness" (Percy's term) of their lives and move—seemingly inadvertently—toward a religious commitment. In these various novels, often the characters cannot logically explain their urge to find something more in life than mere day-to-day existence, yet their need is nevertheless intense. Given the authors' religious concerns, it is probably not surprising that these questers, with their unexplainable motivations, can only find fulfillment in the variety of belief outlined by Buber, a belief beyond the explanation of reasons. They seem to show, in the familiar words of St. Augustine, that "the heart is restless until it finds its rest in Thee." Percy and Malamud employ the quest form to show their characters moving toward this rest.

Ozick's and O'Connor's stories embody the religious mystery that Malamud's and Percy's characters seek to encounter, so their fiction very clearly parallels the Jewish and Catholic practice of giving form to the mystery of belief. Indeed, the sense of the numinous pervades their entire work, through Ozick's use of the fantastic and O'Connor's use of the grotesque. While their specific techniques are somewhat different, it seems useful to link Ozick's and O'Connor's fiction since stories from both authors reveal a breaking with typical "realistic" fictional presentations. Even more, each author is (at least on some level) using her fantastic or grotesque approach in an effort to reach toward a spiritual dimension in her writing. Both the fantastic and the grotesque provide the authors with a way to go beyond traditional, rational forms of fiction—and, I argue, serve as a means to portray the nonrational element of belief. Ozick and O'Connor are especially adept at using concrete—and jarring—images and actions to point toward the numinous. By disrupting the usual narrative conventions, these authors open up space for a recognition of a reality beyond the rational and then point readers toward this mystery by using religiously significant images or dialogue. In Ozick's "Usurpation (Other People's Stories)" and O'Connor's "Parker's Back," for instance, an object or image on a person's skin has apparently supernatural power over the person. Similarly, in Ozick's "Puttermesser and Xanthippe" (from *The Puttermesser Papers*) and O'Connor's "The Enduring Chill," a physical object surprisingly begins to move. In what are perhaps their purest examples of the fantastic and the grotesque, Ozick's "Levitation" and "The Pagan Rabbi" and O'Connor's "Greenleaf" and "A Good Man Is Hard to Find," a violent or shocking action breaks the surface calm of the story, stunning both the characters and the readers. Not surprisingly, their writing often resists an easy interpretation, showing the tendency that Detweiler describes (in a somewhat different context) that "[s]ometimes texts need to be absorbed, taken in and then offered up not to a relentlessly analytical readership but rather to a contemplative fellowship" (34). Ozick's and O'Connor's fiction, in its break with reason, offers readers a physical way to approach a nonrational experience of belief as they enter into the fantastic or grotesque world presented by the authors.

RELIGIOUS BELIEF: BETWEEN RATIONALITY AND INDETERMINACY

Before beginning such an investigation of narrative form, it is necessary to place the kind of religious belief I am discussing in its position between two conflicting poles of thought: Enlightenment rationality and postmodern indeterminacy. A contemporary Jewish philosopher defines faith as "the positive answer, given by way of personal commitment, to existential questions of ultimate significance, which reason can still [in the twentieth century] raise, but no longer answer" (Fackenheim 215). Friedrich von Hugel's assessment in *The Mystical Element of Religion* (1927) is that religion is "rather felt than seen or reasoned about, is loved and lived rather than analyzed, is action and power rather than either external fact or intellectual verification" (52). If one accepts these as valid definitions, then religious belief is quite obviously in conflict with some of the basic tenets of rationality growing out of the Enlightenment.[4]

When the Scriptures were accepted as the final arbiter for any questions about how to understand the world, people had less difficulty embracing those aspects of belief that require a nonrational commitment. Drawing on the work of Copernicus and Galileo, though, Isaac Newton's revolutionary concepts in physics led scientists to begin to see the material world as completely comprehensible through objective observation, thus explaining much of existence that had earlier seemed mysterious. The mechanistic functioning of the universe allowed scientists to determine the natural laws governing matter. Because the universe has a logical certainty, they argued, any observed anomalies are simply evidence that the current theory needs to be corrected through better observation and reason, not that the material world is illogical. Since this emphasis on reason carried over to the work of Enlightenment philosophers, such as Descartes, Spinoza, and Leibniz, reason and faith came to be viewed as conflicting, and the mysterious aspects of religion were often under attack. Even though these writers did not oppose theism, as one historian explains, "with hindsight it is hard to avoid the impression that even as early as the seventeenth century, the 'melancholy long withdrawing roar' of the Sea of Faith had begun" (Cottingham 184–85). To cite one slightly later example, John Locke argued that reason is the only way to know what is revealed: "Nothing that is contrary to, and inconsistent with, the clear and self-evident dictates of reason, has a right to be urged or asserted to as a matter of faith" (qtd. in Davis 73).

Thomas Jefferson's effort to put such ideas into practice is possibly the most famous Enlightenment attempt to remove surgically all mysterious parts of, in this case, Christianity. Jefferson rejected the Trinity as logically absurd and proceeded to analyze rationally the rest of Christianity; he concluded that the central dogmas were not acceptable to an enlightened mind (Sheridan 5). In response to his findings, Jefferson literally cut apart the New Testament, taking out those pieces he found irrational, while mounting on a new sheet his bowdlerized version. As Eugene Sheridan says in introducing the critical edition of Jefferson's extracted gospel, "it seems best to describe Jefferson as a demythologized Christian—as one, that is to say, who rejected all myth, all mystery, all miracles, and almost all supernaturalism in religion" (39). The twentieth-century descendants of Jefferson, trying to apply a scientific method to the Bible, are still hard at work, albeit in a more democratic manner: members of the Jesus Seminar, a group of biblical scholars, meet regularly to decide—by voting—whether words and actions reported in the Gospels actually happened. Among other issues, they have voted over the last years that the virgin birth and Jesus' resurrection never occurred (Gibbs 70). Such efforts at determining through human reason whether or not to believe Scripture tend to undercut a sense of religious mystery since events without a rational explanation do not stand up under scientific analysis—and thus must be excised.

Though the details were obviously quite different, the growing emphasis on using human reason to evaluate sacred writing also undercut rabbinic Judaism. While rabbinic literature itself makes explicit use of reason, it does so "in terms laid down by Torah." The logic of interpretation in these writings "derives from the oral Torah, not from autonomous speculation," so for "classic Judaism, reason serves as a handmaiden to revelation" (Borowitz "Reason" 749). Even for a medieval Jewish philosopher such as Maimonides, who lauded the power of reason, rationality must not undercut Scripture but rather works alongside it (Neusner 44). So, as a generalization, in the time before the Enlightenment, Jewish philosophers as well as the rabbis certainly did argue about how the elements in Scripture work together, but—significantly—they did not question the authority of the revealed biblical texts.

With the Enlightenment, Jews found new freedoms in Europe to move in the larger society as they came to be recognized as citizens, a process begun shortly after the French Revolution. The additional effect of this Emancipation, along with its commendable result of making Jews full citizens, was to lead Jews to considerable assimilation with the dominant culture. With this lessening of the Jewish community's overarching influence in all of life, Jews came to see themselves as "a man abroad and a Jew at home" (Ozick *Metaphor & Memory* 234). Besides these cultural changes, the new emphasis on reason affected Jewish thought as well, leading some to question "the artifacts of the tradition which had formerly been accepted as part of the given, or the revealed reality of the world. . . . The values they projected were those of the neutral society, which they saw as the 'wave of the future'" (Neusner 61–62). Thus, many Jewish intellectuals were left believing the ethical parts of Torah but rejecting the ritual elements, deciding for themselves what aspects of Scripture to embrace (Ariel 171). Accepting the supreme value modernity places on human reason "means adopting stands in opposition to the God-given truths of traditional Judaism and the way of life which enshrines them" (Borowitz *Choices* 22–23). Carrying on into the nineteenth and twentieth centuries, "the desire to preserve the autonomy of human reason continued to undermine the authority" of Jewish law (Ariel 172).[5]

The tradition of rationality being antagonistic to the nonrational parts of religious belief has indeed continued on into the twentieth century. Bertrand Russell, one of the more outspoken advocates promoting the scientific method over religion, said, "We have seen that, in the period since Copernicus, whenever science and theology have disagreed, science has proved victorious" (244). Less trenchantly, but just as assuredly, Ernest Gellner in *Postmodernism, Reason, and Religion* (1992) argues against religious belief:

> To those of us who have deeply internalized . . . the Kantian or Enlightenment ethic of cognition, the obligation to treat all evidence impartially, and all occasions as equally unprivileged, the notion of a Revelation is morally unacceptable. The idea of a unique

and final Message, delivered at one place and one time, exempt from scrutiny, from the disaggregation into its constituent claims, and from the need to subject those claims to questions—this violates the rules of that cognitive ethic which . . . constitutes the fixed point in our world-view, and the only one. (84–85)

As Stephen Nathanson explains in *The Ideal of Rationality* (1994), if a religious believer has a numinous experience that forms the basis of his or her beliefs, rationalists argue that such encounters "are not self-validating and need to be supplemented by some form of argument" (6).

This emphasis on scientific verification and rationality leaves little room for beliefs that cannot be tested and corroborated, so traditional Catholicism and rabbinic Judaism must be seen as going beyond reason. Buber explains how religious belief cannot be subsumed under the powers of reason: "My rationality, my rational power of thought, is merely a part, a particular function of my nature; when however I 'believe,' . . . my entire being is engaged, the totality of my nature enters into the process, indeed this becomes possible only because the relationship of faith is a relationship of my entire being" (7). Unaided reason cannot explain a believer's faith.

Because an emphasis on rationality raises certain difficulties for religion, believers may have initially felt cause to cheer at the startling paradigm shift that occurred in physics in the first part of the twentieth century. Drawing on the work of several earlier physicists, Werner Heisenberg in 1927 set out his uncertainty principle, arguing that the observation of subatomic particles is indeterminate. Specifically, both the position and motion of quantum particles cannot be accurately measured because the scientist's very act of observation disturbs the object, leading to distortion in the measurement.[6] This idea, widely accepted by physicists today, radically altered the view of science—and the universe. Since "[n]ot a single feature [of Newtonian physics] . . . remains unchallenged, either directly or implicitly, by contemporary physics" (38), Milic Capek, in *The Philosophical Impact of Contemporary Physics* (1961), argues that "the effects of these theories on the imagination of physicists, philosophers, and even laymen was truly shattering" (xi). When the scientist, whose method has long been seen as exemplifying objective observation, becomes a central figure in affecting measurement, "the entire set of relations between mind and world has changed" (Strehle 13). At least on the subatomic level, no longer is there stable, identifiable "truth" for scientists to discover. The question still being debated, however, is what effect this uncertainty principle has for daily life experience. Even though Einstein's theory of relativity paved the way for Heisenberg's principle, Einstein refused to accept the broader implications of the uncertainty principle, arguing in his now-famous quotation that "God does not play dice with the world." On the other hand, P.C.W. Davies and J.R. Brown suggest that "[f]ollowing the logic of quantum theory to its ultimate conclusion, most of the physical universe seems to dissolve away into a shadowy fantasy" (30).[7]

Although physicists still debate the implications of the uncertainty principle, the indeterminacy at its core has many parallels in the theory espoused by postmodern philosophers and literary critics as they argue that the powers of reason have been overstated. In his seminal study *The Postmodern Condition* (1984), Jean-François Lyotard argues that the "grand narrative," the overarching attempt to unify understanding into a coherent truth, "has lost its credibility, regardless of what mode of unification it uses" (37). To this end, Geoffrey Hartman suggests, "Indeterminacy functions as a bar separating understanding and truth" (*Wilderness* 272). But for many postmodern theoreticians, the concept of indeterminacy or undecidability goes beyond a simple interrogation of the powers of rationality. Jacques Derrida, arguably the most influential contemporary literary theoretician, asserts that the Western "logocentrism," the emphasis on reason, should be replaced by a recognition that no text has authority over another. Instead, all writing is an interpretation, so that there can be only a "freeplay" of texts—an interaction among various discourses—without any one having supremacy.[8] This deconstructive strategy has had a profound influence on postmodern literary theory, particularly with its emphasis on indeterminacy.[9] As Jonathan Culler explains the difference between a structuralist and a poststructuralist approach, "[s]tructuralists are convinced that systematic knowledge is possible; poststructuralists claim to know only the impossibility of this knowledge" (22). In other words, rather than looking for patterns to organize a coherent view, the deconstructive impulse of postmodernism "bends all its efforts to stretch beyond these boundaries, to transgress these confines, to interrupt and disjoin all such gatherings" (Caputo "Commentary" 31).

This resistance by advocates of indeterminacy to the Enlightenment assumption that all "reality" can be explained through reason may at a glance seem compatible with certain aspects of religious mystery. Like many postmodern theoreticians, religious believers reject the notion that all parts of life can be understood rationally. Indeed, in his more recent writing, Derrida—and one of his preeminent interpreters, Villanova University philosopher John Caputo—has suggested that there are significant parallels between his deconstructive approach and religious faith. While still rejecting religion as a set of beliefs, Derrida embraces faith as "presupposed by the most radical deconstructive gesture. You cannot address the other, speak to the other, without an act of faith, without testimony" (22). Caputo goes even further, affirming that he believes "[d]econstruction is a blessing for religion, its positive salvation, keeping it open to constant reinvention, encouraging religion to reread ancient texts in new ways, to reinvent ancient traditions in new contexts" ("Commentary" 159). Rather than being antithetical to religious belief, Caputo and Derrida argue, the undecidability of postmodernism provides space for religious voices to be heard and reinvigorated. Resisting the argument that postmodern undecidability undercuts ethics by removing religious moorings, Caputo and Derrida insist that justice—reaching out to the "other"—is "undeconstructible" (Caputo "Commentary" 128). Derrida says, "Justice in itself, if such a thing exists, outside or beyond law, is not deconstructible" (qtd. in Caputo "Commentary" 131). This striving for justice sounds almost like a Platonic goal, but Caputo insists it is rather the opposite, since the deconstructive approach is to look for the singular instance of justice that serves as an exception to the law rather than an overarching Platonic ideal (Caputo "Commentary" 135).

Yet while this appeal to justice may seem to parallel a search for God, Caputo reminds us that for Derrida (and deconstruction) there is "at bottom, no bottom," "no deep essence to keep things on course" ("Commentary" 122 and 117). And it is this profound difference between the undecidability of postmodernism and the mystery of religious belief that finally reveals that the two are at a most basic level incompatible. For, as Linda Hutcheon explains, the indeterminacy of postmodernism "raises questions about (or renders problematic) the common-sensical and the 'natural.' *But it never offers answers that are anything but provisional and contextually determined (and limited)*" (xi, emphasis added). Or in the words of another important interpreter, Ihab Hassan, indeterminacy is characterized by "heterodoxy, pluralism, eclecticism, randomness, revolt, deformation" (9). Because of this questioning, any assessment of a positive meaning for a text is impossible since it remains "uncertain in its communication, obscure in its truth" (Bahti 216). Caputo notes the seeming linkages that exist between Derrida's resistance to make positive assertions and negative theology, the belief that it is only possible to speak about God through negation—saying what God is not. Yet Caputo insists that while the resemblances are strong between deconstruction and negative theology, "still deconstruction is no negative theology. That is because negative theology is always a higher, more refined way of affirming that God exists, or hyperexists, or exists-by-not-existing, that God is really real or hyper-real or sur-real. . . . Way down deep, negative theologians know what they are talking about; they have not entirely lost their way or their balance" (*Prayers* 7 and 11). In his discussion of negative theology and deconstruction, Caputo has, it seems to me, put his finger on the basic incompatibility of religious mystery and postmodern indeterminacy. While a postmodern stance acknowledges that truth is ultimately unknowable, much as believers recognize that God is beyond human comprehension, postmodern thinkers seem to confuse an epistemological problem with a metaphysical one: just because humans cannot adequately articulate knowledge about the divine does not mean that there is no center, no God to encounter.[10] Advocates of indeterminacy not only question the power of rationality but insist that no transcendent truth is possible; all knowledge is constrained, all understanding is subjective.

The initially plausible correspondence between religious belief's nonrational aspects and the postmodern critique of rationality thus collapses on closer examination. For even though belief cannot be locked into rationally defined compartments, both Catholicism and rabbinic Judaism insist that religious mystery has a solid foundation, that (at its most basic) an infinite God is in charge of the universe. This emphasis that a center for belief does exist is a vast difference from a "play of surfaces" (Gitlin 35), a distinction Roger Lundin succinctly articulates:

> Whereas mystery speaks of a truth that encompasses men and women even as they fail to comprehend it fully, indeterminacy has to do with the vertiginous play of interpretation that has given up on truth and seeks its only comfort in the game-playing potential of language. (204–5)

Although not necessarily setting out their beliefs in terms that a rationalist would accept, religious believers do hold that the nonrational, unexplainable aspects of their religion are a matter of human's imperfect insight, of "seeing through a glass darkly," rather than a result of there being only heterodoxy, pluralism, and randomness.

Some theoreticians writing from a Jewish perspective, though, find a greater affinity between Judaism and indeterminacy than I have outlined here. For them, Hartman's suggestion that deconstruction's play with words is "as consistent and extravagant as that of the midrashic rabbis" ("State of Criticism" 100) provides an illuminating way of linking indeterminacy and Jewish tradition. The most prominent proponent of such a position, Susan Handelman, argues in *The Slayers of Moses: The Emergence of Rabbinic Interpretation in Modern Literary Theory* (1982) that while earlier criticism had a more "Christian" outlook, contemporary theory follows a midrashic approach:

> Christianity claimed it had the final and validating interpretation of the now "Old" Testament text. . . . The Rabbinic tradition, by contrast, based itself on the principles of multiple meaning and endless interpretability, maintaining that interpretation and text were not only inseparable, but that interpretation—as opposed to incarnation—was the central divine act. (xiv)

Focusing on this concept of "endless interpretability" that she sees in rabbinic thought, Handelman finds "*structural* affinities" between rabbinic patterns of interpretation and writers such as Freud, Derrida, and Bloom (xv). For Handelman, then, Judaism is as open to "differentiation, metaphorical multiplicity, multiple meanings" (33) as is postmodern theory.

Daniel Boyarin in *Intertextuality and the Reading of Midrash* (1990) also sees considerable play in rabbinic interpretation, but he limits the open-endedness more than does Handelman. Specifically, Boyarin believes that the "biblical text as written is characterized by hiatus and indeterminacy on many points. The work of midrash, similar to all reading of narrative, is the filling of the gaps" (92). Yet, even though an appeal to the author's intention as a control on interpretation is disallowed, Boyarin, unlike Handelman, recognizes that not "anything at all can be said to be the meaning of the text. Such hermeneutical anarchy is clearly *not* the way that midrash presents itself." Instead, "the majority of the community which holds cultural hegemony controls interpretation" (35). So rather than relying on a divine message, the exegesis is established by "the ideology of the interpretive community" (36). But such a culturally defined and limited view of "truth" still seems a distance from the solidity behind religious mystery.

In response, Daniel Stern in his illuminating article, "Midrash and Indeterminacy," argues that theorists such as Handelman (and Boyarin, although his book was not published when Stern wrote) are misunderstanding midrash. Rather than being open to indeterminacy, "midrashic polysemy is predicated precisely on the existence of . . . a perspective [outside the flux of time], the divine presence from which all the contradictory interpretations derive" (141). Because rabbinic Judaism emphasizes that both the oral (Talmud) and written Torah were revealed on Sinai, they "together form a unified, timeless entity with a single origin in the divine revelation" (148). Instead of seeing the rabbis' opinions as being in contradiction, the multiple interpretations are rather an effort to represent "an idealized academy of Rabbinic tradition" with the varying opinions recorded as "part of a single divine conversation." Therefore, "[o]pinions that in human discourse may appear as contradictory or mutually exclusive are raised to the state of paradox once traced to their common source in the speech of the divine author" (155). Stern thus shows that even though midrash has certain surface characteristics that make it appear compatible with indeterminacy, the emphasis on the "divine author" sets apart rabbinic Judaism from postmodern theory.[11]

The religious mystery of both Catholicism and rabbinic Judaism, then, occupies a middle position between rationality and indeterminacy. Religious adherents assert that a meaningful part of life—their beliefs, their relationship with God—cannot be explained in entirely rational terms. At the same time, they insist that their rejection of a complete reliance on reason does not mean that they have cut themselves loose from all moorings. It is this nonrational element of belief—beyond final explanation yet with a firm foundation—that is the subject of my study.

NOTES

1. I use this term not in a specific, technical sense of differentiating between "rationalism" and "positivism" but rather in the more general sense of relying on reason as the supreme arbiter of ideas.

2. Fletcher and Bradbury are not discussing religious mystery but are rather describing the important role form plays in the experimental Modernist novels in the early part of the twentieth century. The similarity, however, between their emphasis on formal considerations for understanding these novels and my study of religious mystery's impact on narrative form suggests a potentially rich comparison between the role of form in Modernism and in contemporary religious writing.

3. Since I compare the work of two men and then two women, it would of course be possible to consider the role that gender plays in the differences between the pairs. One wonders, for instance, how O'Connor and Ozick were differently affected by being women from minority religious groups, or how their status within each religion (each of which is sometimes characterized as not particularly congenial to women) had an impact on their writing. While interesting questions, such considerations are outside the scope of my study.

4. Various Christian theologians, such as Paul Tillich, have tried to articulate a faith that limits nonrational elements. In a somewhat different way, many contemporary Jews have moved from seeing their Judaism as a religious commitment to viewing it as simply a cultural identification. Neither position is acceptable to traditional Catholicism or rabbinic Judaism, and so neither seems germane to this study.

5. This tension between the rational and the nonrational is exemplified within Judaism by the conflict, beginning in the late eighteenth century, between *Haskalah* and Hasidism. Supporters of the *Haskalah* movement, founded in western Europe and initially influenced by the French and German Enlightenment, focused on rectifying "the alleged backwardness of Jewry and eliminat[ing] the supposed irrational features of Judaism" by "reforms of Jewish education, livelihood, and religious practice" (Seltzer 171). In contrast, Hasidism, primarily in Eastern Europe, was a pietistic and mystical (and generally anti-scholarly) revival movement that sought to revitalize the spiritual dimensions of Judaism.

6. My treatment of the discoveries leading up to Heisenberg's principle and the later developments from his ideas is necessarily limited. For a more complete discussion, see P.C.W. Davies and J.R. Brown, *The Ghost in the Atom: A Discussion of Quantum Physics* (1986). The first chapters of Susan Strehle's *Fiction in the Quantum Universe* (1992) and Gregory Connes's *The Ethics of Indeterminacy in the Novels of William Gaddis* (1994) also contain helpful summaries of quantum physics.

7. See Davies and Brown's *The Ghost in the Atom*, pages 31–39, for a summary of the explanations given to understand the implications of quantum theory. Jean-François Lyotard also discusses quantum physics in *The Postmodern Condition: A Report of Knowledge* (1984), page 55ff.

8. See Arkady Plotnitsky's *Complementarity: Anti-epistemology after Bohr and Derrida* (1994) for a study of the relationships between quantum physics and Derrida's ideas.

9. Since the number of competing definitions of postmodernism is roughly equal to the number of interpreters of this phenomenon, I am not trying to construct my own full-scale definition of literary postmodernism. This task has been undertaken by others, such as Brian McHale in *Postmodernist Fiction* (1987) and *Constructing Postmodernism* (1992), Linda Hutcheon in *A Poetics of Postmodernism* (1988), and Ihab Hassan in "Desire and Dissent in the Postmodern Age" (*Kenyon Review*). Sociologist Todd Gitlin considers postmodernism on a broader, societal scale in "Hip-Deep in Post-modernism." Nor am I even engaging all the aspects of postmodernism. My focus is solely on one part of postmodernism—indeterminacy—and its relationship to religious belief.

10. My thanks to philosopher Caleb Miller at Messiah College for discussions that helped elucidate these ideas.

11. It is also worth noting that the multiplicity of interpretations applies only to the biblical narrative; rabbinic Judaism is not polysemous concerning Jewish law.

2

Making Physical the Mystery: Jewish *Mitzvot* and Catholic Sacraments

Since the role of religious belief in fiction is the focus of this study, it seems appropriate to begin with a brief overview of Jewish and Catholic theology before examining the fiction of Malamud, Percy, Ozick, and O'Connor. My emphasis will be on those aspects of theology that highlight religious mystery, the nonrational aspect of belief. After an initial, general discussion about beliefs in Judaism and Catholicism that move beyond the rational, I have narrowed my presentation to examine two specific, but very important, elements of the two religions: Jewish commandments (*mitzvot*)[1] and Catholic sacraments. I have chosen to focus on these aspects of Judaism and Catholicism for two reasons. First, *mitzvot* and sacraments are central to the practice of the respective religions, so it seems valuable to consider how they relate to mystery. Second, and most important for my study, such an examination shows that these two practices serve to make physical the nonrational, an approach that the authors I discuss mirror in their own work.

My focus on the nonrational in religion may lead readers to assume I am speaking of mysticism. Although both Judaism and Catholicism have aspects that are mystical and both religions encompass distinctive strains which emphasize mystical experiences—such as Kabbalah in Judaism and the Desert Fathers in Catholicism—my primary focus is not on these specifically mystical groups. R.A. Herrera helpfully distinguishes between mysticism and theology in his introduction to *Mystics of the Book* (1993):

> Both theology and mysticism are subsumed under the umbrella of religion. What distinguishes the two is mysticism's claim to be uniquely wedded to experience and to teach a deeper mystery, to probe alien heights and depths, to uncover hidden meanings, and transcend the natural order. If we take the mystics at their word, they aspire to "polish the

mirror of the soul". . . . They aspire to arrive at proximity with the Prime Reality, God, even [attain] union. (3)

Certainly a firm boundary between theology and mysticism is impossible since mystical experience is a part of more mainstream theology. But this chapter is primarily concerned with how central beliefs in traditional Jewish and Catholic theology encompass nonrational aspects. More specifically, the goal of mainstream theology is much the same as for the mystics—to invoke a sense of the numinous or, to use more traditional language, to encounter God. But the process to achieve that relationship in standard Jewish and Catholic practices generally involves imbuing regular activities or rituals with a sense of the holy without the ecstasy or displacement of the physical that is commonly associated with mysticism.

First, a caveat about outlining Jewish theology. Determining basic Jewish religious beliefs is somewhat difficult because even the rabbis of the Talmudic period do not set out clear doctrines; rather, they participate in an ongoing dialogue with each other concerning the proper way to act and think. As Daniel Stern says, "If all the statements about faith that characterize Rabbinic Judaism were collected, they would more closely resemble the anthologies of multiple interpretations for a single verse found in Rabbinic exegesis than a systematic exposition of religious beliefs" ("Midrash and Indeterminacy" 145). To a certain extent, Maimonides' 13 Principles serve as a doctrinal basis for rabbinic Judaism, but the primary emphasis centers on following God by obeying his commandments (as will be discussed more fully later).[2]

Nevertheless, certain fundamental understandings of religious mystery in rabbinic Judaism do become clear. As noted in the Introduction, religious believers can experience tension concerning the role of reason in their beliefs. Maimonides, in the medieval tradition of joining together faith and reason, is often cited as putting much emphasis on reason's power. But even he recognized that reason is finite when discussing religious beliefs, noting that certain concepts must be accepted without rational proof. In his *Guide for the Perplexed*, a book especially designed to help those feeling caught between philosophy and Judaism, Maimonides explained that "for the human mind there are certain objects of perception which are within the scope of its nature and capacity; on the other hand, there are, amongst things which actually exist, certain objects which the mind can in no way and by no means grasp" (40). A present-day interpreter of Maimonides gives an example of Maimonides' understanding of the limits of reason: "Reason cannot decide the question of whether the cosmos was created or whether it was eternal; it can only determine that the scales are equally balanced. The Torah . . . must be allowed to tip the scales in favor of creationism" (Agus 575).

The tension between reason and religious belief continues today, with Jewish theologians differing in their articulations of the relationship of rationality and mystery. Marvin Fox points out that reason plays a significant role in rabbinic Judaism: "While Judaism admits the limitations of man's intellect and the presence of certain cosmic mysteries, it does not lay its primary stress on this side of things. Instead, one finds in the rabbinic sources a rather steady inclination to make sense out of the apparently senseless" (117)—to work toward rational understandings. On the other hand, post-Holocaust theologian Emil Fackenheim, in his outline of a modern Jewish theology, places a much greater emphasis on the nonrational, saying that reason can still in the late twentieth century raise a question about existence, "but it can no longer answer it." To answer such questions, "we require a leap, an act of decision and commitment" (215). Louis Jacobs, defining a position he calls "liberal supernaturalism," says he does not necessarily accept all the earlier commentators' interpretations of Scripture. Nevertheless, what a contemporary believer gains from these writings is "the appreciation that the true nature of God is bound to be a mystery beyond the grasp of the human mind" (10). Samuel Cohon, an important theologian in Reform Judaism, places a high value on reason, saying that faith must "justify itself before the bar of reason." Yet even for him, nonrational belief has a central role in keeping a person from a sterile rationality: "In the religious sense, faith represents personal avowal of the values of religion: the purposefulness of life, the reality of God, and the rightness of his will; and speaks commitment to these truths, whether they be disclosed by reason, grasped by intuition, or delivered by tradition" (26). Coming from their disparate positions, all these theologians still recognize the role that nonrational beliefs play in rabbinic Judaism.[3]

In Catholicism, perhaps even more obviously than in Judaism, the concept of religious mystery is central to belief: the core doctrine, salvation through Jesus' death and resurrection, cannot be rationally understood. Indeed, in the fourth century, Cyril of Jerusalem had such a strong sense of the nonrationality of belief that he implored instructors not to reveal too much to catechumens early in their learning: "For we are entrusting to you a mystery, the hope of life to come. . . . If a catechumen is told of these mysteries by one of the faithful . . . he does not understand what he is told, and he criticizes and jeers: and the faithful is condemned for treachery" (qtd. in Bettenson *Later Church Fathers* 41). St. Thomas Aquinas, who with his detailed exposition of belief performed a similar role for Catholicism as Maimonides did for Judaism, recognized the important position that reason held in making doctrine understandable. But after using reason to "arrive at the knowledge of divine things through creatures," he pointed out that "[t]his way is imperfect," so "[w]e must now deal with those divine things that have been divinely revealed to us to be believed, since they transcend the human intellect" (*Summa Contra Gentiles* 39). For instance, Aquinas says that the trinity cannot be understood rationally: "That God is both threefold and one is solely an object of belief. There is no way of proving it demonstratively . . ." (*Faith* 31). In the present day, Pope John Paul II, too, has underlined the fundamental intersection he finds between faith and reason: "Faith asks that its object be understood with the help of reason; and at the summit of its searching reason acknowledges that it cannot do without what faith presents" (64).

This sense of mystery's central place, of reason's power being limited, has clearly been reiterated in official church dogma. At the Council of Trent, convened largely in response to the Protestant Reformation, the Church affirmed the importance of encouraging a sense of mystery as people celebrate the mass:

And as human nature is such that it cannot easily raise itself up to the meditation of divine realities without external aids, holy mother church has for that reason duly established certain rites . . . by which the majesty of this great sacrifice is enhanced, and the minds of the faithful are aroused by those visible signs of religious devotion to contemplation of the high mysteries hidden in it. (Session 22, Chapter 5)

The service and the liturgy are specifically designed to encourage the believer to develop a sense of religious mystery. As the current Catechism says, the Church's liturgy especially focuses on Christ's death and resurrection: "It is this mystery of Christ that the Church proclaims and celebrates in her liturgy so that the faithful may live from it and bear witness to it in the world" (277). For Catholics, then, recognizing the nonrational aspects of belief—the mystery—is a central part of worship.

But as the Tridentine proclamation acknowledges, mystery is—by its very nature—difficult to grasp. Since one cannot rationally understand it, a believer may have difficulty feeling a connection with the nonrational aspects of his or her beliefs or, even more importantly, with the purpose behind these doctrines: developing a sense of the numinous. Jews and Catholics certainly may experience a personal relationship with God, a feeling of connection, an "I and Thou" affiliation. But such an emphasis on a "personal friend" relationship with God is not the only, probably not even the most important, Jewish and Catholic understanding of how to encounter God. Instead, Judaism and Catholicism provide specific ways to reach the divine, a concrete action or ritual that opens the path to an anagogical level. While there are significant differences, Jewish *mitzvot* and Catholic sacraments both serve as concrete ways for believers to encounter and follow God; believers are not left with merely a mandate to believe but rather are given specific practices that serve as "doors to the sacred."[4] Gersion Appel describes the role that following *mitzvot* has in a believer's life:

The *mitzvot* . . . impart a religious dimension to life. By performing the *mitzvot* in obedience to divine command, man is able to relate to God and to serve Him. Through the involvement of the whole of his physical and intellectual being, of his material and spiritual nature, they afford him the means of attaining an awareness of living continually in the presence of God. (4)

In a somewhat similar way, as David Bourke points out, sacraments provide a way for Catholics to encounter God:

Taken as a whole the sacramental system provides for a worshipping community constituted, preserved, nourished, and restored by a limited number of prescribed rites, all of which derive their efficacy from the fact that they are in some way a re-enactment of the redeeming death of Jesus as the sole source of grace and salvation. (xiv)

Mitzvot and sacraments, then, as concretizations of religious mystery, are the specific practices explored in the remainder of this chapter.[5]

JEWISH *MITZVOT*: SANCTIFYING THE ORDINARY

Mitzvot is the Hebrew word for the commandments found in the Torah and later explicated and expanded by the rabbis in the Talmud. The most famous collection of *mitzvot* was compiled by Maimonides who, following tradition established before him, listed 613 commandments, split into 248 positive and 365 negative commandments. These *mitzvot* regulate people's actions by, for example, giving directions for the Sabbath and kosher eating, prohibiting adultery and incest, and even supplying guidelines for marital relations. Because *mitzvot* regulate all of life, every aspect of a committed Jew's life can serve as an act of worship: "Each small detail of behavior expresses the larger message: the law, in specifying the proper modes of behavior for the Jews, becomes **the** vehicle for morality and ethics, and, more importantly for holiness" (Brooks 19). Rather than wondering how to reach God, the believer, through *mitzvot*, is told the specific way to act—and, by extension, to serve God. Since it may be difficult regularly to "feel" mystery in life, the commandments enable a believer "to experience the mysterium in and through commonplace deeds" by "capturing the mysterium and transforming it into *a way of living*" (Lopes Cardozo 157).

Thus, these guidelines serve a twofold purpose of ordering people's proper behavior with each other and, at the same time, sanctifying these ordinary actions so that they have a spiritual dimension. As Zecharias Frankel points out, *mitzvot* fulfill both purposes since they either "aim at ennobling man or, by reminding man of the divine, strengthen his feelings of dependence on God" (174). At best, following *mitzvot* accomplishes both of these functions at the same time:

> Jewish ritual observance is a way of living "with" God in the sense that "ordinary" actions—eating, sleeping, dressing, doing business—are endowed with symbolic significance and by the modalities of their performance express attitudes toward the holy. . . . [T]hey invest our daily actions with an intention toward the holy and in that sense put us into relation with the transcendent. (Goodman 183–84)

One way of understanding *mitzvot*, then, is that *mitzvot* provide a way for believers to encounter God: even though people are incapable of understanding his essence, by following his commandments, a person may find favor with God (Chavel vol. 1 vii). A slightly different perspective puts a greater stress on an ongoing relationship with God. In this view, because of the emphasis on concrete action, the potential division between body and soul is eradicated since *mitzvot* join together spiritual purpose and conscious intention; a proper attitude toward God is cultivated by continually choosing to follow God's commands (Lopes

Cardozo 161). Whatever the specific conception of how *mitzvot* help a person encounter God, following the commandments is clearly a central element in Judaism for experiencing religious mystery.

Implicit in such a view of *mitzvot* is the understanding that the commandments have a divine basis. The traditional rabbinic position has been that both the Hebrew Bible (the written Torah) and the writings of the rabbis in the Talmud (the oral Torah) were revealed to Moses on Mt. Sinai. Although some groups argue for a literal word-by-word revelation of the Oral Torah, a more common interpretation of the rabbinic view is that not each word but only the underlying answer in the Talmudic discussion was revealed on Sinai (Seidel). The basis for accepting the oral Torah as revealed to Moses on Sinai, and then passed down to future generations orally before being written down in the first centuries C.E., comes from the description of what Moses did when he came down from Sinai: "Afterward all the Israelites came near, and he instructed them concerning all that the Lord had imparted to him on Mount Sinai" (Exod. 34.32). Maimonides accepted such a position, arguing in the Eighth Principle of his 13 Principles that all of Torah was divinely revealed to Moses. Concerning the written Torah, Maimonides declared:

> no distinction is to be made between such verses as *And the sons of Ham: Cush and Mizraim*, *And his wife's name was Metetabel*, *And Tima was concubine*, and such verses as, *I am the Lord thy God* and *Hear, O Israel*—all equally having been received from the Almighty, and all alike constituting the Law of the Lord, which is perfect, pure, sacred, and true. (*Commandments* vol. 1 277)

Maimonides similarly asserted the correctness of the traditional view of the oral Torah, saying Jews should believe "that the traditional Exegesis of the Torah [as handed down to us from Moses through the Sages] is also from the Almighty, so that our present-day observances . . . are exactly the same as those wherein the Lord commanded Moses, who in turn communicated them to us" (*Commandments* vol. 1 278).

Not all religious Jews today accept this explanation of the Talmud's origins, but there is nevertheless a strong sense of the divine basis of *mitzvot*. This understanding in large part grows out of the opening of the law given at Sinai: "I the Lord am your God who brought you out of the land of Egypt, the house of bondage: You shall have no other gods besides Me" (Exod. 20.2). This statement of God's past actions establishes the basis for a covenantal relationship: since God has protected them, the people must act in accordance with his commandments as outlined in the coming verses (Brooks 74). As an Israeli Supreme Court Justice explains, commandments such as "'You shall not render an unfair decision . . . You shall not falsify measures of length, weight or capacity'. . . . are based upon 'I the Lord am your God who brought you out from the land of Egypt,'" so that all laws have "the imprint of religious obligation" (Elon 5). A recognition of the exalted status given to following *mitzvot* as God's law is revealed in the maxim that the greatest value is placed on commandments performed *lishmah*—"for the love of God, because it is God's commandment" (Appel 3).

Moving even further from a traditional perspective, some Jews question the direct, divine giving of the written Torah on Sinai, believing instead that human beings have had a significant impact in shaping the law. For some, this assertion may lead them to apply human interpretation to the law to determine what is a permanent part of Scripture and what is open to change (Gordis 76).[6] But Louis Jacobs, from his stance of "liberal supernaturalism," argues that even if the Torah came from custom, "the custom became the Torah. And because there is a two-way traffic in revelation—from the people to God and from God to the people—one cannot go through the Bible with a pencil and mark some passages divine and others human. The totality that we call the Torah is human imbued with the divine" (50). In Jacobs' view, *mitzvot* are still regarded as divine commands:

> To point to the human element in revelation is a far cry from implying that God is not the Creator of the Torah. On the contrary, it is God who makes Himself known through the human process of redaction. How this can be is a tremendous mystery . . . . (52)

What seems significant about Jacobs' position is that even in the move away from some aspects of rabbinic Judaism, this view maintains a recognition of the divine force behind the law, thus ensuring that following *mitzvot* remains a concrete way to reach God.

Through the centuries of studying *mitzvot,* the rabbis—and more recent commentators—have struggled to determine how reason fits into the divinely ordered commands. Does the fact that these commandments are from God set them completely outside the realm of rationality, or does reason still participate in understanding *mitzvot*? The Talmudic rabbis tended to be wary of giving any explanations besides that the law was from Torah, apparently fearing that emphasizing the basis for the laws would lead people to cease following *mitzvot* in favor of individually working out ways to fulfill the "underlying principles" (Appel 23). The rabbinic writings show a recognition of the "ultimacy of Torah and the subordinate status of general wisdom" (Borowitz "Reason" 749).

Medieval writers, though, saw a "metaphysical link between human reason and cosmic Intelligence," so they were more interested in attempting to determine the reasons behind the divine commandments (Appel 183). A tradition that is articulated by a medieval Jewish philosopher, Saadiah Gaon, divides the commandments into two categories: ordinances (*mishpatim*) and statutes (*hukim*). Ordinances, such as the prohibition of incest, are commonly viewed as having a clearly rational basis; even if they had not been given by God, people would still have a sense that they should follow these guidelines. Statutes, on the other hand, are the commands for ritual actions, such as dietary laws, which would not have been obvious to people if they had not been divinely revealed. Although Saadiah Gaon emphasized that the chief reason behind *mitzvot* is God's will, Gersion Appel points out in *A Philosophy of Mitzvot* (1975) that "his endeavor to ascertain a utilitarian basis even for the revealed laws [statutes] would indicate a desire to impart to them an autonomous character as well" (12). Maimonides had a strong sense that *mitzvot* have a rational basis, but he also recognized that "there are commandments the reason of which is unknown to us, and in which the ways of God's wisdom are incomprehensible" (qtd. in Appel 12). In response to the emphasis on rationality, Rashi, one of the medieval philosophers most opposed to touting the power of reason, argued instead that there are laws "for which there are no apparent reason, but which are the king's decrees and enactments imposed on his subjects"—and thus must simply be followed without question (qtd. in Appel 16).

This debate continues among contemporary writers. L.E. Goodman argues, for instance, that later writers have misconstrued what Saadiah Gaon meant by his division of the *mitzvot.* Indicating that some of them cannot be understood rationally is not saying God wants people to follow "*useless* or *pointless* actions" or that the commandments lack wisdom (116). Instead, "[w]hat might have seemed arbitrary in itself becomes morally right or wrong when commanded by God, not merely . . . *because* it is commanded, but because it is made part of a system of virtues and vices by which we are to be perfected and rewarded or corrupted and destroyed" (119). On the other side, Yeshayahu Leibowitz, discussing the commandments in *Contemporary Jewish Religious Thought* (1987), argues that the desire to follow each law must be seen to grow out of a reverence for God, not from any external reasons. He suggests that the reason behind the command to "Love your fellow as yourself" cannot be separated from the second part of the verse, "I am the Lord" (Lev. 19.18). The basis of the command, and the importance of following it, comes not because of "the status of a person as a person but from his status before God" (71). Explanations cannot be adduced to the commandments, for "[e]very reason given for the *mitzvot* that bases itself on human needs—be they intellectual, ethical, social, or national—voids the *mitzvot* of all religious meanings" (71). Such an assertion seems extreme, but Leibowitz properly points out the danger of relying too heavily on reason. For *mitzvot* to serve as doorways to the divine, a follower must maintain the recognition, central to rabbinic Judaism, that the primary purpose for following *mitzvot* is to fulfill God's commandments.

Even if one accepts that *mitzvot* are imperative because they were divinely given, an issue yet remains for this basic discussion of *mitzvot.* If following *mitzvot* is the way to encounter God, is there a mindset or attitude that must accompany the action? The rabbis seem to have had various teachings, with one tradition even saying that it was better to desire to break a commandment and then still keep the *mitzvah*; such action showed true dedication to God's decrees. This tradition, however, seems not to be the most widespread one. More common is the nuanced view that "where a *mitzvah* entails the performance of a specific act—such as the eating of unleavened bread—one who performs the act without conscious purpose fulfills his obligation; but where no specific act is required, there must be a definite awareness of a desire to fulfil one's duty"

(Chavel vol. 1 284). For example, if a person hears the reading of Scripture, he or she only fulfills the obligation by listening attentively, not merely by hearing the words (Chavel vol. 1 284). Nevertheless, a more pervasive attitude of devotion was certainly praised by the rabbis, so that a maxim in the Talmud says that "the reward is proportional to the exertion"; thus, it is fair to say that there is a connection between the careful thought and intention behind the fulfillment of *mitzvot* and the "reward and spiritual satisfaction from their performance" (Chavel vol. 1 288). But even though such a perspective was praised by the rabbis, the Talmud tends to emphasize act over attitude, since truly pious intention "cannot be demanded, measured, or even reliably observed" (Goldenberg 236).

That recognition does not deny, of course, that fulfilling *mitzvot* can itself bring about good results for the believer. As the medieval author of the *Sefer ha-Hinnuk* points out, the soul is influenced more by actions than by thoughts alone; therefore, "through good deeds we will be inclined to become good and to merit life everlasting" (qtd. in Appel 88). Certainly there is the sense for the rabbis that those who follow the law will become the kind of people that God wants them to become (Goldenberg 236). This connection is not a guarantee, but what following *mitzvot* does is "to lay the subconscious foundation . . . so that if man should wish to capitalize on it, he may" (Lopes Cardozo 159). Rabbi Joshua Haberman, writing in *Contemporary Jewish Religious Thought*, draws together well the issues of righteous thought and action:

> To the Jew, the commandments of Torah are both sacrament and salvation. They are vehicles of divine grace insofar as in their joyful performance the Jew is brought into the closest possible relation with God. New Testament distinctions made by Paul between a righteousness of faith and of works (Rom. 4) appears to the Jewish mind as irrelevant. (835)

A pious spirit is, in rabbinic thought, always inherently connected to right action—specifically, following *mitzvot*. And this insistence on the commandments comes from the understanding that fulfilling God's commandments is the way the Divine has given people to enter into communion with God. *Mitzvot* are, then, the established, ritual expression of religious mystery in Judaism.

CATHOLIC SACRAMENTS: RITUALS CONFERRING GRACE

Catholicism, like Judaism, provides a specific, ritualized method for entering into God's presence. Rather than 613 *mitzvot*, which regulate all of life, Catholicism recognizes seven sacraments, which have a more explicitly religious aura in their performance, but they, too, have an impact on all of life. The seven sacraments are baptism, confirmation, Eucharist, penance and reconciliation, anointing the sick, holy orders, and matrimony. Partaking in these ceremonies is essential for Catholics because it is through them that a believer can get a sense of the numinous, as the Catechism explains: "Celebrated worthily in faith, the sacraments confer the grace that they signify. They are *efficacious* because in them Christ himself is at work: it is he who baptizes, he who acts in his sacraments in order to communicate the grace that each sacrament signifies" (292). Thus, the sacraments serve as a concrete expression of religious mystery; through them, the believer is enabled to encounter God. Aquinas, noting that they make visible what is unseen, pointed out the importance of partaking in these sacraments: "Sacraments are necessary for man's salvation inasmuch as they constitute certain sensible signs of invisible things by which man is sanctified" (*Summa Theologiae* 3a, 61, 3). Sacraments are the central religious action in the life of a Catholic, opening the way for the believer to experience God's grace.

Grace, which is of paramount concern in Catholic theology, is a term that refers to the unmerited gift of God's presence in a believer. The *Catechism* says:

> Our justification comes from the grace of God. Grace is *favor*, the *free and undeserved help* that God gives us to respond to his call to become children of God, adoptive sons, partakers of the divine nature and of eternal life. . . . The grace of Christ is the gratuitous gift that God makes to us of his own life, infused by the Holy Spirit into our soul to heal it of sin and to sanctify it. (483–84)

According to Catholic doctrine, although a person has freedom whether or not to respond to God, even one's inner preparation to receive Christ is a gift of grace (*Catechism* 484–85). Further, since grace "belongs to the supernatural order, grace *escapes our experience* and cannot be known except by faith" (*Catechism* 486). Thus, the sacraments are essential to give Catholics a specific way to receive this grace.

Although all the sacraments are seen to originate in the New Testament, the seven sacraments recognized by the Church were not officially instituted until the Middle Ages. In a manner in some ways parallel to the Jewish attitude toward the Talmud, the Catholic Church does not claim that all revealed truth comes directly from the Bible; rather, "[b]oth Scripture and Tradition must be accepted and honored with equal sentiments of devotion and reverence" (*Catechism* 26). Thus, the writings of the Church Fathers are central to an understanding of the Catholic view of sacraments. When Augustine spoke of the sacraments, he was primarily thinking of two, baptism and the Eucharist (Ganoczy 50). Augustine played an important role in providing a theoretical basis for these sacraments, suggesting the symbolic level of the rituals, with the water of baptism signifying inner cleansing and the many grains brought together in bread symbolizing the Church, even as he emphasized that the sacraments effect what they symbolize (Ganoczy 20, 24). In the twelfth century, Peter Lombard published in Paris a work that listed the seven sacraments. Since this was a popular collection, the seven he listed became increasingly accepted and were eventually set out by the most important voice in Catholic theology, St. Thomas Aquinas (Martos 68). Lombard's definition of a sacrament brought together two aspects of sacraments: "Something is properly called a sacrament because it is a *sign* of God's grace, and is such an image of invisible grace that it bears its likeness and exists as its *cause*" (qtd. in Martos 69, emphasis added).

This conception of sacraments serving as both signs and causes of God's grace is an important aspect of Aquinas' theology. Aquinas argues that it is entirely appropriate that God's grace comes to people in visible signs, for it was through the power of Christ, who came in bodily form, that salvation is possible (*Summa Contra Gentiles* 247). Aquinas gives three reasons why physical sacraments are necessary for salvation: people reach knowledge deductively through experience, so sacraments give a physical sense of faith; because of sin, people have a natural affection for the physical, so sacraments remedy the sickness by means of human tendency; and in general activities, humans tend to enter into physical action, so sacraments are made to be not too difficult for people (*Summa Theologiae* 3a,61,1). More than simply being a sign that human beings can experience, Aquinas also strongly argues that sacraments cause grace. He does, though, differentiate between principal and instrumental causes. Principal causes produce effects by virtue of their power; with sacraments, God alone is the principal cause. An instrumental cause acts not on its own force but by the "impetus imparted to it by the principal agent" (*Summa Theologiae* 3a,62,1). Thus, it is more accurate to speak of the grace coming from a sacrament as an instrument rather than as a vessel, for "grace is in a sacrament in the sense of flowing through it, that is in an incomplete mode of being." There is, therefore, "a divine power acting as co-assistant to the sacrament and it is this that produces the sacramental effect" (*Summa Theologiae* 3a,62,4).

Recognizing that it is the force behind the sacrament that causes grace does not for Aquinas lessen the power of the sacrament itself. Indeed, Aquinas says:

> what is acquired by a thing through consecration persists in that thing forever. . . . Therefore, the power of their orders persists in the ministers of the church perpetually. Therefore, it is not taken away by sin. Therefore, even sinners and evil men, provided they have orders, are able to confer the sacraments of the Church. (*Summa Contra Gentiles* 293)

Because of this abiding power of the sacraments, "a man's being good or bad does not make him able to dispense the sacraments, but suitable or unsuitable for dispensing them well" (*Summa Contra Gentiles* 293). The sacraments, then, have a power outside the realm of fallible humans—either the minister or the participant. Aquinas' strong sense of the mysterious power of the sacraments sparked various responses, but the Church ultimately accepted his position. Duns Scotus and a Franciscan "school" of thought argued against Aquinas' view that the sacraments contained grace. For them, the sacraments prepared a person to receive grace, which God then confers separately (Ganoczy 28). A different response to Aquinas' teaching that sacraments cause grace came from a group identified today as "the canonists." The canonists determined that if grace was conferred through the ritual, it must be extremely important that the sacrament be performed with exacting ceremony to ensure that grace is, in fact, bestowed

(Martos 86). This concern with ritualistic details in part sparked the Protestant Reformation. But even though the Council of Trent responded to many of the reformers' criticism, they retained Aquinas' emphasis on the sacraments' necessity for salvation and their power regardless of the specific merits of any one person. The Council declared, "If anyone says that grace is not conferred by the sacraments of the new law through the sacramental action itself, but that faith in the divine promise is by itself sufficient for obtaining the grace: let him be anathema" (session 7, canon on sacraments 8). And even though the Council insisted that ministers must have "the intention of at least doing what the church does" (session 7, canon on sacraments 11), it also said that even a minister in mortal sin could administer a sacrament (session 7, canon on sacraments 12).

This emphasis on sacraments' power independent of individual participants is carried into the current catechism. Sacraments work *ex opere operato*, which literally means "by the very fact of the action's being performed." In other words, since Christ's death has already accomplished his saving work,

> It follows that "the sacrament is not wrought by the righteousness of either the celebrant or the recipient, but by the power of God." From the moment that sacrament is celebrated in accordance with the intention of the Church, the power of Christ and his Spirit acts in and through it, independently of the personal holiness of the minister. Nevertheless, the fruits of the sacraments also depend on the disposition of the one who receives them. (*Catechism* 292)

As the *Catechism* makes clear, how the grace is received (the "fruits") depends on the believer's personal state. But in any case, a participant in a sacrament can know with certainty that grace is being offered when he or she partakes of a sacrament.

What makes this emphasis on the power of the sacraments so important for an understanding of religious mystery in Catholicism is that it concretely shows the nonrational element of belief. Catholicism proclaims a faith in the efficacy of ritual actions—with little regard for the piety of the minister or the recipient—because of the steadfast belief that the grace of God works through these actions. It is only because of this faith in the power of God that the sacraments have any meaning.

Since sacraments are central to Catholic theology, it seems useful to examine two of them in greater depth. As noted earlier, baptism and the Eucharist were the ones first recognized by the Church Fathers, and Aquinas also emphasized that these two are the most important of the sacraments, because the sacraments grow from the power of Christ's passion: "This is signified by the fact that from the side of Christ hanging on the Cross there flowed water and blood, the first of which pertains to baptism and the second to the Eucharist, these two being the greatest of the sacraments" (*Summa Theologiae* 3a,62,5). Thus, the remainder of this chapter examines in more detail baptism and the Eucharist to work toward a more complete understanding of the sacraments' role in being a concrete outworking of mystery.

The central issue about baptism that the Church Fathers and later theologians have discussed concerns the exact purpose of baptism: what does the action signify and accomplish? The emphasis in Catholic teaching focuses on the importance of baptism for salvation. Tertullian (c. 200) taught that in the New Testament, a different procedure for coming to faith in God was given:

> Granted that in former days, before the Lord's passion and resurrection, there was salvation through bare faith; still, now that faith has been enlarged to include belief in his birth, passion, and resurrection, there is an enlargement added to the mystery, namely, the sealing of baptism: the clothing, as it were, of the faith which before was bare. (qtd. in Bettenson *Early Christian Fathers* 144)

Gregory of Nyssa, in the fourth century, tried to explain the connection between the substance of the water and the action that occurs. He emphasized that it is not the water itself that gives grace, but rather God through his Spirit "comes sacramentally to give us liberty." Nevertheless, the water's importance should not be underestimated since it gives "an outward sign of the purification" (qtd. in Bettenson *Later Christian Fathers* 161). Writing about the same time, Cyril of Jerusalem also attempted to find the balance between inward action and outward sign: "If anyone has been baptized with water, without being counted worthy of the Spirit, he does not have the grace in its completeness; while no one will go into the Kingdom of Heaven, however virtuous in his actions he may prove to be, if he does not receive the seal given by means of water" (qtd. in Bettenson *Later Christian Fathers* 39).[7]

Augustine, Aquinas, and later Church doctrine also attempted to balance the importance of a pious inward spirit with a strong emphasis on the unconstrained power of the act of baptism itself. Thus, Augustine argued that if even a "profane or polluted" man should baptize, that baptism is still valid: "No difference is made to the sanctity of baptism by the demerit of the individual who receives or confers it." On the other hand, though, Augustine also said, "the sacrament of baptism is one thing, the conversion of the heart is another; but the salvation of man is effected by these two" (qtd. in Bettenson *Later Christian Fathers* 243). Similarly, Aquinas held that the symbol of washing in baptism is appropriate since it parallels its spiritual effect (*Summa Contra Gentiles* 250). But he, too, emphasized that the sacrament is much more than symbol, since no salvation is possible without baptism, or at least the desire for it (*Summa Theologiae* 3a,68,2). And the sacrament has power beyond any human qualities, "[f]or the sacrament is perfected not through the righteousness of the minister or the recipient of baptism, but rather through the power of God" (*Summa Theologiae* 3a, 68,8). Likewise, the Council of Trent affirmed the necessity of baptism: "If anyone says that baptism is an option, namely that it is not necessary for salvation, let him be anathema" (session 7, canon on baptism 5). The *Catechism*, too, accepts this high view of baptism, saying that this sacrament "signifies and actually brings about the birth of the water and the Spirit without which no one 'can enter the kingdom of God'" (312). Baptism is central because "the Church does not know any means other than Baptism that assures entry into eternal beatitude" (320). Baptism, then, is taught by the Catholic Church to be the ritual necessary to enter into relationship with God. It is designed to be the point of entry into the mystery of Christ.

The ongoing, regular encounter with God occurs through the Eucharist, the commemoration in which each believer takes into him or herself the elements of bread and wine, miraculously transformed into the body and blood of Christ. This practice is believed by Catholics to have been instituted by Jesus at the Last Supper, when he gave his disciples bread and wine, telling them to eat and drink his body and blood. The Church Fathers focused on two primary questions in their consideration of the Eucharist: how can these elements of bread and wine actually turn into the body and blood of Christ; and what effect does partaking of communion have on the believer? Cyril of Jerusalem, writing in the fourth century, is typical of much Patristic teaching when he urged believers to look beyond the physical qualities of the elements: "For though sense suggests the mere elements, let faith assure you otherwise. Do not judge the matter from taste, but from faith be assured, without hesitation, that you have been granted the body and blood of Christ" (qtd. in Bettenson *Later Christian Fathers* 45). Taking a quite different tack, John Chrysostom, also in the fourth century, urged communicants to have a much more physical experience of the Eucharistic celebration: "What the Lord did not endure on the cross [the breaking of his legs] he submits to now in his sacrifice for his love of you: he permits himself to be broken in pieces that all may be filled." In fact, Chrysostom said, "Not only ought we to see the Lord: we ought to take him in our hands, eat him, put our teeth in his flesh, and unite ourselves with him in the closest union" (qtd. in Bettenson *Later Christian Fathers* 174–75). Chrysostom's very physical sense of the Eucharist was not the more accepted one, however. Cyril of Alexandria, writing after Chrysostom, said that it was necessary for Christ to be brought into human bodies to ensure life with Christ. But he downplayed the fleshly substance of the elements: "so that we should not be struck down with horror, at seeing flesh and blood displayed on the holy tables of our churches, God adapts himself to our weakness and infuses the power of life into the oblations and changes them into the effective power of his own flesh" (qtd. in Bettenson *Later Christian Fathers* 268).

Accepted church doctrine taught that the elements did in fact become the body and blood of Christ, but it emphasized, as Cyril of Jerusalem had, that the change was visible only through eyes of faith. Aquinas dealt at some length with concerns about how the bread and wine could still look and taste like their original forms but contain the body and blood of Christ. In brief, Aquinas' explanation hinged on differentiating between the accidents (the physical form) and the substance (what is really there); in transubstantiation, the substance changes but the accidents remain the same (*Summa Contra Gentiles* 253–68). The Council of Trent was less concerned with elaborate explanations of how Christ becomes present in the elements than in affirming that such a transformation does in fact take place: "after the consecration of the bread and wine, our lord Jesus Christ, true God and true man, is truly, really and substantially contained in the propitious sacrament of the holy eucharist under the appearance of those things which are perceptible to the sense" (session 13 chapter 1). Likewise, the *Catechism* says simply, "The signs of bread and wine become, in a way surpassing understanding, the Body and Blood of Christ" (336). Recognizing the mystery, the Church nevertheless affirms that at each mass a miracle takes place; Christ becomes present in the elements and is thus available to each believer.

Because Christ is literally taken in by each participant of the Eucharist, the Church emphasizes the connection between bodily nourishment and spiritual nourishment that takes place in the Eucharist. As early as the second century, Irenaeus noted that since the communion bread, when it becomes the body of Christ, is both earthly and heavenly, "so our bodies, after partaking of the Eucharist, are no longer corruptible, having the hope of the eternal resurrection" (qtd. in Bettenson *Early Christian Fathers* 96). Taking in the elements, then, mysteriously strengthens a believer's soul since Christ has entered that person's physical body, as Clement of Alexandria made clear: "the eating and drinking of the divine Word is the knowledge of the Divine essence" (qtd. in Bettenson *Early Christian Fathers* 181). Gregory of Nyssa, writing in the fourth century, also emphasized the link of immortality that comes to humans through the Eucharist: "It is for this purpose that by the divine plan of his grace he plants himself in the believers by means of that flesh, composed of bread and wine, blending himself with the bodies of believers so that man also may share in immortality by union with the immortal" (qtd. in Bettenson *Later Christian Fathers* 163). This same teaching of Christ being joined to humans through the Eucharist is reiterated in the *Catechism*:

> As bodily nourishment restores lost strength, so the Eucharist strengthens our charity, which tends to be weakened in daily life; and this living charity *wipes away venial sins*. By giving himself to us Christ revives our love and enables us to break our disordered attachments to creatures and root ourselves in him. . . . The more we share the life of Christ and progress in his friendship, the more difficult it is to break away from him by mortal sin. (352)

The Eucharist, then, serves as a physical way for Catholics to draw near to God.

Baptism and the Eucharist are for Catholics doors to the divine, giving believers a ritualized way to experience the grace of God. These two sacraments are especially important because, as Aquinas explained, baptism is "spiritual rebirth" while the Eucharist is "spiritual nourishment" (*Summa Contra Gentiles* 253). Rather than making believers find their own ways to encounter God, the Catholic Church provides specific rituals in which they can experience the mystery of faith. As the Council of Trent proclaimed, the Eucharist and the other elements are "a sign of sacred reality and the visible form of invisible grace" (session 13, chapter 3). The sacraments are a physical expression of entering into relationship with God.

As this overview of *mitzvot* and sacraments has shown, both rabbinic Judaism and Catholicism have a strong sense of religious mystery. By accepting doctrines that cannot be rationally proven—specifically in this case that *mitzvot* have a divine basis and that sacraments confer grace—believers in both religions recognize the limits of reason in their beliefs. Judaism and Catholicism, then, provide a concrete process to partake of religious mystery, through following the commandments or partaking in the sacraments. Joseph Martos argues that all religions have their own sacred actions, but that these actions are "not revered because of what they are in themselves. . . . [T]hey point to or symbolize something beyond themselves—something mysterious, something which cannot be seen, something special" (13). It is this function that *mitzvot* and sacraments fulfill in Judaism and Catholicism as they point believers to a sense of the numinous. They embody the religious mystery that is at the heart of each religion.

While the similarity in the approach to religious mystery in Judaism and Catholicism has been emphasized, the differences in the specific methods used to move beyond the rational should, of course, not be overlooked. *Mitzvot* are regulations that, though they invoke the numinous, are also obviously important for ordering everyday interpersonal relations. Sacraments, on the other hand, remain on the level of religious ceremony, although their conferring of grace is certainly intended to change the individual's daily actions. This difference has potential implications in the way that the sense of mystery is represented by the authors discussed.

Understanding that both Jewish and Catholic theology do contain a nonrational element is central for a proper reading of the four authors studied here, since each attempts to portray a religious perspective in his or her fiction. For these authors, their religion's understanding of mystery seems to have become a part of their writing so that their fiction portrays a mysterious, nonrational level of belief. More specifically, just as Judaism and Catholicism provide a concrete expression of religious mystery, so these narratives—as the authors embody religious beliefs in literature—represent mystery through the material particulars of the fiction. As the following chapters will show, the forms of these narratives by Malamud, Percy, Ozick, and O'Connor all give substance to religious mystery. Interestingly, the four authors' use of the physical to suggest mystery does not always follow the pattern set out in their religions, with Percy and O'Connor in particular often sanctifying the ordinary in their fiction. Recognizing these methods for giving concrete form to mystery will help readers to make sense of this sometimes puzzling fiction—and to reach for the anagogical level that is so central to these authors' narratives.

NOTES

1. The Hebrew word for commandments is transliterated in various forms. In my study, I will consistently spell it *mitzvot*, even if a source I am quoting uses a different spelling.

2. It may seem that Maimonides, predominantly known as a rationalist in his work with Jewish law, is not a likely source in a discussion about the nonrational. Yet it is significant that even this rationalist recognized the limits of reason in belief, showing that the nonrational holds an important place in rabbinic Judaism. Further, as David Ariel explains, Maimonides "maintained that personal spirituality in addition to faithful practice of the law constituted the proper life for a Jew" (167), suggesting that his emphasis on the law provided Maimonides with a basis for sensing the numinous. Conservative Rabbi Ethan Seidel reiterates this view, saying that while Maimonides was a rationalist, this aspect of his work does not in any way undermine his consideration of the nonrational. In fact, Seidel notes that Maimonides is today popular among those Jews who are emphasizing a more spiritual or nonrational approach to Judaism.

3. Only holding these beliefs is, of course, not sufficient to be considered a good Jew. Performing righteous deeds must always accompany proper thinking.

4. This phrase comes from Joseph Martos' title of his study of sacraments.

5. Judaism certainly has rituals that are a part of its practice, such as circumcision, the Passover seder, and the lighting of the Sabbath candles, all of which function on the nonrational level. A significant number of these practices are directed by *mitzvot* and so are, at least indirectly, a part of the discussion of this chapter. While one could certainly make useful comparisons between Jewish rituals and Catholic sacraments, this chapter focuses on *mitzvot* because they—rather than the rituals themselves—make up the center of Jewish religious life. Since the goal of this chapter is to discuss the importance of religious mystery in the two religions, it seems necessary to focus on the elements of each religion that form its core.

6. Indeed, a famous talmudic story seems to support this point. As Robert Gordis retells the episode,

> the archconservative and highly respected Rabbi Eliezer ben Hyrcanus forcefully presented his view on the question under discussion, but none of his colleagues in the academy agreed. To justify his position, he called upon a series of three miracles, each of which duly took place. When his colleagues remained unconvinced, he asked that a *Bat kol*, "a heavenly voice," pronounce judgment on the issue. It was heard to say, "Who are you to differ with Rabbi Eliezer, for the law is according to his view on every question." Nothing daunted, Rabbi Joshua cited Deuteronomy 30.12, which declares, "'It is not in heaven.' This means that the Torah has already been given on Sinai. We pay no attention to heavenly voices, for You have already written at Sinai in the Torah that we must follow the majority." Rabbi Nathan then met the Prophet Elijah and asked, "What did God do in that hour?" Elijah answered, "He smiled and said, 'My children have overcome me!'" (79)

7. Giving such a priority to one specific sacramental action is a significant difference from Jewish theology, which defines performing proper deeds (as set out in *mitzvot*) as the way to reach God.

3

"Impossible to Say": Malamud's and Percy's Quests for Commitment

At its best our age is an age of searchers and discoverers, and at its worst, an age that has domesticated despair and learned to live with it happily.

—Flannery O'Connor[1]
"Novelist and Believer"

In good fiction and drama you need to go through the concrete situation to some experience of mystery.

—Flannery O'Connor[2]
The Habit of Being

Walker Percy and Bernard Malamud are not often studied together.[3] And because of their differences—southern Catholic as opposed to northeastern Jew, to name just the most obvious—it may seem somewhat incongruous to link them. Even their discussions about their lives are disparate: Malamud tended to be fairly taciturn about his life, revealing that he grew up in a not particularly religious Jewish New York shopkeeper's family, with many parallels to what is represented in *The Assistant*. From an early age he wanted to be a writer, and he pursued the craft while he was earning a living at several different jobs.

As for his religious commitment, Malamud has not said much definitively in his public comments. During one question-and-answer session, he says, "I have had no orthodoxy in my life and very little Jewish living. That is to say, that my father was not a religious man. . . . I know very little of the synagogue life from experience" (*Talking Horse* 124). He emphasizes, though, that there are different ways to think of being Jewish: "By definition, it helps to have had a Jewish mother, but I'm a Jew pretty much because at a certain point in my youth I felt the need to define myself as one. I had consciously related to the Jewish experience" (*Talking Horse* 182). In a 1971 interview, he explains, "I don't live a Jewish life in the religious sense, though I have been influenced by their concern about morality" (*Conversations with Bernard Malamud* 34). Lawrence Lasher finds Malamud's enunciation of "[t]he struggle against self" (*Conversations with Bernard Malamud* 50) as the "core of Jewish ethical experience" for Malamud (Introduction xv). As such, Malamud shows a nonrational commitment to a set of values established outside of himself, particularly in his valuation of humanity: "The suffering of the Jews is a distinct thing for me. I for one believe that not enough has been made of the tragedy of the destruction of 6,000,000 Jews. And I felt the same in 1936 when the Yellow River flooded and six to ten million Chinese were drowned. Not enough has been made of such tragedies. Somebody has to cry—even if it's just a writer, 20 years later" (*Conversations with Bernard Malamud* 5–6). Thus, Joel Salzberg discovers in the fiction "a Malamudian anger directed at the divine indifference in the face of human suffering" (2). Nevertheless, when Malamud is pressed about his belief in God, he observes, "I think it was Carlyle who said whether he believed in God was his business and God's" (*Conversations with Bernard Malamud* 133).

Even though many of the letters and addresses found in the Bernard Malamud Papers of the Library of Congress reiterate Malamud's published comments on belief,[4] we get a rare glimpse into Malamud's thoughts about God through his notes written during his planning for his final completed novel, *God's Grace*. Among his (as always) meticulous notes—including folders of information on primates and even sketched maps of Cohn's Island—Malamud had pages of documentation in a "Biblical-Religious material" folder. Along with careful notes on many sections of the Pentateuch, Malamud took some eleven pages of notes on an essay by Irving Greenberg, "Cloud of Smoke, Pillar of Fire: Judaism, Christianity, and Modernity after the Holocaust," which argues that belief in God must not be static but rather dialectical. While much of Malamud's writing on these pages simply records information, at points he is more reflective. In a marginal comment in his notes, he says of Greenberg's essay, "The argument is basically believe in God" (I:25). More personally, Malamud laments, "Was it mad reasoning that created the Holocaust or impure feeling? Why couldn't man have been created with an ounce more of compassion? That might have made all the difference" (I:25). Although not definitive, these comments and his attention to Greenberg's essay suggest at least that Malamud was engaged with issues of belief and the Creator.

In his early planning for *God's Grace*, though, Malamud was direct about what he was trying to accomplish in the novel—and, by extension, about his sense of God. In a "Religious Statement," dated January 7, 1979, Malamud attempts to articulate to himself the religious implications of the novel—intriguingly mixing seemingly Christian ideas about grace with a negative view of the Church; at the same time, he is also contemplating the novel's characters:

> What would the religious statement be: that civilization fails without God. That God must be reinvented as a spirit of saving grace. But Cohn doesn't believe in God. Is it a gracious thing for a non-believer to teach God (a failed priest? all priests have failed because the

church has failed.) So he sets himself honestly to face God. There is some success until they stop believing in him. Where the representative of God fails to represent him, there is no belief in God. (I:25)

Malamud concludes this statement with a summary of the novel's ending. While these jottings from Malamud are specifically related to his plans for what he identifies earlier in that day's notes as "a religious allegory" (I:25), the belief that God is essential for civilization seems to be a personal stance. Such a belief is underlined in Malamud's further reflections on November 15, 1979, in a document labeled "The Tribe" with his prompting question being, "Why write the book?" In the course of his thoughts, Malamud writes these significant lines about the spiritual life:

What do I truly believe about our society? That we will destroy ourselves? What about God? He doesn't exist in the book, though Cohen [sic] tries to bring him to life. Is the message that there must be a god? What is Cohen preaching?

Why can't he "sell" the spiritual life. His own weaknesses?: He has no God of his own, no God he is passionate about. He succumbs to the instinctual? He hasn't done as much as he ought to do. (I:25)

Although Malamud is dissatisfied with his grasp of the novel, writing at the end of these notes that "I don't think I have it yet," we can see the way that Malamud seems to value belief in God, a God that one is "passionate about." Indeed, Malamud seems almost to reject here the ethical humanism with which he is commonly identified: Cohn failes in his efforts to civilize the other creatures, Malamud suggests, because he attempts to do so without a basis in a belief in God. While one should not make too strong a claim based on these comments, it does seem clear that Malamud believed—at least near the end of his life—that a sense of God should undergird ethical decisions. Not surprisingly, Malamud's moral focus is consistently apparent in his thoughts about the novel; in fact, in a November 16 note, he articulates the novel's message as "You must not be beastly" (I:25).

Yet there is also here an openness in speaking about God that is not found in his public comments. Malamud seems to articulate a need for God as the basis of the moral stance that he so clearly states. These two complementary elements are succinctly stated at the end of a January 7, 1979, outline of *God's Grace*:

Ethically/morally what does the above mean?

1. You can't be against God and try to teach God. But if you are concerned with[?] God it is better for you than not to be concerned.

2. If you are a man you must not act like a beast. You cannot. If you are a man you must—as a leader—a prophet treat (men) beings (morally.) You cannot lie to them or be cruel. (You must be ethical). (I:25)

In these two points, Malamud brings together for himself two themes that seem important not only in *God's Grace* but in many of his novels: whether or not an orthodox stance is possible, one should be focused on and struggling with one's belief in God; and ethical behavior is central to life.

Far from the sleuthing required to understand Malamud's beliefs, Percy has so often repeated in his interviews how he became a writer and believer that the story has nearly reached legendary status: his father committed suicide when Percy was a boy, and his mother died shortly thereafter. He was raised by a cousin, "Uncle Will," who was an adherent to the Southern stoic tradition, much like Aunt Emily in *The Moviegoer*. Percy was graduated from medical school, but while he was fulfilling an internship, he contracted tuberculosis and was sent away for "the rest cure." It was during this time that Percy began to read seriously in some of the important existentialist writers, most prominently Kierkegaard and Marcel. As he read, he began to see that there was more to life than the beautiful simplicity of science:

> What began to interest me was not so much a different question as a larger question, not the physiological and pathological processes within man's body but the problem of man himself, the nature and destiny of man . . . . An extraordinary paradox became clear: that the more science progressed, and even as it benefited man, the less it said about what it is like to be a man living in the world. (*Signposts* 188)

Percy often relates in his essays and interviews that his experience with science paralleled Kierkegaard's sense when he had finished reading Hegel: "Hegel, said Kierkegaard, explained everything under the sun, except one small detail: what it means to be a man living in the world who must die" (*Signposts* 188). Since he found science insufficient, after a time of contemplation Percy joined the Catholic Church, finding faith to be not just a leap into the absurd, as Kierkegaard said, but affirming with St. Thomas Aquinas that "faith is a form of knowledge" (*Conversations with Walker Percy* 204). Percy took his new commitment seriously; he is described by priests and religious women who worked with him as a "'conservative, devout Catholic,' one who tended to accept, witout demanding argumentative motivation, the tenets of his faith" (Samway "Grappling" 18). This faith serves as a central perspective for Percy's writing, since his fiction has gained recognition both for his style, for which he says he is indebted to Sartre and Camus, and for his portrayal of his philosophical ideas in his fiction.

Yet even though the specifics of these authors' lives and perspectives are quite distinctive, the important commonality that draws these novelists together is that their fiction seems to operate on an anagogical level as they present characters who are searching for meaning and commitment. Obviously one can never know with certainty what an author is intending in a novel, but, to use Robert Detweiler's expression, these texts seem to show "an openness to a religious reading" (xiv), suggesting an anagogical dimension. This sense is reinforced by the authors' comments about their understanding of their role as writer, indicating that representing a spiritual dimension is a part of their goal. The anagogical or spiritual level in writing is the final of the four levels of interpretation that Dante sets out, what he calls the "'sense beyond.' This sense occurs when a spiritual interpretation is to be given a text which, even though it is true on the literal level, represents the supreme things belonging to eternal glory by means of the thing it represents" (113). Dante uses Psalm 113.1–2 as an example: "When Israel went out of Egypt, the house of Jacob from a barbarous people, Judea was made his sanctuary, Israel his dominion." On a literal level, the psalm describes "the departure of the sons of Israel from Egypt." On an anagogical level, though, "what is signified to us is the departure of the sanctified soul from bondage to the corruption of this world into the freedom of eternal glory" (99). Malamud's and Percy's novels can be interpreted on an anagogical level as they show a mysterious step toward belief that requires a movement beyond the rational.

Just as the specific religious character of Malamud's life is not immediately obvious, so, too, his novels resist an easy categorization. Rarely do his characters clearly embrace rabbinic Judaism, but they often show a movement toward a moral stance, which Malamud seems to connect to "the metaphorical and moral dimensions of Jewish experience" (Salzberg 1). This perspective is underlined by Malamud's own conception of what an author must do: "The purpose of the writer . . . is to keep civilization from destroying itself. But without preachment. Artists, cannot be ministers. As soon as they attempt it, they destroy their artistry" (*Conversations with Bernard Malamud* 7). He made a similar comment in his address when he won the National Book Award for *The Magic Barrel* in 1959:

> the writer must imagine a better world for men the while he shows us, in all its ugliness and beauty, the possibilities of this. In recreating the humanity of man, in reality his greatness, he will, among other things, hold up the mirror to the mystery of him, in which poetry and possibility live, though he has endlessly betrayed them. ("Writer's Task" 173)

Even more than a general moral sense, though, some of Malamud's characters are wrestling with understanding and relating to God. As Malamud explains in an interview, "Someone said recently that my characters are God-haunted. . . . There are some characters who strongly believe in God. And let me add that I don't feel inhibited in inventing God-haunted characters, which has nothing to do with whether I am or am not religious" (*Conversations with Bernard Malamud* 50). This "God-haunted" quality of Malamud's characters, with its implications of moral actions, seems central for an understanding of religious mystery in his writing. As Daniel Walden suggests, "For Malamud what is supremely important is man's relationship to the Law, meaning doing what is right when it has to be done, no matter the suffering" (156). Although not all his protagonists come to the same final stance, Malamud shows many of his characters on religious quests, attempting to make sense of and put into action their relationship with God.

Percy makes it very clear in his essays and interviews that his Catholicism has a direct impact on his writing—and specifically on his portrayal of mystery. In describing his stance as a writer, Percy says, "As it happens, I speak in a Christian context. That is to say, I do not conceive it my vocation to preach the

Christian faith in a novel, but as it happens, my world view is informed by a certain belief about man's nature and destiny which cannot fail to be central to any novel I write" (*Message* 111). Being a part of the Catholic Church, Percy explains, is not oppressive but is rather liberating because "[i]t puts you in touch . . . with the mystery, and that, in truth, religion has to do with mysteries" (*More Conversations* 5). More explicitly, Percy briefly states, at least in part, his conception of faith: "Faith consists of two or three mysteries: the Incarnation is a mystery, the Trinity is a mystery, and the real Presence in the Eucharist is a mystery. But that is the end of the search, that is the end of the quest, you don't go beyond that. Either you believe that, or you don't" (*More Conversations* 106). Percy feels the importance of his message so strongly that he once wrote to Caroline Gordon, "Actually I do not consider myself a novelist but a moralist or a propagandist. My spiritual father is Pascal (and/or Kierkegaard). And if I also kneel before the altar of Lawrence and Joyce and Flaubert, it is not because I wish to do what they did, even if I could. What I really want to do is to tell people *what they must do and what they must believe if they want to live*" (qtd. in Tolson 301).[5] Nevertheless, Percy recognizes the danger of openly religious language in his fiction:

> James Joyce said that an artist must be above all things cunning and guileful and use every trick in the bag to achieve his purpose. In my view the language of religion, the very words themselves, are almost bankrupt. If you are writing a technical article on philosophy you can use the correct word for the correct meaning. But writing a novel is something different. In my view you have to be wary of using words like "religion," "God," "sin," "salvation," "baptism" because the words are almost worn out. The themes have to be implicit rather than explicit. (*Conversations with Walker Percy* 79)

Indeed, when Percy was revising a section of *The Moviegoer* to be published as a separate story before the novel was completed, he noted, "It is gradually forcing itself upon me in the most painful way that it is almost impossible to Catholicize, pro or con, without falling on your face. . . . My revision will largely consist of removing Catholic licks (and all other licks)" (qtd. in Samway *Life*). Because of his view that novelists cannot use specifically religious language, most of his novels do not detail a conversion using traditional religious terminology, thus leading critics to varying interpretations. As Percy says, he can only take the character to a certain point and then "[y]ou've got to get out" (*Conversations with Walker Percy* 235).

Percy's explanation about the dangers of openly religious commitments suggests that we may need to look elsewhere in the fiction to understand a character's mysterious religious movement. Percy believes that Christianity is especially congenial to the novel "because the novel has to do with narration, and narration has to do with a person born to trouble as the sparks fly up. . . . The whole thrust of Catholic belief is that man is *homo viator*. Man is real and man is in trouble. In theological terms, man is fallen. His life is a journey" (*More Conversations* 123). Malamud's comments, after the publication of his final completed novel *God's Grace*, sound remarkably like Percy's: he notes his sense over the years "that man was in trouble," that "man in many ways was a disappointment to himself" (*Conversations with Bernard Malamud* 112–13).[6] The specific understanding of "trouble" in the two religions obviously differs, with Judaism stressing the divergence from ethical earthly living while Catholicism adds to that the idea of eternal punishments or rewards. Nevertheless, because of their recognition of the human predicament, Malamud and Percy often in their fiction show their protagonists searching for an answer, on a quest for meaning. It is in the course of these quests that Malamud's and Percy's novels embody a sense of mystery as the characters move toward commitment.[7]

As discussed in the previous chapter, Judaism and Catholicism both provide concrete practices—*mitzvot* and sacraments—as a way for believers to participate in religious mystery. Malamud and Percy parallel this approach by giving structure to their presentation of the nonrational: they use the quest myth as an ordering device in their novels. This form gives specific shape to the mystery presented in the narratives so that, without specifically stating a nonrational commitment, the novels can hint at what has occurred. In the course of these quests, the novels contain specific physical actions or images that suggest the anagogical level, again mirroring the way that *mitzvot* and sacraments provide a physical access to the ineffable in each religion. Interestingly, while *mitzvot* emphasize sanctifying the ordinary and the sacraments remain specifically religious ceremonies, Malamud's and Percy's fiction does not show such a clear division. Novels by each author employ both ordinary images that seem freighted with religious significance as well as more overtly religious actions. This mixing may occur because both religions do include elements of religious ritual as well as ethical action, though (as shown in Chapter 2) the emphasis is divergent. Another equally plausible reason may involve simply the requirements of fiction: to communicate, novels need to have concrete details, so any devices that help give solid form to mystery may be used to hint at the ineffable. Often shunning traditional religious language, the authors use such techniques as paradox, irony, mythical suggestions, and biblical overtones that seem to communicate theological meaning. Even though they do not directly state their protagonists' encounter with mystery, their fiction clearly engages such issues.[8] Their narratives exemplify what Flannery O'Connor believes should happen in good fiction: their novels "go through the concrete situation to some experience of mystery" (*Habit of Being* 520).

The specific goal of Malamud's and Percy's quests, as the chapter title suggests, is a movement toward commitment. But though both writers have said that they conceive their task to include a definite moral message in their novels, they intend to present their fiction (to use Malamud's expression) "without preachment." Thus, it is hardly surprising that any religious sense that readers find in their novels may not be presented in traditional religious language—or that the commitment the characters make is not always easily identifiable as religious in nature. The protagonists may, for instance, make a selfless commitment to a person or community. But such a dedication moves beyond humanism and toward religious mystery when it is motivated by the character's following of a biblical moral code, showing an adherence to a set of values that must be simply accepted rather than rationally explained. Even more closely connected to the nonrational, in some instances the protagonist's commitment seems motivated by a sense of the numinous, a response to a feeling of awe from encountering the "wholly other" (Otto 26). In these instances, the narratives suggest through some tangible action that the protagonist's change from self-centeredness to selfless commitment—to others and, by extension, to God—is brought about by a recognition of a divine force. Although the specifics vary among the novels, these quests do portray a sense of the ineffable.

THE ARTHURIAN (AND SPIRITUAL) QUESTS: *THE NATURAL* AND *LANCELOT*

That the quest theme holds a prominent place in each writer's imagination is confirmed by the explicit use of the Arthurian quest myth in a novel by each of the authors, Malamud's *The Natural* and Percy's *Lancelot.* These novels are probably not the most conspicuous examples of religious searching in each author's oeuvre, although there are such hints in the novels, as will be discussed later. More important, though, is their clear use of mythic material, which alerts the reader to watch for some of the less overtly mythical—though perhaps more obviously religious—quests in their other fiction.

The quest pattern in literature is a theme common to almost every culture. Joseph Campbell, one of the greatest interpreters of mythic quests, describes the basic pattern of the quest in *The Hero with a Thousand Faces* (1949): "*A hero ventures forth from the world of common day into a region of supernatural wonder: fabulous forces are there encountered and a decisive victory is won: the hero comes back from this mysterious adventure with the power to bestow boons on his fellow man*" (30, his emphasis). As is obvious from Campbell's description of encounters with the "supernatural" and a "mysterious" adventure, these quests frequently have religious connotations. Based on his study of world religions, Robert Torrance asserts that the quest is central in many religions and should not be seen as an innovation of the Great World Religions (xiii). Even one of the most famous Western quests, *The Odyssey*, where Odysseus seems to have a secular goal of returning home, also depicts "a process by which a 'lost soul' is reconciled with the cosmos, which is represented by the gods" (Leeming 147). More obviously still, the commonly known myths of the Arthurian knights' quest for the Holy Grail—the cup or platter used by Christ at the Last Supper[9]—very clearly link together the quest form and religious seeking. The Grail stories serve as a metaphor for a person's seeking God, since "[l]ife renewal is always the ultimate goal of the quest, and life renewal is both a spiritual and a physical process" (Leeming 147). Thus, it is hardly surprising that, as Malamud and

Percy present characters searching for religious commitment, they make use of the quest form.

The collections of myths that make up the story of Lancelot's quest for the Holy Grail are quite well known, although they have significant variation among them. According to one version, the episodic *Quest of the Holy Grail*, which is a part of the thirteenth-century Vulgate Cycle of Arthurian romances, the Grail briefly appears at one of King Arthur's feasts, and various knights vow to go off to search for it. Fairly quickly in his journey, Lancelot sees the Holy Grail, but he has not confessed his sin in sleeping with Guinevere, so he is unable to speak or draw near to the Grail. Lancelot confesses his sins, does penance, and continues on his journey. Meanwhile, as Perceval is also searching for the Grail, he is tempted and nearly gives in to an evil woman who would have drawn him away from his quest. The knights also have to partake in various jousting matches as they journey. Later, Perceval, along with several knights who have joined him, comes to a body of water and is helped by a good maiden to find safe passage. Eventually, Lancelot, and others—including his son Galahad—do find the Grail. When they are there, they cure the maimed Fisher-King (who was guarding the Grail) by dripping a drop of blood on him from the perpetually bleeding lance that hovers near the Grail.

These elements are quite obviously central to an understanding of *The Natural*. In notes to himself, Malamud wonders how to handle the material: "Baseball when described realistically as a game is boring. How to enrich characterization, humor, and the game itself? . . . decision—treat the material symbolically to give it a more meaningful quality for me" (*Talking Horse* 41). More specifically, Malamud acknowledges his debt to the Grail myth: "Baseball had interested me, especially its comic aspects, but I wasn't able to write about the game until I transformed the game into myth, via Jessie Weston's Percival legend with an assist by T.S. Eliot's 'Waste Land' plus the lives of several ballplayers I had read" ("Reflections" 16). Since the Grail myths have Christian overtones both because the Holy Grail is linked to Christ's Last Supper and because the suffering of the Fisher-King is often symbolically linked with Christ's passion, it may seem somewhat incongruous that a Jewish writer uses this mythic structure—or at least somewhat odd to study his fiction in the context of Jewish spirituality. In part, Malamud's use of the quest myth is understandable simply because it has become a significant component of Western literature, quite apart from its Christian connections. Further, Malamud acknowledges that he draws from various religious traditions: "The heart doesn't have a single religion. It goes where the heart is. I have been influenced by Buddha, Jesus, and Francis of Assisi, as you see in *The Assistant*" (*Conversations with Bernard Malamud* 72). Yet even though such a mixing is evident in his writing—and his own position is at a remove from rabbinic Judaism—the central recurring concern in both Malamud's fiction and his interviews is his emphasis on ethical behavior, which he says comes from his Jewish background. Because that emphasis connects with one part of religious mystery, it remains useful to consider Malamud in the context of Jewish spirituality.

The parallels to the quest myth in *The Natural* have often been noted by critics and are nowhere more thoroughly probed than in Earl Wasserman's essay, "*The Natural*: Malamud's World Ceres": "By drawing his material from actual baseball and yet fusing it with the Arthurian legend, Malamud sets and sustains his novel in a region that is both real and mythic, particular and universal, ludicrous melodrama and spiritual probing" (47). These mythic parallels, with the various knights' adventures combined together, are many and quite obvious.[10] When Roy Hobbs (a name signifying both king and common man) strikes out the reigning king of batting, the Whammer, one observer wondered if it was "David jawboning the Goliath-Whammer, or was it Sir Percy lancing Sir Maldemer, or the first son (with a rock in his paw) ranged against the primitive papa?" (31–32). After this victory, Harriet Bird questions Roy about his ambitions, and he proclaims he wants to be "the best there ever was in the game" (33); in response, she shoots him. Robert Lidston finds her to be a "figure who tests the young knight's motives. He fails and she punishes him" (77). When Roy returns to baseball many years later, he joins the (significantly named) Knights, where the Fisher-King coach, Pop Fisher, has athlete's foot of the hands and wishes he were a farmer, where the water fountain is broken, and where the playing field is parched and dry. The rains come to the land and Pop Fisher is healed when Roy (literally) hits the cover off the ball. This productive season continues until Roy is led astray by another temptress, Memo Paris, the former girlfriend of the man Roy has displaced in left field. He can only be restored by a Lady of the Lake, Iris Lemon, who stands up at a game "to show her confidence in him" (147); after he hits a home run, he goes with Iris to a lake, but subsequently rejects her when he learns she is a grandmother. In his effort to win Memo, Roy gives in to temptation yet again and agrees intentionally to throw a key playoff game. Midway through the game, Roy decides that he was wrong and attempts to win the game for Pop Fisher. As he stands at bat, the pitcher sees him "in full armor, mounted on a black charger" (231). Roy, though, has given in to temptation for too long, so he fails. As he leaves the stadium, a woman remarks, "He coulda been a king" (237). Besides the specific Arthurian parallels, Malamud also makes use of common seasonal archetypes, since Roy's defeat comes in late autumn, while his entry as a rookie was during the spring. Malamud deftly combines mythic details of a questing knight, who must overcome temptations to succeed in his mission, with the national pastime.

But more than being only a modern myth, *The Natural* also suggests the kind of spiritual questing that is prominent in several other Malamud novels. From the earliest part of the novel, Roy has a sharp hunger (10), and that hunger only increases throughout the novel, leading to his eventually eating everything in sight at Memo's buffet (184). Even after he has gorged himself, he thinks, "I am hungry. No, I am not hungry, I am hungry, whatever that means . . . What must I do not to be hungry? He considered fasting but he hadn't fasted since he was a kid.

Besides, it made him hungry" (188). This superhuman hunger signifies Roy's overreaching appetite for fame through records. But especially with the reference to fasting and its connection with religious devotion, the physicality of Roy's hunger also suggests that perhaps he has a deeper, spiritual hunger that he refuses to recognize, a motif that follows throughout Malamud's novels. Roy's rejection of fasting—with his humorous comment that it would make him hungry—shows his unwillingness to submit to controls on his own desires. The sense that Roy does not even know what he needs—or is not in touch with important parts of himself—is emphasized when he is driving with Memo and thinks he sees a young boy that Memo has hit; when he says he is sure they hit someone because he heard someone groan, she responds, "That was yourself" (123). Although it is unclear exactly what happens in the incident, this concrete action seems to show that Roy and Memo may have "killed" an innocent part of Roy, particularly since Memo is associated with evil as she is connected with the crooked team owner and eventually tempts Roy to throw the game.

Roy's lack of knowledge of himself and his acquiescence to his own destructive impulses is underlined by his attitude toward suffering. As in much of Malamud's fiction, suffering—and a person's reaction to it—is a key indication of a character's moral nature. In a selfless sacrifice of her privacy, Iris Lemon stands at the baseball game to show her confidence in Roy even while he is in a slump. Afterward, as Roy complains to Iris about his problems, she instructs Roy that suffering "makes good people better"; Roy responds that he has had enough of suffering. In a telling answer, Iris says, "We have two lives, Roy, the life we learn with and the life we live with after that. Suffering is what brings us toward happiness" (158). All his life, Roy has resisted learning from suffering. His reaction at the end of the novel, then, shows a significant step forward. He first shows a willingness to make a commitment when he learns that Iris is carrying their baby, kissing "her hard belly, wild with love for her and the child" (225). Then, after he fails during the game, he thinks, "I never did learn anything out of my past life, now I have to suffer again" (236). After a boy pleads with him to "[s]ay it ain't true," Roy "lifted his hands to his face and wept many bitter tears" (237). Given his recognition that he has failed to learn before, these tears suggest that Roy is not only mourning his defeat but is also weeping for the evil that he sees in his life. The change occurring *within* Roy is made explicit through the physical description of his weeping. As Ellen Pifer explains, "the end of Roy's bid for glory marks the dawn of moral knowledge" ("Malamud's Unnatural" 148). Thus, although the novel's ending does not explicitly show Roy growing and changing, the progression of his quest suggests that he is *prepared* to take a step toward a new moral understanding. It is therefore not clear that his commitment to Iris signifies a nonrational religious movement, but his joyful acknowledgment of his responsibility to her could presage a more extensive religious awakening since there have been hints in the novel of his spiritual emptiness. In any case, his new realization that suffering must be accepted and commitments must be made are, for Roy, a step toward spiritual enlightenment.

Percy, like Malamud, makes use of the Arthurian myth. His approach in *Lancelot*, however, is somewhat different from Malamud's. This tale is told by Lancelot, held in the "Center for Aberrant Behavior," to a priest-psychiatrist. Nicknamed Percival, this former priest is a childhood friend of Lancelot's who has fallen away from the faith. Rather than closely linking the plot to the Lancelot legend, Percy takes from the myth "an attitude and an approach to life" (Lister 78). As noted earlier, Percy grew up within the Southern stoic tradition, and it seems accurate to see *Lancelot* as "the Broadsword Tradition run wild, carried out to its logical (or illogical) extreme" (Lister 78). There are, certainly, plenty of hints in the novel that the reader is to think of the Arthurian legend, beginning with the protagonist's name, Lancelot Andrewes Lamar. Lancelot says that "[t]he Andrewes was tacked on by [my father] to give it Episcopal sanction, but what he really had in mind and in his heart wanted to be and couldn't have been more different from was that old nonexistent Catholic brawler and adulterer, Lancelot du Lac" (116).

Further, as Lancelot describes the events that led up to his placement in the cell where he is being held, he makes it very clear that he had been on a quest—for the unholy grail. What stirs him from his lethargy is the hint, based on the blood type of the girl he had assumed to be his daughter, that his wife Margot has been unfaithful. In his search to verify this information, he mentally transforms the issue from adultery to a quest for absolute evil. As he tells his friend Percival,

> You should be interested! Such a quest serves God's cause! How? Because the Good proves nothing. When everything is wonderful, nobody bothers with God. . . .
>
> But suppose you could show me one "sin," one pure act of malevolence. A different cup of tea! That would bring matters to a screeching halt. . . .
>
> "Evil" is surely the clue to this age, the only quest appropriate to the age. For everything and everyone's either wonderful or sick and nothing is evil. (138)

But instead of seeing the Grail, as the mythical Lancelot did, this Lancelot tells Percival that he found nothing in his quest. When he crept into Margot's bedroom and found her in bed with another man, he states: "I felt nothing at all. Nothing good, nothing bad, not even a sense of discovery. . . . There is no unholy grail just as there was no Holy Grail" (253). Even though he believes he has not been able to find the center of evil, his outrage at the sins in his own household leads Lancelot to murder Margot's lover and blow up the house, killing Margot and two houseguests. Again, he reports that even as he was cutting the throat of Margot's lover, "Not even the knife at his throat seemed to make any difference. All it came down to was steel molecules entering skin molecules, artery molecules, blood cells" (254). Yet what Lancelot fails to recognize is that he is unable to find the unholy grail because he himself has entered into the evil. His insistence that he saw the murder as being nothing but a mechanistic process reveals that he is entirely emmeshed in the evil that he condemns. Indeed, because of his identification with evil, one could say that Percy does show the reader the unholy grail: Lancelot and his own actions. Percy even acknowledges in an interview that Lancelot's finding nothing when he searches for evil is exactly in line with Thomist doctrine, because Aquinas "defines evil as the absence of essence" (*Conversations with Walker Percy* 155). Therefore, although Lancelot believes his quest has failed, the reader can perceive that, chillingly, Lancelot has been more successful in locating evil than he yet understands.

Since Lancelot's unholy actions do not fulfill our expectations of a modern-day Lancelot, John Hardy finds the Arthurian allusions in the novel "simply as the most flamboyant evidence of Lance Lamar's general disposition to self-aggrandizement" (149). Likewise, Michael Kobre, in his intriguing investigation of narrative patterns at work in the novel, believes Lance's attempt to interpret his past actions as a quest for the Unholy Grail is "entirely an afterthought," since these ideas only appear on Lancelot's recounting of the events (4). John Bugge further interprets the myth as functioning ironically in two ways: first, the mythical correspondences "work a colossal irony upon the hero," for his tale points up "how impossibly at variance with the true quest of the Grail is Lance's action of murderous revenge" (182); and, second, the author plays on our sympathies for the Arthurian legend "only to be brought up short when we discover that Percy is using the Arthurian myth with neither sympathy nor admiration, but portraying it as a distinctly negative force" (178). While Percy is clearly not setting up Lancelot's understanding of the Arthurian myth as exemplary, Bugge's analysis seems overly negative, for the novel's presentation of the adultery, variant sexual connections, and drug abuse within Lancelot's house suggest that the reader is to share Lancelot's outrage at the sin of the present-age—while not, of course, endorsing his diabolic solution.

Percy's use of the Lancelot myth ties in closely with the larger issue of this chapter, namely the presentation of a spiritual quest. Lancelot says numerous times that he had sunken into a rut of drunken television watching. But when he began his search, "I left the worn path of my life" (49). As in other Percy novels, this breaking out of "everydayness" (a term Percy takes from Heidegger) gives the character a chance to make a change—to begin to search. Linda Hobson points out, though, that when Lancelot breaks from his routine, instead of choosing faith he opts for violence (103). His method, as he tells Percival after the priest-psychiatrist suggests that he needs love, is, "Don't talk to me of love until we shovel out the shit" (179). Lancelot cannot stomach the sin he perceives in society, so he feels he must return to a mythic past in which women are clearly either "whores" or "ladies." What suggests that Lancelot may be open to a religious commitment is his insistence, as he tells the (newly reconfirmed) priest near the end of the novel, "It will be your way or it will be my way. . . . it will not be their way" (257). Lancelot's belief that sin is still meaningful and must be resisted points toward a possibility for spiritual growth since a recognition that certain actions are sinful—that not anything is permissible—is a necessary starting point before acknowledging one's own sin and amending one's life.

Moreover, Lancelot has realized that his own way to find meaning has failed—he believes he has found nothing through his quest. In the year since the murders until he relates the events to Percival, he has felt a coldness, so that still "I don't feel anything" (253). William Dowie believes that Lancelot's quest was wrongly directed: "In looking for sin in others, . . . Lancelot was looking for the impossible, for sin is a subjective occurrence existing only within an individual psyche. . . . So taken up with his search for sexual sin in others, Lancelot misses the sinfulness of his own acts, sexual and violent" (254). Gary Ciuba adds, "at the end of his quest Lancelot sees nothing of sin but not the nothingness of sin"; he "misses the invisible nonbeing at the heart of darkness, at the heart of himself" (189). While Dowie's assertion that Lancelot was wrong to look for sin in others seems excessive since the inner subjectiveness of sin is given outer expression through people's actions, the idea that Lancelot needs to look within himself before condemning others is an important one. Lancelot is so full of anger and hatred that he is unable to experience love—from God or from others. The novel portrays, then, Lancelot's "detour—often expressed in terms of the Arthurian legend—in Lancelot Lamar's journey toward wholeness" (Lister 77).[11] That Lancelot will find wholeness is only hinted at the end. At the outset of the novel, Percival has apparently left the priesthood; he even refuses a woman's request to pray for the dead. From his reactions during Lancelot's narrative—his shocked expressions and whispers of "love"—Percival reveals that he is deeply affected by Lancelot's hate-filled rantings. So, in one sense, Lancelot seems to be correct: his revealing of his own evil actions becomes for Percival the unholy grail, leading him back to God just as Lancelot predicted it would. Percival recommits himself to the priesthood and plans, at the conclusion, to take a small parish in Alabama. His change—from refusing to pray for the dead to accepting a church—provides a strong message that Christian belief remains possible.

Whether Lancelot will open himself to grace is not certain, but Percy provides clues to suggest that he may yet come to faith. Because of the novel's mythical connections, it seems highly significant that in the Arthurian legend, Percival and Lancelot do see the Grail. Thus, since in the novel Percival has already been directed to his "Holy Grail," the mythic parallels hint that Lancelot may yet encounter God as well.[12] Further, after being silent throughout the novel, Percival begins to speak at the novel's end. Lancelot says, "Very well. I've finished. Is there anything you wish to tell me before I leave?" The priest answers, "*Yes*" (257). The implication seems to be that Percival will now share the news of Christianity with Lancelot, and he will listen. As Percy says of the ending, "presumably Percival gives him a similar version of the orthodoxy, of the Judeo-Christian tradition, which can't be done in a novel" (*More Conversations* 10). Percy's comment about the novel points to the way that the structure of the quest form can suggest a movement to religious mystery that cannot be rationally spelled out in fiction. From Lancelot's searching and the priest's readiness to speak, we can gather that Lancelot may be spiritually prepared to make a religious commitment.[13]

QUESTS FOR COMMUNITY: *THE FIXER* AND *THE SECOND COMING*

While *The Natural* and *Lancelot* are Malamud’s and Percy’s novels that deal most explicitly with mythical material, the theme of quests is an important one throughout their fiction. Often without fully understanding for what they are searching, the protagonists nevertheless sense that they have, in Pascal’s words, a “God-shaped vacuum” within themselves, and thus they undertake spiritual quests. Probably the most explicit of these religious searches are shown in Malamud’s *The Fixer* and Percy’s *The Second Coming*. For even though the characters are in vastly different situations and come to somewhat divergent conclusions, much of each novel is concerned with Yakov Bok’s and Will Barrett’s overt wrestling with God. Besides the openness of the search, the central theme that draws these novels together is the way that the character’s step toward mystery is represented: by a commitment to community. Malamud and Percy use the quest form to show the protagonist’s searching and then indicate his commitment by showing him accepting his responsibility to community.

The Fixer has a clear historical connection, for Malamud based his novel on the 1911 Mendel Beiliss case in Russia, when a Jew was charged with the ritual murder of a twelve-year-old boy. For two years, Beiliss was held in prison, although not mistreated, before being tried and found innocent (*Conversations with Bernard Malamud* 24). These details connect *The Fixer* to history, but the novel is clearly a fictional version that only takes the Beiliss case as a starting point. Malamud says that he brought in material from the Dreyfus case and from Vanzetti’s insanity and incarceration at Massachusetts General Hospital. Additionally, Malamud notes the novel has resonances with other terrible injustices: “Somewhere along the line, what had happened in Nazi Germany began to be important to me in terms of the book, and that’s part of Yakov’s story. . . . One of the things that I think of now is the Negro, the Negroes who live lives of second-class citizens. Their story is one leading up to a situation that’s revolutionary.” Nevertheless, Malamud stresses that the novel is “an imaginative piece of work” that has a “mythological quality,” so it should not be read as a case study (*Conversations with Bernard Malamud* 19–20). The novel has broad historical resonances, but it also is a specific exploration of one man’s spiritual struggle.

Yakov Bok in *The Fixer* attempts at the beginning of the novel to move away from everything associated with Judaism. He has had a hard life, losing both of his parents very early in his life, being unable to have children with his wife, and then losing her when she runs off with another man. So he decides that he will leave his village and seek a new life in Kiev. He is bitter with his fate, noting that as a carpenter, “I fix what’s broken—except in the heart” (7). On leaving the village, he attempts to break from his inherited Jewishness—shaving off his beard, throwing his prayer things away, and thus being able to pass as a “goy.” In making this move to Kiev, as Lewis Horne points out, Yakov is extremely isolated: “He is separated from his wife (he believes her barren and she leaves him), from his parents (they died in his youth), from his people (he rejects their religion), from his country (he is Jewish), and from God (he does not believe)" (322). Yakov's effort at abandoning his Jewish identity is in large part an attempt to seek a superior socioeconomic position in life, a status denied him as a Jew because of the rabid anti-Semitism of Czarist Russia. As such, the theme of *The Fixer* connects with centuries of prejudice and abuse suffered by Jews in Europe and elsewhere. While he was writing about *The Assistant*, Earl Rovit's assessment seems to fit Yakov Bok's situation, as well: he is "[h]edged in and thwarted by the fatal limitations of human existence, and imprisoned even beyond that by a pervasive sense of being 'alien' in a Gentile world" (7). Because of that sense of alienation—of not fitting in with the dominant culture—one can see a connection between Yakov Bok's sufferings and the trials of Jews in the Diaspora (Robert Alter 40). Such an historical linkage to Jewish persecution, as Malamud himself suggested, also serves to link the novel to the Holocaust. In her examination of the novel's correlations to Nazi Germany, Lillian Kremer finds that Malamud's historical perspective "documents Christian Europe's moral culpability in the Holocaust, clearly demonstrating that centuries of European, anti-Semitic violence prefigures acquiescence to and collaboration in Hitler's genocidal program" (95). Clearly, Yakov's move for a better life points up the overtly hostile dominant culture in which Jews have lived.

Yet Yakov's abandonment of his Jewish past is not motivated alone by a desire to escape prejudice. Yakov is particularly angry that the Jews continue to believe in God even though God seems to have abandoned them. His father-in-law Shmuel exhorts him to stay in the village, saying, "here at least God is with us." Yakov replies, "He's with us till the Cossacks come galloping, then he's elsewhere. He's in the outhouse, that's where he is" (12). In response to another reminder from Shmuel not to forget God, Yakov explodes, "Who forgets who? . . . What do I get from him but a bang on the head and a stream of piss in my face. So what's there to be worshipful about?" (17). Yakov wants to make a clean break from his past and all it has included. He is angry with God for his unending string of troubles and decides that he will begin a new life separate from his community and their religion.

When he arrives in Kiev, he unsuccessfully looks for work, until one day he happens upon a man who is lying face down in the snow. Yakov helps the man, even though he is wearing the symbol of an anti-Semitic group. In return for the favor, Nikolai Maximovitch offers to pay Yakov well to repair some apartments. With some hesitation, Yakov accepts, having to give a false name since the vociferous Jew-hater would not knowingly employ a Jew. Since Nikolai is pleased with Yakov's work, he offers Yakov a permanent job as an overseer of a brick-making factory. The drawback: Yakov would have to live in a section of the city where Jews are forbidden to live. Yakov accepts the job with considerable misgivings, but he hopes that perhaps this is the chance to begin a new life. This illusion is quickly shattered since Yakov is soon arrested on trumped up charges of murdering a boy for a religious ritual. It is ironic that Yakov suffers for doing a good deed, but Robert Kegan points out that it is in some sense appropriate that since he has moved away from Judaism, "what results, rather than a covenant relationship, is a business alliance; rather than an encounter with God, he meets an anti-Semite. Rather than a union with the historic, the *mitzvah* results in a denial of the Old Testament; rather than a union with the spiritual, the *mitzvah* results in a near coupling with an 'unclean woman'" (59). These ironic consequences suggest that Yakov's few isolated good deeds are not an adequate response; what he needs is a completely different spiritual understanding that will transform his entire outlook.

The assertion that Yakov's overt rejection of Judaism in some ways "brings about" his future suffering, though, should in no way be taken to excuse the rabid societal anti-Semitism that makes the murder charges so plausible to the Russians—both in history and in this fiction. Nor should one neglect the fact that even while Yakov is living in Kiev, his Judaism retains more importance than he would like to think. Even the initials of his assumed name, Yakov Ivanovitch Dologushev (YID), hint of his Jewish background (Kegan 53). Further, when Nikolai's daughter Zina attempts to seduce him, Yakov almost gives in—until he sees that she is having her menstrual period. His exclamation, "But you are unclean!" (52), shows that his past following of Jewish commandments, with the prohibition of contact with menstrual blood, is still very much with him. Similarly, when he rescues an old Hasidic man, who had been injured by boys, and learns that it is Passover, his reaction again reveals the importance that his tradition still holds for him: "It came as a surprise to the fixer that it was Passover. He was moved by a strong emotion and had to turn away till it had gone" (65). These hints that Yakov has not as successfully abandoned Judaism as he would like to think make plausible his later religious search.

Yakov Bok's experiment in living as a gentile is startlingly interrupted when he is arrested and imprisoned on allegations that he killed a young boy. The charges are patently false, a fact made clear by the Russian authorities' refusal to indict Yakov and bring him to trial. But Yakov Bok, whose last name means scapegoat in German, is nevertheless held in increasingly brutal conditions. This enforced solitude leads Yakov to examine his life and his beliefs as he tries to make sense of his unjust punishment. When he is first arrested, he admits to being a Jew "by birth and nationality," claiming to be a freethinker and not religious (86). He does, though, say that he is not "ashamed" of his people, even as he is trying to distance himself from them. After his interrogation, he nears despair, believing that "I'm a fixer but all my life I've broken more than I fix" (104). Even at this early stage in his incarceration, however, Yakov refuses to turn his back on the Jewish community. The prosecutor tells him that if he "confesses" that he was put up to his crime by the "Jewish Nation," things will go easier for him; Yakov says, "How could I do such a thing, your honor? I couldn't do such a thing. Why should I blame it on innocent people?" The prosecutor responds that Yakov has tried to distance himself from the Jews and, besides, "What have they done for you?" Yakov says, "At the very least, your honor, they've left me alone" (142). Although he is in misery, Yakov will not open the way for a pogrom against the Jews. His initial standing with his Jewish community, somewhat unexpected given his adamant rejection of all things obviously Jewish, hints at the moral courage and commitment that is so fully developed later in the novel.

After three months in prison, Yakov begins to question himself about God: "He sometimes thought God was punishing him for his unbelief. He was, after all, the jealous God. 'Thou shalt have no other Gods before me,' not even no Gods" (153). At this stage, such ideas are only passing thoughts. Yakov still believes and hopes that he will be able to get out from prison to live his life. He thus puts his hope and faith in Bibikov, the Investigating Magistrate who believes in Yakov's innocence. Bibikov exhorts Yakov to "[t]ake heart in the truth and endure your trials. Sustain yourself on your innocence" (175). He adds that Yakov must believe that the law will protect him, and Yakov does trust that Bibikov will be able to defend "his 'innocence' on the grounds of human law" (Ruotolo 131). It is then a tremendous shock when Yakov momentarily escapes from his cell to peer into the adjoining one and see Bibikov hanged there, also a victim of the state's terror. Since Yakov's last perceived hope is gone with Bibikov's death, he becomes desperate:

> He mourned Bibikov with great sorrow, great bitterness. For weeks he had lived with this potential savior in his thoughts, this just and gentle man; depended on him somehow to free him from prison . . . His only peace had come from these thoughts, that a good man was assisting him, and because of him, when the trial came, he would be judged not guilty. . . . But now these hopes and expectations, these reveries on which he had lived, were gone, snatched from him without warning. Who would help him now, what could he hope for? Where Bibikov had lived in his mind was a hopeless hole. (182–83)

All of Yakov's human aids have been swept away, and he must now look for other means to survive his unjust suffering. Bibikov's death prepares the way for Yakov's spiritual questions since all other supports have been stripped from him.

After the initial agony of Bibikov's loss leaves Yakov, he is in deep despair, still lacking the fortitude he needs to survive. The narrator's description of Yakov that the "minute after he had eaten he was hungry" (196) is certainly a realistic representation of his meager portions. But the statement also has symbolic significance, as it did for Roy Hobbs: "What Bok hungers for is the same thing all of Malamud's principals hunger for, spiritual freedom" (Sandy Cohen 183). Yakov turns to the reading he had done in Spinoza, hoping to find comfort in the freedom that Jewish philosopher had discovered, but he is unable to encounter the independence Spinoza described: Spinoza "was free in his thoughts, his understanding of Necessity, and in the construction of his philosophy. The fixer's thoughts added nothing to his freedom; it was nil" (207). Yakov's understanding of Spinoza's philosophy seems to focus on Spinoza's reasoning to a conception of God, based on a kind of monism: "whatever is, is in God, and nothing can be or be conceived without God" (qtd. in Allison 62). Thus, Spinoza has no belief in the power of God to *cause* anything; rather, he sees only a logical connection between God and the world, with God as the logical starting point for creation (Allison 64). The God Spinoza conceives of is without intellect and without free will in creation since the world is a necessary result from Spinoza's concept of God: "whatever we conceive to be in God's power, necessarily exists" (qtd. in Allison 82). So as John Cottingham points out in his discussion of Spinoza, "Spinoza's God, the self-subsistent and self-creating substance that is identical with the natural universe, seems far removed from the personal God of traditional Judaeo-Christian belief" (179). Although Yakov admires Spinoza's movement away from a traditional Jewish idea of a God standing apart from nature and acting in history, he is unable to create a God through his reasoning as Spinoza did. So he tries to return to a more traditional approach as he remembers some Psalms he had known and hopes to find comfort in them: "He thought of himself pursuing his enemies with God at his side, but when he looked at God all he saw or heard was a loud Ha Ha Ha. It was his own imprisoned laughter" (209). Yakov cannot square the pain of his own life, during which he has sensed no help from God, with the idea in the Psalms that God is on the side of the Jews. Therefore, neither Yakov's attempt to create the Spinozan idea of God nor a more traditionally Jewish conception of God is successful for Yakov; "[t]he Hebrew God Yakov Bok cannot accept; the Spinozan God Yakov Bok cannot create" (Horne 325).

The movement to Yakov's final transformation is marked by a series of specific actions and physical images that serve as hints of the mysterious changes that are taking place in Yakov. His first step comes when he is able to admit that he has wronged others, particularly his wife, Raisl. Since he was frustrated that they were not having children, he began to distance himself from her, choosing to remain in the kitchen and read Spinoza instead of going to bed with his wife. In response, she left him for another man. Yakov reflects, "At first I cursed her like somebody in the Bible curses his whorish wife. 'May she keep her miscarrying womb and dry breasts.' But now I look at it like this: She had tied herself to the wrong future" (213). Although Yakov cites the Bible for his curses instead of his new insight, his acknowledgment of his wrong to his wife carries clear biblical overtones. In the Mosaic covenant, God commands the people to confess their sins before they can return to a covenant relationship (Lev. 26.39–42). Similarly, Yakov's owning of his wrongs prepares him for new spiritual insights. In moving from blaming his wife to accepting his share of responsibility for their difficulties, Yakov has opened the way for spiritual growth.

While Yakov is experiencing the faint stirrings of spiritual change, the Russian authorities—to "strengthen" their case—attempt to make Yakov seem more outwardly religious than he is, so they give him phylacteries and a prayer shawl, the latter of which he wears for warmth. The phylacteries are small, hollow, cube-shaped leather boxes that contain four small scrolls of Scripture; one is to be worn on the forehead and the other on the left arm opposite the heart in response to the commandment to bind the laws on the hand and forehead so that they are always present with the believer (Deut. 6.8). The prayer shawl, a white wrap with fringed edges, is worn to follow the biblical command to wear fringes on the corners of garments; these fringes are commanded to be worn so that when Jews see them, they will remember and follow God's commandments (Num. 15.37–41). One day, Yakov cracks open a phylactery and reads the scrolls from Exodus and Deuteronomy inside of it with "excitement and sadness":

> The bondage in Egypt was over, and in one scroll Moses proclaimed the celebration of Passover. Another scroll was the Sh'ma Ysroël. Another enumerated the rewards for loving and serving God and the punishment for not: the loss of heaven, rain, and the fruit of that rain; even life. In each of the four scrolls the people were commanded to obey God and teach his words. (230)

When the guard discovers the scroll, it is confiscated and Yakov is given a New Testament. Desperate for any reading material, Yakov reads the Gospels and finds particular identification with Jesus' cry of being forsaken by God while on the cross: "There was a man crying out in anguish in the dark, but God was on the other side of his mountain" (232). Instead of becoming a Christian, though, Yakov uses this story to draw strength for his Jewishness, as Josephine Knopp explains: "In a specifically Jewish (as opposed to Christian) interpretation of the Crucifixion, Yakov stresses the culpability of God, identifying Jesus with those Old Testament figures, like Job and Jeremiah, who rebuke God for the suffering of mankind, and, ultimately, with himself" (120).[14] For Yakov, Jesus is significant as an example of a man abandoned by God in his time of need on earth, not as an atoning sacrifice for the sins of humankind.

So even though he gains encouragement from reading the story of Jesus and from chanting the Beatitudes, Yakov refuses to consider the "salvation" offered by a priest who comes to convert him; his response is to stand silently in the trappings of his Jewish religious heritage: "Yakov stood in the dim light, motionless at the table, the prayer shawl covering his head, the phylactery for the arm bound to his brow" (237). Although Yakov does not claim to be a religious Jew, his silent use of the symbols of rabbinic Judaism connect him to that tradition and serve as his response to the debauched Christianity presented to him. Indeed, the phylacteries and prayer shawl are physical items that convey a sense of mystery, since they are part of a specifically religious ritual designed to invoke a sense of the numinous. Yakov's purpose in wearing the prayer shawl is at least in part utilitarian—to stay warm—but his very acceptance of these items that he had earlier thrown in the river before his arrival in Kiev hint at Yakov's return to his Jewishness. However, Yakov still does not recover his belief in God, feeling that he "suffers without either the intellectual idea of God, or the God of the covenant" (240). As he tells Shmuel when his father-in-law manages to bribe his way into the prison, "I blame him [God] for not existing" (256). Yakov adds that he is bitter over what God did to Job: "To win a lousy bet with the devil he killed off all the servants and innocent children of Job" (258). When

Shmuel reminds him that belief is possible for anyone whose heart is open, Yakov responds bitterly, "What's left of my heart is pure rock" (259).

Yet for all of his railing, Yakov has changed. He dreams of Shmuel's death and says when he awakes, "Live Shmuel, . . . live. Let me die for you. . . . Suffering I can gladly live without, I hate the taste of it, but if I must suffer let it be for something. Let it be for Shmuel" (272–73). Yakov then decides that he will do what he can for his people, the Jews: "All he can do is not make things worse. . . . He will protect them to the extent that he can. This is his covenant with himself. If God's not a man he has to be. Therefore he must endure to the trial and let them confirm his innocence by their lies" (274). In many ways, this commitment by Yakov serves as the climax of the novel: without traditional religious language, Yakov's spiritual change is shown through his moral commitment to his community. No longer is Yakov thinking only of himself; he is able to move from being trapped in his own suffering to finding meaning as he suffers for someone else. That Yakov's change is made manifest through his connection to the community ties this movement to religious mystery since the importance of community is at the heart of the Mosaic covenant: God says to the children of Israel, "you shall be to Me a kingdom of priests and a holy nation" (Exod. 19.6). As Yakov decides that he will attach himself to this holy nation, he makes a nonrational commitment to this biblical injunction of caring for others. His struggle with God throughout the course of the novel makes it plausible to see that his change in morality is connected to his religious understanding, even though his conflict with God has not ended. In the context of his decision, his comment that "If God is not a man he has to be" seems to be a statement of anger and frustration at the little help he and the Jews have received from God. Nevertheless, it is intriguing that on a most literal level, Yakov's formulation actually underlines Jewish (as opposed to Christian) theology: God has not appeared as a man but is rather the unnameable one, the holy one set apart from humanity. Yakov probably does not intend such an affirmation in his comment, but his words do suggest rich Jewish resonances. What is most clear is that with his paradoxical decision to live for his community—despite the "evidence" of his horrendous personal experience—Yakov moves beyond the rational to religious mystery.

The abstraction of Yakov's thoughts is quickly given physical form. His wife Raisl visits him in prison and tells him that she has had an illegitimate son (showing that the problem of conception was Yakov's, not hers). She asks him if he is willing to sign a statement that the son is his so that the boy will not be an outcast. Yakov agrees to sign. He has made his commitment to "his" son, to his wife, to his community. This commitment takes on particularly religious significance given the name of the boy: Chaim, meaning "life" in Hebrew. By moving beyond his own self-interest to accept the Jewish emphasis on community, Yakov is confirming that he has chosen life—both physical life by rejecting suicide as well as the ethical life of commitment to community. It is this decision that gives him true freedom: "Once the fixer chooses life, no one can impose his will on him" (Helterman 76).

In some ways, Yakov's shift to a revolutionary political position at the end of the novel seems difficult to understand. Pirjo Ahokas articulates the difficulty by noting the abruptness of the "political conclusions which come unexpectedly in the novel and that, in fact, are in conflict with the explicit ethical claims concerning individual responsibility" in the novel (202).[15] While such a criticism is fair, Yakov's revolutionary sense is really an outgrowth of his commitment to community; because Russia is so corrupt that it threatens the existence of all Jews, Yakov believes that he must work against the state, leading him in his dream to shoot the Tsar.[16] "One thing I learned, he thought, there's no such thing as an unpolitical man, especially a Jew. You can't be one without the other, that's clear enough. You can't sit still and see yourself destroyed" (335). Thus, Yakov becomes political as a way to save his people.[17]

Just before Yakov goes to his trial, there is a hint that despite all of his heterodox statements, he may yet have a sense of the numinous. When the guards tell him to eat, Yakov refuses, saying he is fasting for "God's world," even though he does not believe in God (321). As his attraction to Spinoza's philosophy indicated Yakov's dissatisfaction with the traditional Jewish understanding of God, his denial of God even as he fasts for "God's world" may indicate that Yakov has a sense of the Divine—particularly through his commitment to other people—even though he cannot fit that numinous feeling into traditional religious language. Although only a hint, his concrete action of fasting suggests a sense of religious mystery.

Yakov's movement toward religious mystery, then, does not clearly end in his acceptance of rabbinical Judaism. Rather, his change, using Shmuel's teaching about morality as his standard, focuses on "his attitude and behavior toward his fellow man" (Knopp 124) based on the Jewish covenant. Thus, this commitment moves beyond what can be explained as self-interest as he suffers for his people and acknowledges as his own a son he has not sired. Yakov has shown a mysterious movement to an acceptance of an external divinely instituted moral code.

Walker Percy's *The Second Coming*, a cheerful love story set in the United States around 1980, is at a far remove from *The Fixer*'s claustrophobic imprisonment. In fact, Percy says in an interview, "I make only one small, single modest claim for this book; it's the first unalienated novel since *War and Peace*" (*Conversations with Walker Percy* 235). Yet Will Barrett's quest for meaning has many important parallels to Yakov Bok's.

Will Barrett was a successful New York lawyer who "made more money than some, married a great deal more money than most" (72), and then retired early to North Carolina. After his wife's death, he is drifting through life, with little purpose beyond playing golf. Just as Lancelot Lamar had fallen into a routine, Will is a typical Percy protagonist who, for no apparent reason, finds his life purposeless and futile: "For some time he had been feeling depressed without knowing why. In fact, he didn't even realize he was depressed" (3). One day, he develops a bad slice in his golf stroke and falls down on the golf course when he remembers forgotten memories—concrete evidence that something is wrong in his life. Besides forcing him to reflect on his life, this falling is an amusing manifestation of the Christian doctrine that humanity is fallen and sinful; only when Will comes to belief (and receives proper medication) will he stop falling. His despair is made clear in his thought about shooting himself:

> Then it was that it occurred to him that he might shoot himself.
> First, it was only a thought that popped into his head.
> Next, it was an idea he entertained ironically.
> Finally, it was a course of action which he took seriously and decided to carry out. (4)

Although he does not shoot himself, he has found that the only thing that can break his "spells" is shooting his Luger—feeling the buck of the gun and smelling the gunpowder.

As Will understands, it is ironic that he is in despair since he lives in "the most Christian nation in the world, the U.S.A., in the most Christian part of that nation, the South, in the most Christian state in the South, North Carolina, in the most Christian town in North Carolina" (13). Yet this characterization of Will's town is in significant measure ironic, for Percy presents a wide range of different beliefs in the novel, a divergence that is instrumental in Will's confusion about what to believe. As Gloria Cronin explains, Will's father was a nihilist who committed suicide; his former wife Marion was a debased Christian—"a merely ethical, patriotic Christianity stripped of its sacred healing power"; his daughter Leslie is an individualistic "born-again" Christian; his former girlfriend Kitty Vaught is an advocate of reincarnation; his cook Yamaiuchi is a Jehovah's Witness; Jack Curl is an unfocused Episcopal priest; and Will's acquaintance Lewis Peckham is a humorous Renaissance man (114). What breaks Will from his stasis and forces him to confront these competing ideologies is that he comes to a gradual realization—during his fits of falling—that his father had tried to kill him just before his father's first attempted suicide. Will's father "was obsessed with the absurdity of life, could not bear to see his son trapped in that absurdity, took the moral law into his own hands, and put his son and himself under a death penalty that would save them both from a galling existence among ignoramuses, racists, bigots, charlatans, fanatics, and the like" (Magaw 80). In a twisted way, Will's father thought he was protecting his son, leading Will to wonder about his father's unsuccessful attempted murder, "Was it love or failure of love?" that led his father not to kill his son (148). Will must now himself struggle with the strange love of death that he inherited from his father.

In this new search to understand what is happening in his life, Will's initial thoughts about Christianity are that he is unattracted to both belief and unbelief. He starkly sets out his dilemma: "If belief is shitty and unbelief is shitty, what does that leave?" (151) Or as he says a bit later:

> It has taken me all these years to make the simplest discovery: that I am surrounded by two classes of maniacs. The first are the believers, who think they know the reason why

> we find ourselves in this ludicrous predicament yet act for all he world as if they don't. The second are the unbelievers, who don't know the reason and don't care if they don't. (190)

Will settles, he thinks, on the perfect solution to his dilemma: he will conduct the ultimate scientific experiment that must prove whether or not there is a God. Will admires Pascal's wager—"One makes the bet that God exists, though one doesn't know for sure"—but says that wager is frivolous; Will's father's solution, shooting himself, is problematical because it "yields no answers" (191). What Will has determined is that he will go into a cave and wait to be rescued by God. If God rescues Will, it proves there is a deity; if Will dies, there must be no God. As Will says, this experiment, much like Jacob's wrestling with God, should have the benefit of yielding a clear response. But the problem with Will's "conducting research into the mechanics of mystery," Gary Ciuba points out, is that he "naively overlooks the paradox that if Pascal's wager was a rationalist's attempt to show the logic of belief in God, it was formulated by a scientist and mathematician who continually recognized the limits of reason" (216). Moreover, because Will assumes that he can force God to make manifest his presence at his own demand, Will is "intently seeking salvation through his own efforts" (Prochaska 100) instead of recognizing that it is only through God's grace that he can find redemption. Rather than the religious mystery of faith, Will wants scientific certainty; he wrongly believes that the mystery of God can be examined in a test tube.

For about a week, Will's experiment proceeds satisfactorily. Then, whether "it was God's doing or ordinary mortal frailty," Will developed a terrible toothache (213). The narrator notes, "It is astonishing how such a simple and commonplace ailment as pain and nausea can knock everything else out of one's head, lofty thoughts, profound thoughts, crazy thoughts, even lust" (223), so Will attempts to leave the cave. The problem is that he is very weak and has lost his way. Eventually, he falls out through a hole in the cave wall and into a greenhouse occupied by Allie, an escapee from a mental institution, who made "straight A's [in school] and flunked ordinary living" (93). Besides the outrageous hilarity of the bat-dung-covered Will falling through the roof of a greenhouse, this end to Will's experiment sets up a wonderful irony: even though it seems that his experiment has failed to produce an answer, it is through Will's encounter with Allie that he is eventually able to find reason to live. Thus, without explicit narratorial comment, the irony suggests that Will's "scientific" experiment is hokey and his real hope will come through its failure. This sense, of course, is underlined by the fact that it is a greenhouse where Will recovers from his cave ordeal, a place of new life.

The imagery of Will's coming out of the cave to Allie further supports the sense that this is a rebirth for him. On his way into the cave, there were places where the ceiling and floor were so close that "he had to turn his head sideways like a baby getting through a pelvis" (209). Additionally, when Will comes to consciousness in the greenhouse, he sees the colored light from a stained-glass window that Allie had used to repair a hole in the roof and assumes that he is in a church (227). Allie notices that Will smells "of a freshly dug ditch. A grave" (234), and Will's gaunt body reminds her of "some paintings of the body of Christ taken down from the crucifix, the white flesh gone blue with death" (236). Although he has by no means settled his quest, his recovery time with Allie, as they quietly talk and lie together, is a reminder to Will that there may be reasons to continue living. Thus, it seems that God has not so much denied Will's request for a sign, but rather that "He declines, as is His wont, to let the human seeker determine the time, place, and manner of His appearing" (Hardy 192). Since the experiment is an attempt to find a scientific answer to an unscientific question, the conclusion reasserts that God resides in mystery, far beyond human control.

Throughout the novel, though, this mystery is incarnated in very concrete ways, especially through the attraction between Allie and Will. Even though Allie was unable to look at or speak to people—leading to her placement in the institution—she is able to deal lovingly with Will since his glances are soft rather than impaling. Indeed, she finds such pleasure in their conversations that she wonders, "Was this a way of making love?" (262), and she realizes that "I do not want him not being here" (253). Will, however, is not yet ready to make a commitment since he continues to struggle with the despairing love of death he inherited from his father. So he boards a bus and heads for the Georgia woods, to complete the job that his father had unsuccessfully attempted. On the bus to Georgia, though, Will sits beside a loan Associate who tells him about his work. As Will listens, he suddenly realizes that he does not have to choose dying; he can find comfort and hope in working and in living with Allie:

> But as he listened to the Associate talk about his work—talk with pleasure! he enjoyed his work! enjoyed walking twenty blocks down West Peachtree, sitting behind his desk for ten hours, making loans, good loans! . . .—his eye traveled along the ridge and came to a notch where in the darkness of the pine and spruce there grew a single gold poplar which caught the sun like a yellow-haired girl coming out of a dark forest. Once again his heart was flooded with sweetness but a sweetness of a different sort, a sharp sweet urgency, a need to act, to run and catch. He was losing something. Something of his as solid and heavy and sweet as a pot of honey in his lap was being taken away.
>
> "I'm not going back to Georgia," he said, rising. (297)

Through the Associate's recounting of his pleasures of work and Will's glimpse of light on a tree that reminds him of Allie, he is able to understand that life is possible. Rather than the blinding light referred to in conversion accounts such as Saul's experience on the road to Damascus, Will sees only "a single gold poplar which caught the sun"; yet like a traditional conversion narrative, this concrete image, which reminds Will of Allie, is sacramental, serving as a moment of grace for Will. In pointing to Allie, the light on the tree becomes a vivid symbol suggesting that Will must find God through his connection with other people, not through a solo experiment. Similarly, the Associate is a human vehicle of God's grace for Will, again showing "that salvation is possible, that life is good and work can be enjoyed" (Prochaska 113). With that realization, Will forces the bus driver to stop, is pushed off the bus, and ends up in a hospital.

Because of this accident, Will's decision that life is possible when it is lived with others finds different actualization than he had intended. The doctors discover that Will's falling is caused by his body's unstable pH. To monitor and adjust this level, Will is placed in "St. Mark's Convalescent Home taking pills and shots and having blood drawn every hour" (278), since, as Ciuba notes, "scientific abstraction understands the search for love and God only as the symptoms of an imbalance in body chemistry" (238).[18] Will's doctor and daughter want to keep him in the home, maintaining him in a comfortable environment where he is no danger to himself or others. It is during his time here, as he gets to know the talented retired men who have been shuttled off to this home, that Will reaffirms that he can—indeed must—live in community. Having learned that the authorities are coming to take Allie back to the institution, he confronts his father's death wish, which is still at the back of his mind, and realizes that he must take action.

When he finds Allie in the greenhouse, she is happy to see him. In their bizarre but fresh way of speaking, begun by Allie since she had forgotten speech because of her electric shock treatments, they profess their love for each other:

> "Are you fond of me besides?" she asked.
>
> "Yes, yes. I must be sure you're all right. Are you?"
>
> "Similarly and moreover. Do you feel a smiling ease with me as well as a sweetness for me in the deepest regions?"
>
> "Yes, in the deep regions, a sweetness, as well as the smiling ease."
>
> "Is it possible that there is such a life?"
>
> "As what?"
>
> "As a life of smiling ease with someone else and sweetness for you deep in me and play and frolic and dear sweet love the livelong day, even at four o'clock in the afternoon turning the old yellow green-glade lonesomeness into a being with you at ease not a being with you at unease?"
>
> "Yes, it's possible." (328–29)

With this commitment, Will acts on his choice for life and relationship by making arrangements so that Allie will not be reinstitutionalized and by taking a job. In his final confrontation with death, Will once more hears his father's suggestion that he commit suicide, but he answers that temptation once for all by throwing away the guns he has inherited from his father.

From the description of Will and Allie, it is clear that he has made the right choice in his mysterious step of commitment. He and Allie make love and spend time "kneading and poking" (341) each other's sore muscles, an intimacy that suggests that they are not only soothing the other's physical aches but also massaging a deeper pain—the spiritual emptiness that their commitment to each other is beginning to fill. This sense is reinforced by the narrator's comment: "It had come to pass, for reasons which neither could have said, that he now knew what needed to be done . . . . She looked like a survivor on the mend" (343). With Will newly able to act and Allie a healing survivor, their committed relationship is clearly salutary for spirit as well as body. Will solidifies his commitment to community by returning to the convalescent home and his new friends. He proposes to Mr. Arnold, who used to build log cabins, and Mr. Ryan, who was a contractor using gypsy labor, that they together form a business, using Mr. Ryan's work crew and Mr. Arnold's cabin knowledge to build well-constructed cabins for people with little income. He also hires Mr. Eberhart, a retired gardener, to work in Allie's greenhouse. In all these cases, the proposals both benefit society by the work being done and—perhaps more importantly—give these retirees significant work to do.

In the final movement of the novel, Will still claims that he is not a believer and does not want to enter the church. But he sees two orderlies showing tenderness as they work with a frightened old woman, and this physical action—a sanctification of the ordinary—leads him to make the connection between the centrality of relationships and the possibility of belief in God:

> Then how does it add up in the economy of giving and getting, he wondered, that the two orderlies cared nothing (or did they?) for the old woman, that even in the very act of their offhand reassurances to her they were probably cooking up something between themselves, that they, the orderlies, who had no reason to give her anything at all, gave it because it was so little to give and so much for her to get? 2¢=$5? How?
>
> Does goodness come tricked out so as fakery and fondness and carrying on and is God himself as sly?
>
> In the hall he stood gazing after the three of them. Young big black mammy, Sugar Ray, and the sick woman, the great machinery of her heart socking away so hard at her neck, it made her nod perceptibly as if she understood and agreed, yes, yes, yes. (349)

Will is beginning to understand that one cannot logically explain grace or prove God's existence through scientific experiment. Just as Will began to move toward God through his relationship with Allie instead of through a private revelation, it is the paradox of selfless giving which shows Will the mystery of grace (Ciuba 243). This paradox that "2¢=$5" suggests the kind of unmerited gift St. Paul articulates when he describes Christ's atoning death for all sinners: "rarely will anyone die for a righteous person—though perhaps for a good person someone might actually dare to die. But God proves his love for us in that while we still were sinners Christ died for us" (Rom. 5.7–8). Will's inability to make logical sense of the charity he sees the orderlies give suggests the "unreasonableness" of Christ's sacrifice, a gift mysteriously repeated at each celebration of the Eucharist.

Later, Will goes to Father Weatherbee, a retired and slightly addled Episcopal priest, and requests that he perform Allie and Will's wedding ceremony. Although Weatherbee initially declines, suggesting that Will should speak instead with Jack Curl, the Episcopal priest with more time for humanistic love centers than for faith, Will insists that even though he is not a believer, he wants Father

Weatherbee for "I perceive that you seem to know something—and by the same token Jack Curl does not" (358).[19] Will senses that the spiritual knowledge of this devout priest is what he needs to hear. His description echoes Percy's imagery in an essay in which he describes humanity as castaways on an island, waiting for "someone who delivers the news and who speaks with authority" (*Message* 148). And what happens when such a person comes to the castaway? "[T]he castaway will, by the grace of God, believe him" (*Message* 149). In the novel, the priest begins to reflect on his experiences as a missionary to the Philippines, an account that indicates that he does, indeed, speak with authority. He remembers that when he went to a village, "They believed me! They believed the Gospel whole and entire, the teachings of the church. They said that if I told them, then it must be true or I would not have gone to so much trouble" (359). During this testimony, Will is becoming increasingly excited. He stares at the old man's face and thinks of Allie waiting for him at the greenhouse: "What is it I want from her and him, he wondered, not only want but must have? Is she a gift and therefore a sign of a giver? Could it be that the Lord is here, masquerading behind this simple silly holy face? Am I crazy to want both, her and Him? No, not want, must have. And will have" (360). Will has taken the mysterious further step from a commitment to community to a belief in God. Malcolm Magaw, though, believes the ending of the novel is ambiguous because Will "is drawn ambivalently toward an existential Second Coming in the countenance of his beloved Allie and a contrasting divine Second Coming which he sees prefigured in the mystical countenance of Father Weatherbee" (84). What Magaw seems to miss is that these attractions are not contradictory but rather paradoxically complementary, working in much the same manner as Catholic sacraments. Allie is for Will both a material, corporeal being as well as a sign of something more, a suggestion of the numinous; she is both a wonderful mate for him on earth as well as an indication that God is the giver of all good gifts. Instead of undercutting his conversion, Will's ability to accept these paradoxical impulses is a central indication that he is properly moving toward an acceptance of mystery instead of requiring scientific certainty before he can believe. Will's religious search has come to its conclusion.[20]

The direct presentation of both Yakov Bok's and Will Barrett's religious searching comes through the structure of their spiritual quests. What happens on those quests, though, is often buried behind a character's action or a passing observation since these authors, in their effort to avoid "preachment," will usually not explicitly state a movement to mystery but rely instead on irony, paradox, and biblical hints to convey this understanding. In these two novels, these suggestions are augmented by the concrete presentation of a movement to mystery through the protagonists' commitment to community. Both Yakov and Will must emerge from their isolation—in the prison or in the cave—to connect with society. Although they experience it in significantly different ways, both Yakov and Will undergo alterations that can only be understood as a mystery.

THE INEFFABLE QUESTS: *THE ASSISTANT* AND *THE MOVIEGOER*

While *The Fixer* and *The Second Coming* can be identified as Malamud's and Percy's most explicit examples of spiritual quests, Malamud's *The Assistant* and Percy's *The Moviegoer* are arguably their most skillful presentations of religious mystery through a quest, of reaching for the ineffable. Once again, in *The Assistant* and *The Moviegoer*, Malamud and Percy present protagonists who have not domesticated despair but are rather on a quest—although neither knows (or at least admits) that he is dealing with a religious question. Frank Alpine and Binx Bolling each have an urge to find more than day-to-day existence, and Malamud and Percy portray Frank's and Binx's searches, finally leading to their religious commitment. But as in *The Fixer* and *The Second Coming*, because of the difficulty of explicitly portraying this mysterious step to belief, Malamud and Percy rely on their narrative form—the quest—to represent this nonrational commitment with only a brief hint of the change at the conclusion, making the completion of the search seem ambiguous if the movements of the characters throughout their quests have not been properly understood.

Malamud is much more reticent about discussing his writing than is Percy, being very wary of any comments that might seem to "explain" his fiction.[21] Nevertheless, as his comment that his characters are "God-haunted" implies, it seems appropriate to see that another level is at work in *The Assistant* besides the finely developed world of a Jewish grocery store in New York City. As occurs in several other Malamud novels, *The Assistant* shows the protagonist, Frank Alpine, beginning to realize that he can possibly find "a fuller existence than the one he has been living[,] and that awakening begins a quest for existence" (Handy 68). One can even import Percy's Kierkegaardian language to describe Frank's quest: he moves from an aesthetic to an ethical to finally a religious sphere. Initially, it seems Frank wants only his piece of the American dream. After Frank has somewhat unwillingly participated in holding up Morris Bober's grocery store, he feels the need to go back to Morris to try to make amends. As they talk, Frank tells the grocer about the disappointments he has experienced as he has tried to make something of his life: "I've been close to some wonderful things—jobs, for instance, education, women, but close is as far as I go. . . . Don't ask me why, but sooner or later everything I think is worth having gets away from me in some way or other" (36). Frank's baffled assessment that "close is as far as I go" and that everything "gets away from me" points toward the fact that he may be reaching for the wrong goals—or at least selling himself short by making those his ultimate dreams.

Nonetheless, Frank hopes that he can find just the kinds of things he wants by working at the grocery store—and he wishes to soothe his conscience for his part in the robbery. But even though Frank is drawn to Morris' honesty and generosity, he still tries to fill the emptiness inside him through physical pleasures. Since Helen, Morris' daughter, seems inaccessible to the "goy" Frank, he attempts to fulfill his desires by peering at her bathing, thus objectifying her: "But in looking he was forcing her out of reach, making her into a thing only of his seeing" (75–

76). Eventually he does manage to begin a relationship with her, but he shows that he is still in the aesthetic sphere by neglecting her identity and focusing on the physical parts of their relationship: once as they went out, Helen says to him, "Don't forget I'm Jewish." He replies, "So what?" Later, as he thought about his response, "he felt this elated feeling, as if he had crashed head on through a brick wall and hadn't bruised himself" (121). Frank feels that he is breaking Helen away from her Jewish identity and thus is getting closer to the physical intimacy he desires. His surreal image of crashing through a wall without harming himself, particularly in the context of Helen's mentioning her religious heritage, has intimations of mystical religious experience: the devotee is able to burst the boundaries of physical existence to reach for the ineffable. But in Frank's case, these religious overtones ironically suggest that he is placing sex as his highest goal, making physical intimacy his god.

Yet even as he tries to satisfy his desires through the physical pleasures of the aesthetic sphere, there are clues that he senses that such a solution is inadequate. As his desire for Helen continues to go unfulfilled, his waiting becomes less patient: "He was the victim of the sharp edge of his hunger" (135). This description, which clearly refers to his sexual longings, also carries implications of a deeper hunger inside Frank, especially when linked with Frank's earlier comment to Morris: "I'm always hungry" (51). That Frank's never-satisfied appetite is an indication of his religious emptiness is emphasized by the novel's insistence on connecting Frank with St. Francis of Assisi. This parallel between Frank and his namesake is suggested from the beginning of the novel, underlining the idea that Frank's search is for more than sensual pleasures. Indeed, when we first learn his name, Frank immediately tells his listener a story about St. Francis' rejection of physical comforts, saying, "he gave everything away that he owned, every cent, all his clothes off his back. . . . Every time I read about somebody like him I get a feeling inside me I have to fight to keep from crying. He was born good, which is a talent if you have it" (31). Actually, St. Francis was more accurately "born good" in a material, rather than a spiritual sense: he grew up in a worldly and wealthy family. But he felt that he was called to rebuild the Church, so he literally did take off his elaborate clothes and handed them to his father, indicating that he was about to begin a new life of devotion and service to others, especially lepers and other neglected sick people. St. Francis' deep care for God's creation extended to nature as well; one of the best known stories about him concerns his preaching to "his sisters," the birds, telling them to "strive always to praise God" (Foster and Smith 314–17).

Frank's admiration and deep feeling for the saint hint at his own spiritual longing. He is further identified with St. Francis through additional stories he tells of the saint and through Helen's linking him to St. Francis in her mind. After he describes the saint's creation of a "wife" out of snow, Helen reflects of Frank, "Who was he making into a wife out of snowy moonlight?" (102). Helen's connection of Frank and St. Francis is reiterated through her perception of him at the park: "Helen saw a man squatting by one of the benches, feeding the birds. . . . When the man rose, the pigeons rose with him, a few landing on his arms and shoulders, one perched on his fingers, pecking peanuts from his cupped palm. Another fat bird sat on his hat" (118). Because of Frank's identification with St. Francis—and here specifically his love for birds—the reader can sense that more is at work in Frank than he articulates. Frank reveals that he has a spiritual longing which, like St. Francis', will only be filled when he is "beyond caring for his physical wellbeing" (Sandy Cohen 43). As Robert Kegan suggests, we think that Frank is staying at Morris' store because of guilt for his part in the robbery and his attraction for Helen, but that is not an entirely adequate understanding: "There is a force growing here, about which we have no knowledge whatever" (39). Or, perhaps more accurately, our knowledge of Frank's increasing sense of his religious need is supplied only through brief hints of his search in the novel.

This growing moral force is at times hard to recognize because Frank is learning from the principled Morris even as Frank is still engaged in the aesthetic sphere. But his discomfort with dishonesty—especially in his initial return to Morris after the holdup—shows that Frank has not domesticated his negative qualities but still wishes for change. Frank even acknowledges to himself that he will not find peace until he starts "shoveling out the load he was carrying around in his mind by admitting to Morris that he was one of the guys that had held him up" (89). Nevertheless, he begins to steal small amounts of money from the cash register, attempting to justify himself; yet even when he thought he had "settled it in his mind" he found himself "remorseful" (69). He suggests to Morris that he cheat the customers. Morris responds in surprise, "Why should I steal from my customers? Do they steal from me? . . . When a man is honest he don't worry when he sleeps. This is more important than to steal a nickel" (84). What Frank has not admitted to himself is that there is a conflict between American materialism and the moral improvement that he desires (Iska Alter 94). Instead, Frank needs to learn from Morris about a higher law than his own desires.

When Frank asks Morris what it means to be a Jew, he replies, "The important thing is the Torah." But Frank presses Morris, pointing out that Morris does not keep kosher laws or observe the Sabbath, so Morris spells out his understanding of the Law: "Nobody will tell me that I am not Jewish because I put in my mouth once in a while, when my tongue is dry, a piece of ham. But they will tell me, and I will believe them, if I forget the Law. This means to do what is right, to be honest, to be good. This means to other people." Frank persists, asking,

> "What do you suffer for, Morris?" . . .
> "I suffer for you," Morris said calmly. . . .
> [Frank's] mouth ached. "What do you mean?"
> "I mean you suffer for me." (125)

This kind of understanding of Judaism is reinforced by the rabbi's words at Morris' funeral. The rabbi acknowledges that Morris did not follow the "formal tradition," but he was a Jew because he "lived in the Jewish experience" with "the Jewish heart" (229). Frank cannot understand the kind of morality and relationships that Morris is spelling out, a relationship of love and commitment. As critics have pointed out, though, Frank is correct in arguing that Morris' interpretation of the law does not stand up to rabbinical standards. Morris' picking and choosing among the commandments seems almost an individualized, Americanized version of Judaism, a middle ground between separatism and assimilation (Nilsen 45). David Hirsch, for instance, insists that for Morris, "apparently, the Law is an abstraction that does not seem to be in any way connected to a Divine revelation, and he does not seem capable of conceiving that by obeying himself he may be disobeying God." Instead, "Both Morris and the rabbi cling to what may be called sentimental cliches of Jewishness: a true Jew has a 'Jewish heart'" (48–49).

Nevertheless, even though it is accurate that Morris' conception falls short of rabbinic Judaism, his explanation of Judaism fits in with certain Jewish traditions. The Jewish sage Hillel, when asked by a gentile to define Judaism, did so in much the same way as Morris, saying, "What is hateful to yourself do not do to your fellow man. That is the whole of the Torah. All the rest is commentary" (qtd. in Neusner 87).[22] While Hillel did not eliminate this "commentary" as Morris does, Hillel's formulation does put the emphasis on the parts of Judaism that are important to Morris. Additionally, as many critics have noted, the names Morris Bober and Martin Buber are strikingly similar, seeming to suggest that Malamud may have had Buber's philosophy in mind as he wrote. However, in a May 12, 1963, letter to Mr. [Sidney?] Richman, Malamud writes, "I read my first Martin Buber book after I wrote *The Assistant*. He has not in the least influenced me, though I do like what he writes" (Bernard Malamud Papers II:1). Yet even if Malamud did not deliberately borrow from Buber, the ideas of Buber do seem to relate to *The Assistant*. The most well-known feature of Buber's philosophy is the contrast he outlines between "I–It" relations, where a person treats others as objects, and "I–Thou" relationships, which are characterized by openness and mutuality. This conception seems to correspond with Morris' sense of connection to fellow human beings—of seeing, for instance, even the poor Polish woman, who demands her daily roll of bread while Morris is still in bed, as a worthwhile person who must be treated with respect. For Buber, such a relationship is in some way holy, for "every approach to another's Thou [is] . . . an approach to God, the Eternal Thou" (qtd. in Hays 24). So even though Morris' Judaism does not meet rabbinical standards, he does model for Frank what it means to live out Jewish ethics.

Frank finds it difficult to change in the ways that he wants, though, sinking to what is his lowest point in the novel. When Helen arranges one night to meet him in the park, Frank is hopeful it means she will offer herself to him—as, in fact, Helen is planning to do. But on arriving at the park, Helen is attacked by a would-be rapist and is narrowly saved by Frank. Although Helen is distraught and begs Frank to wait, "he spoke of his starved and passionate love, and all his endless waiting. . . . Afterward, she cried, 'Dog—uncircumcised dog!'" (168). Too late for his relationship with Helen, Frank realizes his need to move beyond his own desires. As he shifts more fully into the ethical sphere, he recognizes the stench of his own behavior: "He smelled garbage in his bed and couldn't move out of it. He couldn't because he was it—the stink in his own broken nose. What you did was how bad you smelled" (147). Replacing a traditional discussion of "sin" with this linkage of behavior and odor seems to be Malamud's concrete way of introducing a theological concept without using worn-out religious language. Admitting his wrong to Helen, Frank attempts to make it up to the Bobers through his hard work in the store, keeping the family afloat financially. His moral change is made clear through his attitude toward a poor family in the neighborhood. When he goes to their home to collect an old debt to the store, Frank recognizes the squalor of their living and, as Morris might have done, decides to give them money instead of collecting what is owed (190). He also confesses to Morris his part in the holdup, a clearing of his conscience that he had wanted to do throughout the novel. He insists to Morris, "I have changed" (198).

Frank's final movement to a religious commitment is a gradual one. Although, as we have seen, Frank throughout the course of the novel has been searching, his entry into the religious sphere begins the day of Morris' funeral. Frank inadvertently falls onto Morris' coffin in the grave; "Frank scrambled out of the grave, helped by the diggers. I have spoiled the funeral, he thought. He felt pity on the world for harboring him" (232). As Frank symbolically dies to his old life and rises to become a new man in the pattern of Morris, he admits that his old efforts at succeeding were worthless. No longer does he feel that he can succeed just with his efforts at discipline and love (184); instead, he has recognized a deeper spiritual need, as is evidenced by his sense of unworthiness at the funeral. This new acknowledgment does not mean he has reached perfection. At one point, he returns to spying on Helen bathing and to cheating customers (242).[23] "Then, one day, for no reason he could give, though the reason felt familiar, he stopped climbing up the air shaft to peek at Helen, and he was honest in the store" (242). Helen realizes that he has changed and thanks him for keeping the store solvent. With little fanfare, the narrator notes that Frank was reading the Bible and continuing to think of St. Francis. Finally, "One day in April Frank went to the hospital and had himself circumcised. For a couple of days he dragged himself around with a pain between his legs. The pain enraged and inspired him. After Passover he became a Jew" (246).

This understated conclusion has given rise to varied interpretations of what takes place. Sanford Pinsker finds Frank coming to "a Judaism he does not understand and which cannot possibly sustain him" (53). In a somewhat similar way, Jonathan Baumbach believes that "Frank becomes a Jew, not out of religious conviction but because he elects to be like Morris, a good man," choosing to suffer for others (117). Baumbach adds, "Ironically, Frank's rebirth leads him only to the assumption of Morris' living death in the tomb of the grocery store" (121). Paradoxically, though, rather than this "tomb" having a deleterious effect on Frank, it is only when Frank is imprisoned in the store that through suffering and commitment he opens the way for a religious conversion. Thus, while suffering is clearly a part of what Frank accepts when he becomes a Jew, Philip Roth's assessment seems closer to the mark than Baumbach's: "We might almost take what happens to the bad goy when he falls into the hands of the good Jew as an act of enraged Old Testament retribution visited upon him by the wrathful Jewish author—if it weren't for the moral pathos and gentle religious coloration with which Malamud invests the tale of conversion" (99).

This "religious coloration" throughout his quest does indeed set the stage for Frank's conversion. But, as discussed earlier, Malamud is wary of explicitly articulating a religious commitment, so there is a lack of directness about the conversion. Critics, however, have not fully understood this representation of the ineffable. Sidney Richman, for example, observes: "Ultimately, at the heart of Frankie's conversion—as well as Morris Bober's identity—is a transcendent mystery. But, curiously, there are none of the features of mystery. Assuredly, there is nothing of the intensity of the mystical states which can answer for the horror of the immediate world" (*Bernard Malamud* 70). Richman seems not to realize that such a calm, indirect presentation, not the ecstasy of mysticism, is Malamud's way to present religious mystery. Malamud uses the quest form to indicate that Frank is moving toward a nonrational religious commitment, showing "the wandering, the moving to the edge" (Kegan 48). It is up to the reader, after recognizing Frank's search, to understand what is finally happening. Malamud will not be explicit, as he acknowledges in a conversation: "My job is to create mystery. Exemplification of mystery is the creation of mystery" (qtd. in Kegan 41). This religious mystery is most clearly hinted at in the description of Frank's final abandonment of his spying and stealing, when he acknowledges that he changes "for no reason he could give, though the reason felt familiar." An attempt at a rational analysis of this statement shows that it makes little logical sense: how is it that Frank cannot give a reason for his transformation but still know the reason feels familiar? This paradoxical assertion gets at the ineffable quality of a religious conversion, exemplifying perfectly the difficulty of directly articulating religious mystery. Malamud only implies why Frank has changed, leaving to the reader to understand the enigmatic comment that "the reason felt familiar." Since we have followed Frank's sense throughout the novel that he is looking for something more, his turning to a religious commitment does indeed feel comfortable and right.

His circumcision then becomes a physical, external symbol—both for Frank and for the reader—of the mysterious change that is happening within him. By partaking in this ceremony, which was instituted in God's original covenant with Abraham, Frank becomes connected to the larger community of Jews as he enters into the covenantal relationship. Within the novel, the circumcision also serves as Frank's symbolic repentance for raping Helen; she had called him an "uncircumcised dog," so his decision to be circumcised (along with his long hours of working in the store) shows his repentance and his desire to renew his relationship with Helen. It seems significant, too, that Frank's official conversion to Judaism takes place shortly after Passover, the commemoration of God's sparing the Israelites when the firstborn were killed at the time of the Exodus. On a personal level, Frank's conversion to Judaism indicates that he has experienced God's mercy, mirroring the deliverance the Israelites received. It then becomes clear that even if he does not understand all of Jewish law, Frank is making a sincere conversion to Judaism.[24]

In *The Moviegoer*, as in many of his novels, Percy, too, shows a man searching. Percy has made it clear in various conversations and essays, though, that he sees himself as a "diagnostic" novelist, not one who supplies answers: "The physician-novelist is not himself a news-bearer, and he is not in the business of writing edifying tales. . . . It is enough for him to have discovered and put his finger on the peculiar lesion of the age" (*Signposts* 195). Alfred Kazin, picking up on this theme, says of Percy, "Faith for him seems to express a search rather than something found, a *way* of seeing, not an end" (103). While such an observation is not inaccurate, one must be careful not to swing too far toward seeing Percy's characters as only on the way. For even though he recognizes the dangers and difficulties in representing a Christian commitment, Percy subtly infuses Binx Bolling's quest with religious significance so that it is clear that he has encountered "the infinite mystery and the infinite delight" (*Conversations with Walker Percy* 175).

More explicitly than Frank Alpine, Binx Bolling tells of his search and its beginnings when he was injured in Korea, lying in a ditch and watching a dung beetle. "As I watched, there awoke in me an immense curiosity. I was onto something. I vowed that if I ever got out of this fix, I would pursue the search. Naturally, as soon as I recovered and got home, I forgot all about it" (11). Actually, Binx tells us later that he had for a time undertaken what he called a "vertical search," which involved reading "fundamental books" to learn about the universe (69–70). In a passage obviously parallel to Percy's own frequent paraphrases of Kierkegaard's assessment of Hegel, Binx thinks, "The only difficulty was that though the universe had been disposed of, I myself was left over. There I lay in my hotel room with my [vertical] search over yet still obliged to draw one breath and then the next" (70). Echoing Percy's own views, Binx realizes the insufficiency of assuming that science can answer all questions about human existence—the danger of seeing people only as "specimens" (73)—and thus leaves his vertical search.

In the present of the novel, Binx has just begun, again, to search—this time horizontally. Binx's often-quoted definition of the search is "what anyone would undertake if he were not sunk in the everydayness of his own life" (13).[25] The horizontal search involves a looking around him "for clues to grace—the presence of God in the world" (Hobson 29). But, at the beginning, even though Binx is awakening again to the possibility of a search, he does not admit he is looking for God; instead, being very much caught in the aesthetic sphere, he attempts to find fulfillment in "the Little Way, not the big search for happiness but the sad little happiness of drinks and kisses, a good little car and a warm deep thigh" (135–36). With his succession of girlfriend-secretaries and his incessant moviegoing, Binx is trying to drown his sense of unease in a flood of physical pleasure and distraction. Later in the novel, though, Binx acknowledges that the "search has spoiled the pleasure of my tidy and ingenious life in Gentilly" (191). The course of the novel charts his increasing dissatisfaction with other answers until he is finally thrust into the religious sphere.

Even when Binx was involved in the "vertical search" through his work in a laboratory, he became much more interested in the wonder of a summer afternoon than the work he was doing in the laboratory, unlike his partner who was "no more aware of the mystery which surrounds him than a fish is aware of the water it swims in" (52). From his observation, it is clear that Binx has a sense of mystery, but he is unable—or unwilling—to break out of his neatly organized life as a stockbroker to reach beyond simple existence. His discomfort is made obvious by his remark: "I have not slept soundly for many years" (83). Even though he appears on the surface to have a fulfilling life, Binx recognizes an emptiness. Yet he refuses to acknowledge that he may be searching for God:

> My unbelief was invincible from the beginning. I could never make head or tail of God. The proofs of God's existence may have been true for all I know, but it didn't make the slightest difference. If God himself had appeared to me, it would have changed nothing. In fact, I have only to hear the word God and a curtain comes down in my head. . . . Abraham saw signs of God and believed. Now the only sign is that all the signs in the world make no difference. Is this God's ironic revenge? But I am onto him. (145–46)

Binx is insisting that he has no use for God—is indifferent to him. But even in this nonchalance, Binx may be showing that he has a sense of God. As Gary Ciuba observes, "Binx's recognition of God's trickery finally turns on himself and then turns him toward God. If the only sign is the lack of interest in signs, Binx transforms human carelessness about God into a testimony of the divine presence: the mind can only be indifferent to God because God already exists" (70). If this is so, then even as Binx denies any interest in God, he is showing his hand, indicating that God's existence does matter to him. Similarly, Binx mentions throughout the novel that he has always been interested in Jews; perhaps he identifies with Jews because he seeks for knowledge of God, as Jews do, even if Binx has not consciously acknowledged his search (Futrell 169).

Just as Binx's interest in God suggests that he is aware of the Divine, some of his interactions with other people demonstrate that he is capable of deeper attachments than his cool, ironic surface might imply. Even in his moviegoing, he enjoys engaging the employees at the theater in conversation: "I have discovered that most people have no one to talk to, no one, that is, who really wants to listen" (64). Binx is interested in listening to people who are usually overlooked by much of society. More important for understanding Binx's search is recognizing the significance of his relationship with his devout and diseased half-brother Lonnie. Binx says:

> we are good friends because he knows I do not feel sorry for him. For one thing, he has the gift of believing that he can offer his sufferings in reparation of men's indifference to the pierced heart of Jesus Christ. For another thing, I would not mind so much trading places with him. His life is a serene business. (137)

Binx's profound love and respect for Lonnie show a depth not easily evident in much of his surface existence. He can tell that Lonnie has a peace which he finds attractive.

Binx's final movement toward a religious commitment begins when he goes off to Chicago with his Great Aunt Emily's stepdaughter Kate, who is seeing a psychiatrist and had (not too seriously) just attempted suicide. Kate has found Binx to be someone she can talk to, someone who can reach her even at those moments when, as she says, "it's bad" (61). Binx had suggested that they marry, and Kate decides that perhaps she could marry Binx if he would promise always to tell her what to do. It is at Kate's suggestion, though, that they sleep together on the train on the way to Chicago, but this pleasure, which had been central in Binx's aesthetic sphere, is not particularly successful. Binx says, "Flesh poor flesh failed us. The burden was too great and flesh poor flesh, neither hallowed by sacrament nor despised by spirit . . .—flesh poor flesh now at this moment summoned to be all and every thing, end all and be all, the last and only hope—quails and fails" (200). Binx recognizes "[w]hat a sickness it is . . . this latter-day post-Christian sex" (207). The physical image of Binx's impotence serves as an indicator that all is not well within him. His aesthetic sphere is being smashed, but he has nothing with which to replace it. Since Binx can see the emptiness in others (and eventually in himself) without adequately understanding how to fill his void, he is, as Ralph C. Wood explains, "in danger of becoming a diagnostician without a cure" (163).

Much like Frank Alpine, who found the grace to turn when he felt he was beyond hope, Binx reaches the depths on his return from Chicago. His Aunt Emily, a representative of the stoic tradition, lectures him about how he has failed in his responsibilities to Kate. Kate, who was listening to the conversation, calls Binx "stupid" for not defending himself. When he leaves his aunt and while he is waiting, hoping that Kate will arrive, Binx despairs on this, his birthday, about the state of his life:

> Now is the thirty-first year of my dark pilgrimage on this earth and knowing less than I ever knew before, having learned only to recognize merde when I see it . . . . Nothing remains but desire, and desire comes howling down. . . . My search has been abandoned; it is no match for my aunt, her rightness and her despair, her despair of me and her despairing of herself. (228)

Believing that Kate has been persuaded to abandon him, Binx decides to try once more to lose himself in physical pleasure, and thus he calls his secretary to attempt to arrange a tryst. Just as he is setting up a meeting—actually with his secretary's roommate—Kate appears, and Binx regains hope that the search is possible (Lawson 887–88). Binx thinks, "Is it possible—that it is not too late?" (231).

Binx commits himself to Kate, promising to stand by her and tell her what she should do. He then seals this covenant by kissing her bloody thumb, which in her anxiety she picks apart, thus partaking in a form of the sacrament at the heart of Lonnie's Catholicism (Ciuba 90). Just after he realizes that Kate is indeed coming back to him and as he is trying to decide what he should do with his life, he thinks, "There is only one thing that I can do: listen to people, see how they stick themselves into the world, hand them along a ways in their dark journey and be handed along, and for good and selfish reasons" (233). While he is talking with Kate, he observes a "Negro" entering a nearby church since this is Ash Wednesday. At first, Binx thinks cynically that the man is at church as part of a plan for social advancement. But then he realizes that something else could be at work:

> It is impossible to say why he is here. Is it part and parcel of the complex business of coming up in the world? Or is it because he believes that God himself is present here at the corner of Elysian Fields and Bons Enfants? Or is he here for both reasons: through some dim dazzling trick of grace, coming for the one and receiving the other as God's own importunate bonus?
>
> It is impossible to say. (235)

Finally, in an Epilogue, Binx briefly reports that he and Kate have married. He refuses to speak of his search, citing Kierkegaard and saying that it is "much too late to edify" (237). Binx relates that on the day when Lonnie died, he went to his half brothers and sisters to talk with them. One asks him, "When Our Lord raises up on the last day, will Lonnie still be in a wheelchair or will he be like us?" Binx answers, "He'll be like you" (240). The novel ends with his giving directions to Kate about a trip downtown she is to take. She nervously asks him,

> "I'm going to sit next to the window on the Lake side and put the cape jasmine in my lap?"
>
> "That's right."
>
> "And you'll be thinking of me just that way?"
>
> "That's right."
>
> "Good-by."
>
> "Good-by." . . .
>
> I watch her walk toward St Charles, cape jasmine held against her cheek, until my brothers and sisters call out behind me. (242)

As with the ending of *The Assistant*, critics have interpreted what happens to Binx in varying ways. Ted Spivey believes, "Except that he is married, the end of the book finds him in much the same condition as the beginning, still bound to pleasures arising from the contemplation of images" ("Religion and Reintegration" 73). Similarly, Emory Elliott argues that we may wish to believe that Binx has found new meaning; "[t]he problem with this reading, however, is that it is not borne out by the text, especially that of the final chapter and epilogue" (36). John Hardy's assessment that Binx properly calls his half brothers and sisters full siblings in Christ is helpful, but even he finds that "[t]he trouble with the Binx of the epilogue is not that he has changed too much, or too abruptly or unaccountably, but that he has not changed enough," especially in his relationship with Kate (50, 55). On the other hand, Kieran Quinlan believes that the ending does show a change—but that alteration does not grow naturally from the rest of the novel: "to a degree an ending consistent with Percy's own philosophical and theological views has been imposed upon the narrative rather than allowed to arise naturally from it" (97). Wood's analysis seems more on the mark: "Through his love for Kate Cutrer, Binx Bolling discovers that his cynical contempt for the world's unconscious despair will not suffice" but rather finds that ethical and religious reality "begins at the point where self-absorption ends—namely, in true community" (172).[26]

Just as Malamud only suggests Frank's change, Percy also refuses to be too explicit about what happens to his characters, recognizing the difficulties of directly representing a conversion. He says he does not give a firm direction to his endings: "Maybe I give the ending a certain tilt. But I take it as far as I believe a novelist can take it" (*More Conversations with Walker Percy* 69). More specifically, when discussing the problems of representing grace, he says, "I have to be very careful when I talk about grace. I have to be extremely allusive. I think Caroline Gordon said, 'The novelist is entitled to use every trick of deceit and underhandedness at his or her control'" (*More Conversations with Walker Percy* 239). It is just this allusiveness that allows for the range of interpretations concerning *The Moviegoer*'s conclusion. But again, by focusing on Binx's quest throughout the novel, it is possible to see the inexorable direction of his search. His recognition of the inadequacy of his aesthetic search, his studied lack of interest in God, his deep relationship with Lonnie all lead up to his final commitment to love and care for Kate. Even more, he makes clear that he acknowledges his "vocation" of helping others along the way—and with his earlier listening to those usually ignored, he is clearly ready for such a calling. But most important, Percy gives a strong hint that grace is at work in Binx's life since—on Ash Wednesday, the beginning of Lent—Binx is able to understand that maybe, just maybe, the Negro has experienced God's grace. The incident suggests that perhaps Binx, too, has received a sense of the numinous.

The Epilogue simply underlines that understanding. Even the formal structure of a nineteenth-century-style epilogue suggests a difference from the disjointed opening of the novel (Ciuba 91). With Binx's statement of faith to his siblings that Lonnie will be raised up and with his caring for Kate—as she had asked him to do—we can see that Binx has in fact made a religious commitment.[27] Martin Luschei is indeed correct when he says that "Percy suggests this without moralizing and without grandiose claims, by his elliptical approach and the language of understatement" (110).

Such is the task of any novelist attempting to represent a movement to religious mystery. Both Malamud's and Percy's novels show that for them, a portrayal of a character's encounter with the Divine must be set up by a fully developed search and then hinted at only briefly. In a 1962 letter to Caroline Gordon, Percy writes about the threadbareness of religious words: "When the holy has disappeared, how in blazes can a novelist expect to make use of it? . . . Perhaps the craft of the religious novelist nowadays consists mainly in learning how to shout in silence" (qtd. in Brown 173). That silence is never more thundering than in the time when a character experiences a moment of grace and reaches toward God. Like Binx Bolling, these authors seem to realize of such transcendent moments, "It is impossible to say."

As shown in these six novels, the quest form provides a structure through which Malamud and Percy can present a sense of religious mystery. That specific form is augmented through other concrete actions during the course of the novels, which, mirroring the function of *mitzvot* and sacraments, serve as tangible evidence of the nonrational. A technique that recurs in these novels to convey this sense involves giving added significance to the relationship between the protagonist and a woman. These romantic attractions, though, can serve either to indicate his spiritual needs or to point toward his sense of the numinous. For instance, Frank Alpine's rape of Helen, along with his attendant realization that he smells garbage in his bed, provides a very physical sense of Frank's need to change. On the other hand, it is through Will Barrett's relationship with Allie—both emotional and physical—that he is able to affirm life and, eventually, become a believer. It may be more than coincidence that erotic relationships are often freighted with religious significance in these novels. Rudolf Otto points out that love relationships are in certain ways analogous to a religious consciousness, for in such relations, there is a level of friendship and attraction, which can be explained, as well as the feeling of love, which resists articulation (46). As the example of romantic relationships suggests, Malamud's and Percy's quests contain religiously significant actions that serve as physical links to mystery.

NOTES

1. "Novelist and Believer," *Mystery and Manners*, New York: Farrar, Straus and Giroux, 1962, page 159.
2. *The Habit of Being*, ed. Sally Fitzgerald, New York: Farrar, Straus and Giroux, 1979, page 520.
3. Percy, though, did regularly mention Malamud when asked to cite authors he admired. And in his notes for *God's Grace*, Malamud mentions that "Bob [presumably Robert Giroux, his editor] suggests I read Walker Percy's 'The Message in the Bottle'" (Bernard Malamud Papers, part I, container 25). The Bernard Malamud Papers at the Library of Congress are divided into parts I and II. Future references to this collection will be cited in the text by listing part number followed by container number, e.g., I:25.

4. For instance, in a March 1963 letter to Phil Baum turning down an invitation to participate in a "Dialogue" in Israel, hosted by the American Jewish Congress, Malamud lists the private nature of his beliefs as one of his reasons for declining to come: "First of all, I feel that how my Jewishness operates in me and my works is a private matter and one that I ought to limit to my fiction. I can't easily make it a matter of public autobiography or confession" (I:1).

5. Such a sentiment is just what Harold Bloom finds objectionable. He writes that even though he experiences delight in reading *The Moviegoer*, that pleasure is "perhaps somewhat darkened by intimations in the novel of the moral and religious obsessions that have made each subsequent fiction by Walker Percy rather more problematic than before" (*Walker Percy* 1).

6. Malamud's religious concerns in *God's Grace* have been a subject of controversy. See Elaine B. Safer's "The Allusive Mode, the Absurd, and Black Humor in Bernard Malamud's *God's Grace*" and Sydney Richman's "Malamud's Quarrel with God" for discussions of this theme. Joel Salzberg believes that *God's Grace* brings "to the surface what seems to have been a private conflict implied in his earlier stories—Malamud's quarrel with God" (2). While the issues raised in *God's Grace* could certainly fit within this study, Malamud is drawing in this novel on a different narrative form—the fable—rather than the quest, so a detailed examination of this, the last of Malamud's completed novels, is outside the scope of my discussion.

7. Percy's conception of the distinctly religious intimations of setting a character on a quest underlines the reasonableness of examining the quests in his fiction: "any novelist who begins his novel with his character in a life predicament which is a profound mystery to which he devotes his entire life to unraveling . . . is a closet Jew or Christian whether he likes it or not" (*Signposts* 178).

8. Percy's novels can, without exception, be seen to work on an anagogical level. Some of Malamud's later novels, such as *Dubin's Lives*, have a less obviously spiritual dimension. Nevertheless, Andrew Furman sees a basic similarity between Malamud's earlier writing and *Dubin's Lives*. In all of the novels, Furman believes, Malamud's central question is, "are we responsible only for ourselves, or must we bear responsibility for our family, our friends, even strangers?" (44).

9. Although in the common imagination the Grail is associated with the cup, according to the description in the Grail accounts, it seems more likely to have been the dish on which Christ served the Passover lamb (Matarasso 276).

10. In an October 23, 1951, letter in the Bernard Malamud Papers, Malamud spells out many of these mythical connections to his agent, pointing out ways that the symbolism of the first chapter sets up the remainder of the novel's symbolic quality.

11. Lister's conception, though, that the novel portrays Lancelot as a "devil" and that the novel is really a "book-length exorcism" seems excessive (84–85). Although Lancelot is far from entirely admirable, his insistence that actions do matter, that sin is still around, show him to be at least praiseworthy on that count. Percy himself said that Lancelot's actions are "partly admirable and partly crazy" (*Conversations with Walker Percy* 209).

12. Percy notes this connection, saying, "the reader may remember in the legend it was only Percival and Lancelot, of all the knights, who saw the Grail" (*More Conversations* 146). Although some versions of the myth show more knights seeing the Grail, Percy's comment that Percival and Lancelot are among them is still illuminating.

13. While many critics see Lancelot prepared to change, that view is by no means universal. In a review, Joyce Carol Oates excoriates the novel, feeling only scorn for Lance: "Though the plot of *Lancelot* is a tired and contrived one involving a cuckolded husband's revenge upon his wife and her decadent friends (for whom we feel, perversely, far more sympathy than we feel for the garrulous and self-righteous central character), it is nevertheless preferable to the empty rhetoric that fills page after page of the novel" (64).

14. Readers disagree over how "Christian" is *The Fixer*. Harold Fisch believes that the novel moves from a "suffering servant" conception to "the more traditional Jewish exegesis which sees the servant as the persona of the whole Jewish people, suffering the trials of its history" (164). But Cynthia Ozick believes that the theme of *The Fixer* is Christian: "Its theme is vicarious suffering, which is by no means a Jewish idea" (Ozick with Kauvar 1993 378).

15. One way to understand the shift is to see it in an historical context as exemplifying the movement of Jews away from religious concerns to political causes.

16. Yakov's dream when he confronts the Tsar has invited a vast range of interpretations, a number of which can function at the same time without contradiction. Sheldon Hershinow points out that this "murder" only takes place in a dream, not in actual action, and that distinction is important: "the tsar insists that he is a kind person who loves his people, including the Jews. Yakov, however, condemns the tsar to death for failing to rule with justice and mercy. The implied conclusion is obvious: thoughts and intentions are not the most important measure of a man's character" (73). In a similar vein, both Lucio Ruotolo and Jeffrey Helterman believe that Yakov "executed" the tsar because the tsar claimed neutrality and, in Ruotolo's words, "Yakov sees that neutrality masks compliance, that in doing nothing Nicholas is equally guilty" (137). Finally, Arvindra Sant believes that "what Bok does is execute a man already dead to human feelings and the needs of his dependent subjects, especially those who must look to him for justice" (186).

17. Interestingly, *The Fixer* itself became a political issue when several school boards banned the novel from libraries. In an undated comment about the banning, Malamud notes both the absurd comedy of the situation—suggesting that perhaps an Art Buchwald article is in order—and the seriousness of censorship. He notes also how odd it is that his novel was banned: "It's ironic that *The Fixer* was chosen as one of the books to be excluded from school libraries. If you don't read it you don't know that, among other things, it's a defense of the Jews in Czarist Russia against antisemitism; and a defense of man's right to justice" (II:1).

18. Peter Hawkins accurately points out, though, that there is some confusion in the novel concerning Will's religious longing. The narrator seems to link Will's looking for "signs" to his unbalanced pH level, so the novel apparently suggests that his longings are just a physical problem: "This dismissal goes against everything that Percy believes to be true about the deepest longing of human nature, and yet it is the narrator who makes the connection" (85).

19. John Hardy argues that Will is wrong in his effort to differentiate between the two priests' "authority": "If Weatherbee does have the authority to instruct, in this context, then he has it as a consequence of his ordination; and, 'by the same token,' Jack Curl has identical authority, Barrett's intuitions notwithstanding" (221–22). What Hardy seems to miss is that Jack Curl has been shown throughout the novel to be much more interested in Will's money than in his soul. Thus, Will is completely justified in believing that the old, but sincere, priest is the one to listen to.

20. Not all readers see such a clear movement toward connection to community and to belief. Doreen Fowler agrees that the message of the novel is that people must live in society, but "the society he [Percy] pictures is an inferno of sordid passions and discontent," so the pledge to the community seems impossible (16–17). While the society is far from ideal and Will and Allie will no doubt have difficulties, their ability to break free from their constricting roles—of mental patient and rich retiree—suggests that they will not be overwhelmed by society. Fowler simply seems to miss Percy's point that an apostle has authority to tell the good news when she criticizes Will for not accepting the limits of human knowledge but rather seeks "absolute knowledge" from the priest (20). In the world of the novel, this knowledge of the gospel is what Will needs to live.

21. See, for instance, his reaction to Joel Salzberg when Malamud felt that he was being led to describe his fiction: "You know one thing that I don't like about what we're doing is that I have begun to explain my fiction, and I don't like to do that" (*Conversations with Bernard Malamud* 143). Similarly, in an August 20, 1970, letter to Michael Frank, Malamud declines to explicate his writing: "A writer of fiction works to create mysteries, not to explain them" (Bernard Malamud Papers II:1). At times, though, especially in response to student queries, Malamud is more willing in his letters to discuss his writing.

22. Sandy Cohen makes a similar point in *Bernard Malamud and the Trial by Love* (38).

23. Jonathan Baumbach finds Frank's pattern of wrongdoing to be a test and even punishment for himself: "Since he wants more than anything else to be a good man, his crimes are a means of self-punishment; each time he pockets money from Morris' register, he torments himself with guilt. . . . As a penitent he must fall deeper and deeper into his interior hell before he can allow himself salvation" (120). While Frank's actions are no doubt psychologically complicated, his backsliding seems more a sign of human weakness than a deliberate act of self-punishment.

24. Sandy Cohen points out that since Morris' Judaism is not especially orthodox, "Frankie's conversion is really a confirmation of belief not different in kind from the belief of his Francis of Assisi. Malamud is using Morris' 'Jewish Law' as a symbol for the moral objective of any good man" (38–39). While such a connection is useful, Malamud understood Frank's conversion to tie in more specifically with Judaism. In his note to readers in the Norwegian translation of the novel, Malamud writes that even though Frank sees the Jew as a symbol, "I doubt that his view of the Jew is limited only to the man who has suffered. I think he has begun to understand the meaning of the Law, and since he is engaged, at the end of the book, in reading the Old Testament, perhaps he will appreciate the Prophetic quality of the Jewish religion. As for the Christian elements in Judaism, ideas flow backwards and forwards, and it is ridiculous to define love, charity, endurance, as the particular quality or province of one religion over another. I would want Frank to continue to love St. Francis as much as he may love Isaiah" (*Talking Horse* 86–87).

25. Although most critics agree that Binx is in fact pursuing a metaphysical search, Stanley Edgar Hyman says in a review of *The Moviegoer*, "There are occasional pretentious attempts to make Jack's search seem not neurotic but deeply spiritual, along the lines of Percy's unfortunate statement on receiving the National Book Award that his novel shows Judaeo-Christian man as 'a wayfarer and a pilgrim'" (38).

26. Percy's observation that "Binx jumps from the esthetic clear across the ethical to the religious" seems to be supported by the novel (*Conversations with Walker Percy* 66). Binx appears to have no separately identifiable period of ethical behavior.

27. Jim Van Cleave's assertion that we can learn little about Binx's change from seeing him commit to Kate at the end of the novel and from the Epilogue seems far off the mark: "What Binx says about the intervening time is presented in the past tense [in the Epilogue]. It is a past event. . . . The intervening year, that is, only exists in Binx's consciousness in the way that his years in Gentilly before this awakening into consciousness do. There is no indication that his awakened consciousness continued during that year, or that it will continue after the day of the Epilogue" (1010). This kind of literalness, arguing that we can make no inferences from the glimpses of a changed Binx, seems to assume that we must have record of a character's entire life before we can draw any conclusions. Binx has shown in significant ways that he has changed—and has given no evidence that his alteration is only long enough to be recorded in the novel.

4

Throwing Everything Off Balance: Ozick's Fantastic and O'Connor's Grotesque Portrayals of Mystery

As a writer I absolutely wallow in mystery religion.

—Cynthia Ozick[1]
"An Interview with Cynthia Ozick"

The serious fiction writer will think that any story that can be entirely explained by the motivation of its characters, or by a believable imitation of a way of life, or by a proper theology, will not be a large-enough story for him to occupy himself with.

—Flannery O'Connor[2]
Mystery and Manners

As we have seen, Bernard Malamud and Walker Percy represent mystery by showing characters who are on quests, moving toward a nonrational commitment. In these novels, the reader can encounter religious mystery by following the progression of the protagonists. Cynthia Ozick's and Flannery O'Connor's portrayals of the ineffable involve a very different approach: their fiction thrusts the reader into a direct confrontation with mystery through their use of the fantastic or the grotesque. Ozick's and O'Connor's protagonists do not necessarily experience a change or conversion at the end of the tale. Rather, these authors draw readers into a seemingly "realistic" story only to shock them through a bizarre or supernatural occurrence. By disrupting usual expectations in their stories, Ozick and O'Connor push their readers to recognize that more is at work than can be rationally understood—to see that reality is ultimately mysterious.

Like Malamud and Percy, Ozick's and O'Connor's biographies are quite distinct. They, too, are separated by religion and region: Ozick is a New York Jew while O'Connor is a Georgia Catholic. And while each early decided to become a writer, their careers diverged sharply. Ozick labored for seven years on a first novel, *Mercy, Pity, Peace, and Love*, which she wryly says became abbreviated to "Mippel." It was, as she notes with self-deprecating humor, "An endless suck on that Mippel" (Ozick with Rainwater and Scheick 257), particularly since the novel never was published. Under the spell of Henry James, she worked almost as long again on her first published novel, *Trust* (1966). After these nearly fourteen years with only one book published, Ozick decided to turn to shorter fiction—stories and novellas. As late as 1983, Ozick still says that she struggled to find publishers and acknowledges, "I have never recovered from early neglect" (Ozick with Rainwater and Scheick 257). But clearly her recognition is growing, particularly since she has won several prestigious awards, including the Mildred and Harold Strauss Living Award, which provides an author an annual $35,000 grant for five years. Ozick has published a total of eight novels or collections of stories along with four volumes of nonfiction. She is an exacting stylist and claims that "[m]y first draft is the last. I must perfect each sentence madly before I go on to the next" (Ozick with Kaganoff 34). She adds, "I write in terror. . . . I have to talk myself into bravery with every sentence, sometimes every syllable. I have a raven perched on my right shoulder at all times that says, 'That's not good, that's ugly or confusing'" (Ozick with Kaganoff 33). This concern with getting each sentence exactly right results in memorable phrases in both her fiction and essays.

O'Connor, too, is a precise writer, although her approach was to spend long hours revising manuscripts, often in response to criticism from her mentor, Caroline Gordon. Even her description of what drives her to revise sounds much like Ozick's formulation: "When I sit down to write, a monstrous reader looms up who sits down beside me and continually mutters, 'I don't get it, I don't see it, I don't want it.' Some writers can ignore this presence, but I have never learned how" (qtd. in Feeley 45). Already when she was eighteen, O'Connor recorded in her notebook that she wanted to write fiction that is informed by her Catholicism (Fitzgerald 80). Unlike Ozick's long early novels, O'Connor concentrated on short fiction from the beginning of her career; for her Master's thesis in Paul Engle's Writing Workshop at the University of Iowa, she wrote six stories. And her recognition came fairly early: although critics did not know what to make of the stories, they did notice O'Connor's fresh and startling fiction when it appeared in popular and academic publications. O'Connor spent a short time in New York at Yaddo, living with a group of other writers while she was working on her early fiction. The onset of lupus, the degenerative disease that had earlier killed her father, forced her to return home to her mother in Georgia, where she remained except for brief excursions until her death at thirty-nine in 1964. Since her life was cut off in the midst of her writing career, O'Connor's publications consist of two short novels, two collections of stories, and a volume of her essays; her stories (including some not published in her two earlier volumes) have since been gathered into *The Complete Stories*, and collections of her letters and book reviews have been published.

In evaluating the religious nature of Ozick's and O'Connor's fiction, one is faced with seemingly opposing problems: Ozick is somewhat enigmatic, sometimes even contradictory, in her explanations about how religious issues affect her stories while O'Connor is insistent (some would say overly much so) that her fiction should be read as religiously informed.[3] Indeed, even determining how Ozick would describe her religious affiliation is a difficult task. Ozick would seem to be an Orthodox Jew: she and her husband attend an Orthodox Jewish synagogue and maintain a kosher home. But Ozick rejects the "Orthodox" label. When an interviewer asks her if she is Orthodox, Ozick responds, "Ugh! That's not a Jewish word. It's a post-Enlightenment word. 'Ortho-dox'—'right belief?' That's not Jewish." The interviewer wonders if she is observant of the commandments. Ozick says, "I wouldn't even say I'm observant because I'm not observant. I'm a traditional Jew. . . . I know when I'm violating" (Ozick with Grossman 6). Another time she describes herself as "a covenanted Jew," and she explains that she rejects terms such as "'religious' or 'believing' because all these terms lead us to some kind of substantive declaration about the Godhead" (Ozick with Haberman 155). But "God has no Jewish definition; God is *the* question about the universe. Deuteronomy says your job as a human being is simply to discharge your obligations to your fellow human beings—i.e., to keep the Commandments—and you mustn't think about the nature of the Creator. . . . I must be agnostic, and Judaism *is* agnostic, about the nature of God" (Ozick with Kauvar 1985 395–96). Ozick insists that God is intrinsically beyond human understanding: "The ways of true God cannot be penetrated" (*Fame & Folly* 72). Nevertheless, Ozick does say she senses the presence of God on Yom Kippur: "That's the day when I probably can call myself a believer. Year after year this happens; it may be that result of fasting and of immersing oneself, saturating oneself, in prayer and poetry all day long" (Ozick with Haberman 156). She adds that sometimes she has a sense of the numinous during Sabbath services: "It sometimes comes flying out of the text" when Scripture is read (Ozick with Haberman 156). Clearly, being Jewish is very important to Ozick, since "[a]s a Jew I'm free. I feel enormously grateful to be a Jew. . . . I'm shaped by ethical monotheism, by Torah" (Ozick with Haberman 167).

If a term to describe her religious stance is somewhat difficult to pin down, Ozick's sense of the intersection between her writing and her Jewishness is even more complicated. In an often quoted essay, "Toward a New Yiddish" (1970), Ozick calls for a "Jewish liturgical literature," which "gives its strength to its peoplehood and the whole human note is heard everywhere, enlarged" (*Art & Ardor* 175). She has also insisted that literature must have a moral sense, that "*[w]hat literature means is meaning*" (*Art & Ardor* 247) because self-referential literature is idolatry: an idol is "a thing that can only lead back to itself and hasn't got any connections outside of itself" (Ozick with Kauvar 1985 392). So in Ozick's view, literature should not exist for its own sake but for the sake of humanity (*Art & Ardor* 247).[4] Ozick's concern with the moral sense in literature in many ways echoes Malamud's concept that literature must have a moral base, must recreate "the humanity of man" ("Writer's Task" 173).

More recently, Ozick has backed away from her earlier suggestion that English is the new Yiddish, but she has maintained that literature must have a moral basis. Yet even with that stipulation, her struggle over the role of literature has led her to the sense that any literature may be idolatry. She thus wonders "whether Jews ought to be storytellers. . . . Does the Commandment against idols warn even ink?" (Preface to *Bloodshed* 10). Although this concern figures heavily in several of her stories, by the middle of the 1980s Ozick had moved to the position that "the idol-making capacity of imagination is its lower form, and that one *cannot* be a monotheist without putting the imagination under the greatest pressure of all. To imagine the unimaginable is the highest use of the imagination. I no longer think of the imagination as a thing to be dreaded. . . . Only a very strong imagination can rise to the idea of a non-corporeal God" (Ozick with Teicholz 167). She has even gone so far as to say, "Art cannot blaspheme because it is not in the power of humankind to demean or besmirch the divine" (*Fame & Folly* 190). It seems puzzling, then, when she says in a 1992 interview:

> [W]hat happens when I write is that I am not then a Jewish writer. I think that is an oxymoron . . . . Because the Jewish part refers to a philosophic heritage and a mode of conduct. . . . But an imaginative writer does not have a system of any kind. And so, for a writer to be a Jew is definitely a contradiction in terms. If you are a good Jew, or a good Christian, a good Muslim, a good Hindu, you have a code of behaviour to which you must adhere. But a writer is a *wild* person. . . . I think writing and conscience are very often contradictory. . . . I imagine things against my conscience. (Ozick with Materassi 90–91, 96)

Yet as Susanne Klingenstein points out, Ozick's insistence of a strict divide between Judaism and her writing is not fully convincing: she does bring the parts of her life together "by writing within the moral and intellectual framework of rabbinic Judaism about the subject that compels her, the unsettling nature of the creative imagination" ("In Life" 55). In her newest collection of essays, Ozick seems to reaffirm her growing ease with literary art: "Something there is in poetry that clings and clings to what we lamely and tamely call the metaphysical—the questions that are beyond our capacity to formulate" (*Quarrel & Quandary* 168). In fact, Ozick seems comfortable enough with literature's ability to hint at mystery—and avoid idolatry—to insist, "There is no Second Commandment to inhibit the imagery of the invisible in words" (*Fame & Folly* 169).

O'Connor, however, is more outspoken about the connection between religion and literature. She has made abundantly clear her sense of her vocation as a Catholic novelist. Describing herself as a hillbilly Thomist, she accepts the traditional, orthodox dogmas of the Catholic Church as the basis of her beliefs: "I see from the standpoint of Christian orthodoxy. This means that for me the meaning of life is centered in our Redemption by Christ and what I see in the world I see in its relation to that" (*Mystery and Manners* 32). The Catholic sacraments were particularly important to O'Connor, so when she was at a dinner party where people began to speak of the Eucharist as a symbol, she reports that she said "in a shaky voice, 'Well, if it's a symbol, to hell with it'" (*Habit of Being* 125). There is thus a natural carryover from O'Connor's beliefs to her writing; she notes, "The Catholic writer, in so far as he has the mind of the Church, will feel life from the standpoint of the central Christian mystery: that it has for all its horror, been found by God to be worth dying for" (*Conversations with Flannery O'Connor* 45). Therefore, although most of O'Connor's stories focus on Protestants—often Fundamentalists—rather than Catholics, she is drawn to these sometimes outlandish characters because they, like her, recognize the mystery and power of faith.[5]

Rather than experiencing a tension in her role as writer and believer, O'Connor finds that her Catholicism serves as a foundation for her fiction:

> I write the way I do because and only because I am a Catholic. I feel that if I were not a Catholic, I would have no reason to write, no reason to see, no reason ever to feel horrified or even to enjoy anything. I am born Catholic, went to Catholic schools in my early years, and have never left or wanted to leave the Church. I have never had the sense that being a Catholic is a limit to the freedom of the writer, but just the reverse. (*Habit* 114)

So central is her belief to her fiction that O'Connor says, "All my stories are about the action of grace on a character who is not very willing to support it, but most people think of these stories as hard, hopeless, brutal, etc." (*Habit* 275). In large part, O'Connor believes that her readers misunderstand her stories because the readers are "wingless chickens": "the moral sense has been bred out of certain sections of the population, like the wings have been bred off certain chickens to produce more white meat on them. This is a generation of wingless chickens, which I suppose is what Nietzsche meant when he said God was dead" (*Habit* 90).

WALLOWING IN MYSTERY

Whether doubtfully or assuredly, both Ozick and O'Connor acknowledge that their religious viewpoints influence their writing. Since mystery is a part of those religions, the question—as it was for Malamud and Percy—is how these authors portray the nonrational in their stories. What makes Ozick and O'Connor intriguing to study together is their similar method for representing religious mystery: they distort the surface to get at a deeper truth.[6] By disrupting the usual verisimilitude of fiction, these authors attempt to show the more profound religious truth that for them more accurately reflects reality. Since fiction that conforms to usual representations of everyday life is typically referred to as "realism," discussing the kind of religious mystery that appears in Ozick's and O'Connor's fiction can be somewhat confusing. With the bizarre occurrences in their fiction, their stories verge rather far from the usual conception of literary realism with its emphasis on non-sensational depictions of the everyday lives and conversations of characters. But, on a different level, the mystery that is an element of Judaism and Catholicism is also a part of a larger sense of reality. Therefore, when I am referring to the usual concept of literary realism, I will use the term "verisimilitude" to distinguish it from the fuller view of reality presented in Ozick's and O'Connor's fiction. As O'Connor explains, "I think that every writer, when he speaks of his own approach to fiction, hopes to show that, in some crucial and deep sense, he is a realist; and for some of us [writers with a religious sensibility], for whom the ordinary aspects of daily life prove to be of no great fictional interest, this is very difficult" (*Mystery* 37). Although Ozick articulates her understanding differently, she, too, seems to have a sense that the weird occurrences in her fiction are in some way a part of a larger sense of reality. For even though her stories often contain startling and mysterious incidents, she insists that her goal as a writer is to be clear for her readers: "surely one doesn't set out to weave a veil 'for the mystery behind.' Speaking for myself, I want to reveal, not to conceal!" (Ozick with Rainwater and Scheick 262). Yet in actuality, the events in Ozick's stories often go beyond the rational and thus resist easy explication. If it is fair to juxtapose Ozick's assertion that she is attempting in her stories to reveal rather than to conceal with the actuality that her stories' fantastic elements resist easy interpretation, one gets the sense that for Ozick a part of the reality of existence is on some level mysterious: her view of reality includes occurrences beyond most readers' understanding of reality, which leads her to find stories clear that others find difficult.

Even more obviously than in Malamud's and Percy's novels, Ozick's and O'Connor's fiction follows the pattern of *mitzvot* and sacraments to use physical actions or images to suggest religious mystery—or, more specifically to their fiction, often to evoke a sense of the numinous. Like Malamud and Percy, Ozick and O'Connor both seem to use a combination of specifically religious rituals as well as more commonplace actions to suggest mystery. For through Ozick's fantastic tales and O'Connor's grotesque stories, each thrusts readers into a seemingly usual experience of verisimilitude, only to shock them by a bizarre or supernatural action. In these stories, then, Ozick and O'Connor break from common expectations and, by presenting these surprises in the context of dialogue or images freighted with religious significance, push the reader toward the numinous. Indeed, in Rudolf Otto's discussion of the numinous, he notes that direct transmission of the numinous is impossible; it must rather be "'awakened' from the spirit" (60). Of the indirect means for awakening this sense of the holy, Otto points out two methods that have a very direct bearing on Ozick's and O'Connor's narrative strategies. Otto says that in art, "the magical is nothing but a suppressed and dimmed form of the numinous, a crude form of it which great art purifies and ennobles. In great art the point is reached at which we may no longer speak of the 'magical,' but are rather confronted with the numinous itself, with all its impelling motive power, transcending reason, expressed in sweeping lines and rhythms" (67). As we shall see, this concept of magic pointing toward the numinous is borne out in Ozick's fantastically magical fiction. Otto also suggests an indirect entrance to the numinous that has implications for O'Connor's stories. He points out that "the 'fearful' and horrible, and even at times the revolting and the loathsome" can suggest the numinous since "their outlets and means of expression may become indirect modes of expressing the specific 'numinous awe' that cannot be expressed directly" (62). With her use of the grotesque, O'Connor's fiction appropriates this feeling of horror as a link to the numinous.

But even though her fiction is magical, Ozick draws a sharp distinction between the mystical or fantastic elements in her stories and her own beliefs. She says that "in rabbinic Judaism (which *is* Judaism) there aren't any miracles or bizarre contrary-to-nature beliefs, that inquiry is encouraged, that rationalism rules, that textual study is primary, an absolute *sine qua non*. . . . And that's all there is" (qtd. in Strandberg 21). More specifically, she distances her own beliefs from the fantastic elements of her stories: "I myself am hostile to the whole mystical enterprise. I'm a rationalist and a skeptic. But there's something in me that is fascinated by this surrender to the mystical blur between the creator and the created. It's really a fictional theme for me. I reject it intellectually and emotionally. But it's where the stories come from" (qtd. in Ottenberg 68). Or, as she says in another interview, "as a writer I absolutely wallow in mystery religion" (Ozick with Kauvar 1985 400).

Yet one wonders if this rejection of mystery is as complete as Ozick would have us believe. Ozick has cited Leo Baeck's essay "Romantic Religion" as influential in her adult commitment to Judaism.[7] In this essay, Baeck focuses on the difference between the emphasis on faith and grace in Christianity and the stress on reason and the commandments in Judaism (211). Yet Baeck points out that even in a classical religion such as Judaism, "the irrational is the profound truth of life and therefore also the profound source of the Law, the profound guarantee of certainty, the 'arm of eternity' which embraces everything. In classical religion, the irrational appears as the holy, the covenant between the Eternal and man" (291). Ozick herself acknowledges a sense of mystery in a specific instance: "I think on Friday nights when I do the blessing over the Sabbath candles, that's also a kind of letter to the universe, a making rational of an irrational moment" (Ozick with Kauvar 1985 400). So on some level, Ozick's stories reflect an engagement with the ineffable found in Judaism.

The fantastic in literature, as Tzvetan Todorov explains in his definitive study of the fantastic, forces the reader to confront an alien event and attempt to make sense of it. Rather than instantly knowing how to assimilate the information, the reader hesitates "between a natural and a supernatural explanation of the events described" (33). It is in this uncertainty that the fantastic resides: "Once we choose one answer or the other, we leave the fantastic for a neighboring genre, the uncanny or the marvelous. The fantastic is that hesitation experienced by a person who knows only the laws of nature, confronting an apparently supernatural event" (25). Malamud, who has written numerous fantastic stories, suggests that the reader of such tales "experiences the poetry of the unearthly strange and mysterious; he senses the effect of the supernatural whether he believes in it or not; he enjoys the fact that the impossible happens" (*Talking Horse* 50).[8] Todorov explains that the uncanny occurs when the fantastic event receives a rational explanation; the marvelous is present when the reader ends with accepting the existence of the supernatural (44, 52). What makes several of Ozick's stories so intriguing is that they end without a clear sense of an explanation for the fantastic event; the reader is left in the fantastic realm. Although he is not speaking of religious mystery, Todorov's comment that "the fantastic permits us to cross certain frontiers that are inaccessible so long as we have no recourse to it" certainly seems to apply to the difficulty in portraying the spiritual nonrational (158).[9]

While there are competing strains in Judaism between the rationalists and the mystics, events beyond rational explanation make up a significant portion of Jewish folktales and are even present in rabbinic literature. The ambivalence toward magic comes from Scripture itself, where the biblical injunction against sorcery in Deuteronomy 18.10–12 is followed by King Saul's consultation of a witch (1 Sam. 28). Sorcery is also found in rabbinic literature, and the magic is not only performed by witches but "even by some of the most respected rabbis" (Schwartz *Lilith's Cave* 2). Jewish magic was in fact often connected with sacred texts, with individual letters of words or their numerical value having special powers (Schwartz *Gabriel's Palace* 22). Since most of the magic in Jewish texts centered on the power in the names of God, mystics through their meditation were thought to bring "to light awesome and puissant truths" (Trachtenberg 12). So even though Ozick is intellectually opposed to this mystical strain of Judaism, she seems, as the following analysis of her stories shows, to have taken it into her fiction as a way to express the nonrational side of more mainstream belief.[10]

For O'Connor, the idea that there are parts to Catholicism that are beyond rational explanation is a central aspect of her belief. To one correspondent who had questions about Catholicism, O'Connor briefly describes the Catholic doctrines of the Immaculate Conception and the Assumption. She concludes:

> Now neither of these doctrines can be measured with a slide rule. . . . We don't know how the Assumption or the Immaculate Conception were brought about nor is this a matter for science in any way. Dogma is the guardian of mystery. The doctrines are spiritually significant in ways that we cannot fathom. . . . The Church stands for and preserves always what is larger than human understanding. . . . All around you today you will find people accepting "religion" that has been rid of its religious elements. This is what you are asking: if you can be a Catholic and find a natural explanation for mysteries we can never comprehend, you are asking if you can be a Catholic and substitute something for faith. The answer is no. (*Habit* 365)

As she succinctly says in another letter, "I find it reasonable to believe, even though these beliefs are beyond reason" (*Habit* 479). But because she was convinced that many of her readers would not understand the mystery she found so central to her faith, O'Connor decided that she needed to shock her readers into confronting mystery through the grotesque.

The term "grotesque" has had various definitions, and even in O'Connor studies, critics argue about how the grotesque operates in her work. Without using the term, St. Bernard of Clairvaux in the Middle Ages saw the gargoyles and other art decorating churches as "a wonderful sort of hideous beauty and beautiful deformity" (qtd. in Muller 2). More recently, Wolfgang Kayser has suggested that the grotesque involves a transformation of the world we know: "Suddenness and surprise are essential elements of the grotesque" (184). Thus, since our usual categories are disrupted, this technique suggests that "the categories which apply to our world view [have] become inapplicable" (185). Often, Kayser says, comedy is a part of the caricature associated with the grotesque, and this humor is used for mocking and satiric purposes (187). This linkage is a central aspect of the grotesque, with presentations of distorted physical appearance having "an effect at once humorous and disturbing" (Gentry 10). Further, the contorted physical appearance or action of a character is often shown to be a concrete manifestation of some nonquantifiable characteristic.

In describing her technique, O'Connor points out that the grotesque grows naturally out of her view of the world: "My own feeling is that writers who see by the light of their Christian faith will have, in these times, the sharpest eye for the grotesque, for the perverse, and for the unacceptable. . . . The novelist with Christian concerns will find in modern life distortions which are repugnant to him, and his problem will be to make these appear as distortions to an audience which is used to seeing them as natural" (*Mystery* 33). Or again, O'Connor says that she (and other Southern writers) show freaks in their fiction "because we are still able to recognize one. To be able to recognize a freak, you have to have some conception of the whole man," which, for O'Connor, means seeing from a theological perspective (*Mystery* 44). Latching on to such a conception of O'Connor's grotesque, critics have endlessly quoted her memorable description of her technique: "When you can assume that your audience holds the same beliefs you do, you can relax a little and use more normal means of talking to it; when you have to assume that it does not, then you have to make your vision apparent by shock—to the hard of hearing you shout, and for the almost-blind you draw large and startling figures" (*Mystery* 34). Too many critics, though, have assumed that the shock of her stories is designed only to show the deformity in contemporary humanity. For example, Delma Eugene Presley says that the "distortions function as indicators of how far man has drifted from his true image as a creature of God" (39).

But O'Connor's vision is much more complete than simply to show deformity. Just as Edmund Burke recognized a sublime quality in forces beyond human understanding, O'Connor uses the grotesque to transcend the limitations of a created fiction (Raiger 249). She is seeking to use the shock of the grotesque to get readers to see beyond the surface: "in a good novel, more always happens than we are able to take in at once, more happens than meets the eye" (*Mystery*

71). Thus, she finds the perfect action in a story to be one that is "both totally right and totally unexpected; it would have to be one that was both in character and beyond character; it would have to suggest both the world and eternity. The action or gesture I'm talking about would have to be on the anagogical level, that is, the level which has to do with the Divine life and our participation in it" (*Mystery* 111). Or again, in a comment that points to the sacramental nature of her fiction, O'Connor says that the writer of grotesques is "looking for one image that will connect or combine or embody two points; one is a point in the concrete, and the other is a point not visible to the naked eye, but believed in by him firmly, just as real to him, really, as the one that everybody sees" (*Mystery* 42). For O'Connor, then, the grotesque functions as a sign pointing toward the divine—the numinous—with its shock "designed to pierce the seared conscience of the post-Christian world, opening it up to the possibility of the supernatural grace found in the Son of God" (Edwards 72). Insisting that reality consists of more than the verisimilitude of surface appearances, O'Connor startles "her readers into an awareness of a realm of experience beneath or beyond that which is rationally demonstrable" (Nisly 46).[11]

More than through abstract discussions of the fantastic and the grotesque, the nonrational power of these approaches will become most clear through an examination of Ozick's and O'Connor's fiction. I should first acknowledge the obvious: these are sophisticated, tightly written stories, so certainly more is at work than only a presentation of mystery; I do not, therefore, claim that my examination of the stories is exhaustive but rather selective in focusing on how these tales represent the nonrational. I have paired together several of Ozick's and O'Connor's stories because they seem to show similar approaches in portraying religious mystery. Specifically, in Ozick's "Usurpation (Other People's Stories)" and O'Connor's "Parker's Back," a material object placed on a person apparently takes on supernatural power during the course of the story. In Ozick's "Puttermesser and Xanthippe" and O'Connor's "The Enduring Chill," inanimate objects or figures seem to come to life. And the final grouping of stories, Ozick's "Levitation" and "The Pagan Rabbi" along with O'Connor's "Greenleaf" and "A Good Man Is Hard to Find," all seem to contain the most complete examples of a fantastic or grotesque action, laden with religious meaning, breaking the surface calm and suggesting the numinous.

"USURPATION" AND "PARKER'S BACK": THE BODY'S SURFACE AFFECTS THE SOUL

"Usurpation (Other People's Stories)" is quite possibly the most complicated of Ozick's stories, in large part because the tale is, in fact, made up of other people's stories. Ozick (and her narrator in the story) use Malamud's "The Silver Crown" and *The Tenants*, Israeli writer S.Y. Agnon's story about the Messiah, and a tale by a character within Ozick's story; additionally, she includes Jewish poet Tchernikhovsky, particularly making use of his reputation of having little religious commitment (Friedman 108). In part what makes the story disconcerting is that the opening almost seems to be a nonfiction essay: the unnamed first-person narrator tells of hearing a story read by a famous author; anyone familiar with Malamud's tales will recognize her summary—of a false rabbi selling a silver crown that supposedly would heal the sick—as being a description of Malamud's "The Silver Crown." Since it is quite plausible that Ozick could have heard Malamud read his story, the reader of "Usurpation" is unsure whether or not this account is fiction. The narrator then describes how she would have rewritten the story that Malamud drew from a newspaper account, a story, she claims, that should rightfully have been hers: she would have included more magic, for "[m]agic—I admit it—is what I lust after."[12] Just as she is lusting after this story and magic, a would-be writer, whom the narrator identifies as a "goat," approaches her and asks her to take his story to the famous writer (Malamud) or, failing that, at least to read it herself. Reluctantly, she accepts the story.

In her self-consciousness about telling this story, she addresses the reader, begging him or her not to put down the account "in fear of another plot-summary" (139). But even as she retells the goat's story, she acknowledges: "Here I will interrupt the goat's story to apologize. I would not be candid if I did not confess that I am rewriting it; I am making it my own, and that will never do for an act of plagiarism" (142). Such insistence that the narrator is creating her own story occurs throughout the early portion of the tale, and even toward the end, Ozick has fun with the verisimilitude of the fiction. Once in anger the goat says, "I looked up one of your stories. It stank, lady. The one called 'Usurpation.' Half of it's swiped, you ought to get sued" (175).[13]

Given that Ozick claims that "'Usurpation' is a story written against story-writing; against the Muse-goddess; against Apollo" (Preface to *Bloodshed* 11), this self-conscious narration has several possible interpretations. Qualifying the author's power by insisting the story is a literary creation, as Ellen Pifer points out about another Ozick story, shows the author to be a "fallible mortal, not an omniscient god" ("Ozick" 90). Thus, by undercutting any effort to make the narrative appear as a perfect creation, the story resists the possibility of becoming a self-existent idol. From the opposite perspective, one can argue that since the narrator's "own biases and artistic difficulties" are the focus of the story, the story does indeed become self-enclosing and thus an idol (Burstein 94). In a certain sense, Ozick seems to be having it both ways: the story both undercuts the authority of the external author while, at the same time, makes the narrator the god of the story. However one resolves this discrepancy, it does seem clear that the potential idolatry of writing is a concern of the story.

But of most interest from the standpoint of representing mystery is the silver crown itself that continues to appear in the story. In Malamud's story, as the narrator retells it, a teacher's father is ill and in the hospital. Responding to an advertisement for a silver crown that will heal a person, the teacher buys a crown, even though the rabbi who will make it tells him that the crown cannot be seen, only believed in. When the teacher learns that his father is no better, he returns to confront the rabbi, only to find him dressed as a dandy, presumably having used the teacher's money to buy clothes. As they battle over the apparent fraud, the teacher unintentionally confesses that he actually hates his father. The next day his father dies. Since, in Ozick's tale, Malamud admits that he has taken the story from a newspaper account, it does not seem too surprising when the goat claims that he is a cousin of the rabbi's wife.

The crown next appears in the narrator's adulterated retelling of the goat's story. In that account, which the narrator changes to suit her fancy, a young American attending a Jerusalem yeshiva is desperate with ambition. He decides to visit a famous poet to find out how he, too, can become a celebrity. The poet tells him that he must become a "*ba'al ga'avah*," a "self-righteous, self-idolator" (141). To help him on his way, the poet offers the student a gift that he says was given to him by the ghost of Tchernikhovsky: a magic crown which makes the wearer immediately as famous as the giver of the crown. When the student puts it on, he is instantly recognized and praised by crowds wherever he goes. But he is also visited by the ghost of Tchernikhovsky, who points out that as he has become like the other poet, he has also become old and about to die. In anguish, he attempts to get the crown off but is unable to until, in his struggles, he dies.

Within the world of "Usurpation," these two accounts are presented as fictions. In the present of the story, after the narrator finishes her retelling of the goat's story, she decides to visit him, although she has not admitted to herself why she has searched him out. Quickly, the goat says, "'You came because of the crown.' I was amazed: instantly it coursed in on me that this was true. I had come because of the crown; I was in pursuit of the crown" (161). When she meets the cousin, she is forced to read through the false rabbi Saul's papers. Eventually, she is given a crown to wear: "It felt lighter than I imagined. It was easy to forget you were wearing it" (166). Although the narrator insists that "[t]here are no miracles" (169) and learns that the rabbi was a rationalist who "ridiculed everything" (173), she realizes an amazing coincidence when she sees Saul's picture: he looks just like Tchernikhovsky's ghost whom she had imagined in the story. As she is refusing to work to publish Saul's writing, suddenly she feels the weight of the crown:

> It pressed unerringly into the secret tunnels of my brain. . . . Every point of it was a spear, a nail. The crown was no different from the bone of my head. The false rabbi Tchernikhovsky tore himself from the tin prison of his [picture] frame and sped to the ceiling as if gassed. . . . He was solid as a doll; I was not so light-headed as to mistake him for an apparition. His voice was as spindly as a harpsichord: "Choose!"
>
> "Between what and what?"
>
> "The Creator or the creature. God or god. The Name of Names or Apollo."
>
> "Apollo," I said on the instant.
>
> "Good," he tinkled, "blessings," he praised me, "flowings and flowings, streams, brooks, lakes, waters out of waters."
>
> Stories came from me then, births and births of tellings, narratives and suspenses, turning-points and palaces . . . . (176)

As the stories continue to well out of the narrator, they overflow the kitchen, knocking off the crowns of the goat and the cousin. "[M]y own crown in its coat contended with the vines and tangles of my hair, the false rabbi's beard had turned into strips of leather, into whips, the whips struck at my crown, it slid to my forehead, the whips curled round my arm, the crown sliced the flesh of my forehead. At last it fell off" (177). The narrator leaves the cousin's house and walks through the devastated streets of the surrounding Jewish neighborhood.

The role of the crown is the central fantastic element in this story, and it increases in complexity as the story progresses. In the initial account (from Malamud), the silver crown can be rather easily dismissed as a criminal effort at defrauding people of money. In the story which the narrator adapts from the goat, the crown seems at times to verge on the fantastic, but the narrator so insistently ruptures the verisimilitude of that account that the telling seems more like a fairy tale or fable than the fantastic. The narrator repeatedly insists that she is making up the account, and Todorov explains that if "we take the words not in their literal meaning but in another sense which refers to nothing supernatural, there is no longer any space in which the fantastic can exist" (63–64). But when, within the verisimilitude of the story, the narrator visits the rabbi's wife and herself receives a crown, the reader is thrust into the fantastic as he or she hesitates "between a natural and supernatural explanation" (Todorov 33). The obvious power of the crown disrupts the breezy atmosphere of the self-conscious narration and forces the reader to assimilate this event which is outside the realm of common experience, to recognize that—at least in the world of this story—reality includes forces beyond what is obvious on the surface. Since an object placed on the head does have genuine potency to effect change in a character, the reader is pushed toward a sense of the numinous.

With this magical crown rupturing the expected verisimilitude of the story, other elements in the narrative can help direct how this bizarre event should be interpreted. Most important to understand the significance seems to be the choice the narrator has to make between the Name of Names or Apollo. That she is forced into such a decision when she puts on the crown suggests that the crown is in some way related to a religious question. Her immediate decision for Apollo, with the attendant outflowing of stories, implies that following the God of Torah cannot be linked with seeking the god of poetry, that the Crown of Torah must not be confused with the laureate wreath. As the Jewish sage Hillel said, "he that puts the Crown of the Torah to his own use shall perish" (qtd. in Kauvar *Tradition and Invention* 104). Further, the battle that is waged on the narrator between the "strips of leather" (or "whips") and the crown underline this conflict. Since these strips of leather hit her forehead and wrap around her arm, they seem to suggest phylacteries, the leather boxes containing verses of Scripture that believers tie on their arm and forehead in response to the biblical injunction to keep God's word near to their hearts and minds. Thus, the phylacteries' attack on the crown again points out the conflict between following Torah and being devoted to poetry. Another result of the narrator's wearing the crown also reflects this warning; when the narrator leaves the cousin's house, she sees the destroyed Jewish neighborhood, possibly alluding to the destruction of Jewry in the Holocaust but also suggesting what happens when Jews select other gods (Gitenstein 200).

Imparting a sense of the mystery of God's power and insistence on being the sole deity is not easily accomplished within a narrative. With this fantastic crown, the story shocks the reader into realizing that there is real power in the Name of Names, as well as tangible danger in pursuing the idol of art. This sense of awe, evoked by a character's interaction with a tangible object, the crown, suggests an intriguing combination of religious ritual and everyday action. The crown clearly takes on supernatural power, but the consequences for the narrator are made manifest in the commonplace activity of writing. Thus, Ozick links the concrete representation of the numinous—the crown, which seems to have almost sacramental power—with the Jewish emphasis of everyday living within the divine presence.

The epilogue of the story carries on the theme that a Jew can never forsake God without consequences. It opens, "When we enter Paradise there will be a cage for storywriters, who will be taught as follows: All that is not Law is levity" (177). Then follows a description of what has happened to several of the characters—a vanity press will publish the false rabbi's papers, the goat continues to live in an abandoned synagogue. Only the old writer from Jerusalem and Tchernikhovsky have ascended to the Afterlife. The old writer murmurs psalms and polishes his Nobel Prize; Tchernikhovsky is looking resplendent, eating nude and without restraint at the table of the nude gods while ignoring the Sabbath, certainly underlining the connection between idolatry and poetry that Ozick develops in the story. Yet even as he turns his back on the faithful, "the taciturn little Canaanite idols call him, in the language of the spheres, kike" (178). This disturbing conclusion, with its jarring derogatory slang, is in some ways parallel to one aspect of O'Connor's use of the grotesque: Ozick uses the ugliness of the expression to surprise the reader into seeing that Jewish efforts at assimilation are not successful or, apparently, appropriate. This ending suggests that even in the Afterlife, however much Tchernikhovsky (or presumably any Jew) renounces his Jewishness, he cannot erase where his true loyalties should lie (Criswell 96). On the other hand, since Agnon, the old writer from Jerusalem, has refused to accept the crown of poetry in place of the Crown of Torah, he has been able both to receive a Nobel Prize and remain pious—hinting that a writer does not need to renounce God to write. Yet the overall message of the conclusion pushes the fantastic elements of the story toward an affirmation of the mysterious power of religious commitment.

O'Connor's "Parker's Back," which features the grotesquely tattooed O.E. Parker, also shows a specific image on a body having strange powers over the person. But rather than a crown, Parker experiences the mysterious effect through the eminently secular image of a tattoo. This story, like "Usurpation," starts with a seemingly ordinary, albeit comic, scene: O.E. Parker and his wife

Sarah Ruth are sitting on their porch. Sarah Ruth is snapping beans; Parker is wondering why he continues to stay with his plain, pregnant wife. From a series of flashbacks, we learn that Parker seems not to have much control over what he does. Parker had been deeply moved by a sight he saw at a fair when he was fourteen: a man "tattooed from head to foot," who flexed "his muscles so that the arabesque of men and beasts and flowers on his skin appeared to have a subtle motion of its own. Parker was filled with emotion, lifted up as some people are when the flag passes. . . . Parker had never before felt the least motion of wonder in himself."[14] Responding to this mysterious sense of wonder, he begins to get tattoos, but each time he finds his new tattoo satisfying for only a short time before he needs another. After bumping from job to job, he is attempting to fix his truck when he first sees Sarah Ruth. To get her attention, he swears a mighty string of oaths. "Without warning a terribly bristly claw slammed the side of his face and he fell backwards on the hood of the truck" (511): Sarah Ruth, a fundamentalist Christian, has struck him with a broom to punish him for his swearing. Worse yet, she does not seem to be impressed with his tattoos, seeing them as an offense. Still, even though he cannot understand why, Parker continues to court her. She refuses to sleep with him and, when he reaches for her, pushes him away so hard that he is flung out of his truck. "He made up his mind then and there to have nothing further to do with her. They were married in the County Ordinary's office" (518). Thus, partly because he is dissatisfied and partly because he hopes to impress Sarah Ruth, he decides in the present of the story to have a tattoo placed in the one open spot on his body: his back.

To reach his wife, Parker decides that he must get some impressively religious symbol. While there are other elements in the story that are comic or odd, it is this final tattoo that has the most bizarre and startling effect—on both Parker and the reader. Parker looks through the tattoo artist's collection of images until he comes to a picture of "a Byzantine Christ with all-demanding eyes" (522). He continues past this picture, but "there was absolute silence. It said as plainly as if silence were a language itself: GO BACK" (522). Following on this initial indication that this tattoo is especially compelling, the story insists that the tattoo has a deep effect on Parker. While he is working on the tattoo, the artist asks Parker, "why do you want this on you? Have you gone and got religion? Are you saved?" Parker responds, "Naw, I ain't got no use for none of that." Yet even though he insists that he rejects salvation, "[t]hese words seemed to leave his mouth like wraiths and evaporate as if he had never uttered them" (524–25). Although he does not want to look at the finished image on his back, the artist forces him to examine it in a mirror: "Parker looked, turned white and moved away. The eyes in the reflected face continued to look at him—still, straight, all-demanding, enclosed in silence" (525–26). Unsure what to do, Parker heads to a pool hall. There, although he tries to avoid it, the men demand to see his new tattoo. Initially stunned into silence, one eventually says, "O.E.'s got religion and is witnessing for Jesus, ain't you, O.E? . . . An o-riginal way to do it if I ever saw one" (526). After a scuffle, the men toss Parker out the door, and he sits in the alley "examining his soul. He saw it as a spider web of facts and lies that was not at all important to him but which appeared to be necessary in spite of his opinion. The eyes that were now forever on his back were eyes to be obeyed. He was as certain of it as he had ever been of anything" (527). In ways that he cannot understand, Parker senses that the tattoo has a power over him.

That an image should exert such a force may be bizarre. Yet Parker's experience of the all-demanding eyes along with the witness of the men in the pool hall suggest that something mysterious has happened with this latest tattoo. Parker—and the reader—are thrown off balance by this surprising effect of the tattoo. Although emotional and psychological explanations can be offered, the tattoo's effect cannot be interpreted solely on these grounds. Parker has gotten tattoos initially as art and, in this final case, to please his wife. Whatever his motivation, as Lorine Getz points out, when he gets this tattoo of Christ, "Parker's natural intention ceases. The outcome reveals a divine will which has intervened, replacing Parker's natural desire with supernatural intention" (78). This physical image, in some way that exceeds logical explanation, pushes Parker to an encounter with the numinous.

Understanding the startling effect of the tattoo of Christ as a representation of God's mysterious power is validated by the religious imagery present throughout the story. Parker has throughout his life refused to use his given name, using only the initials O.E. With a hint of flirtation, Sarah Ruth manages to learn that his name is Obadiah Elihue, a name that combines an Old Testament prophet with a name meaning "He is God." Further, Parker's attraction to tattoos has religious overtones. His sense of wonder begins with seeing the man at the fair, and getting a tattoo, which "hurt very little, just enough to make it appear to Parker to be worth doing" (513), hints at the suffering that is commonly associated with being a prophet for God (Orvell 167–68). Yet rather than being satisfied with his tattoos, he feels that they are not "an arabesque of colors" but "something haphazard and botched" (514). This dissatisfaction grows so that Parker perceives that the various creatures on his flesh have "penetrated his skin and lived inside him in a raging warfare" (514), a significant connection to the final invasion of his soul by the Christ on his back. Parker finally decides that he must get the tattoo of Christ because of a cataclysmic accident he has while driving a tractor. With a "ferocious thud," Parker hits a tree and is thrown into the air: "he heard himself yelling in an unbelievably loud voice, 'GOD ABOVE!'" When he lands, he sees the tree, the tractor, and his shoes on fire; "if he had known how to cross himself he would have done it" (520). With the burning tree, Parker's exclamation, and his removed shoes, the scene has clear parallels to Moses' call at the burning bush (May 117). The religious connections of this scene are underlined by Parker's twice collapsing to his knees as he runs away, suggesting the genuflecting that is often a part of religious devotion. Parker is linked to another Old Testament figure, Jonah, after he receives his final tattoo. When the men at the pool hall throw Parker out, "a calm descended on the pool hall as nerve shattering as if the long barnlike room were the ship from which Jonah had been cast into the sea" (527). The men's response, as with the pagan crewmen in the Jonah story, show that his friends "can tell he is more serious about the Jesus on his back than he admits" (Ragen 37).

With this biblical imagery, it seems fitting that the shocking tattoo of Christ has deep religious significance for Parker. In the final movement of the story, Parker returns to Sarah Ruth, believing that she "would know what he had to do" (527). That the tattoo has indeed altered his vision is underlined by his feeling like "a stranger to himself, driving into a new country though everything he saw was familiar to him" (527). Angry at his being gone for a couple of days, however, Sarah Ruth initially refuses to open the door to him, insisting that he identify himself by his full name. While he is at the door, "a tree of light burst over the skyline" and he feels pinned by a lance (528), a rather clear allusion to Christ's crucifixion. When he does whisper his name, "all at once he felt the light pouring through him, turning his spider web soul into a perfect arabesque of colors, a garden of trees and birds and beasts" (528). By acknowledging his full name with its prophetic implications, Parker seems to move into an acceptance of his call to be a prophet, and so his soul, with this final tattoo, becomes the wonderful arrangement of colors that he had earlier unsuccessfully sought for his body. Because Carol Shloss does not want to admit a religious reading of the story, she finds the meaning "being forced into the unwilling mold of unrelated events, or actions having to carry disproportionate moral weight" (118). What Shloss seems not to see, or at least to accept, is that the jarring lack of connection is what pushes the reader to look beyond psychological verisimilitude toward a religious understanding. With her desire to reach what she perceived as a hardened audience, O'Connor created narratives that force readers, in their bafflement and perturbation, to enter into the story almost as much as the characters themselves (Johansen 67).

But the story does not end with this image. Rather, Sarah Ruth, who eschews any images of Christ as idolatrous, is angered by the tattoo and beats Parker with the broom: "Parker was too stunned to resist. He sat there and let her beat him until she had nearly knocked him senseless and large welts had formed on the face of the tattooed Christ" (529). The final image of the story is from Sarah Ruth's perspective, when she looks out the window and sees under a pecan tree, "There he was—who called himself Obadiah Elihue—leaning against the tree, crying like a baby" (530). This surprising conclusion has led to various interpretations. Most critics agree that, given the power the image of Christ has had for Parker, the story indicts Sarah Ruth for refusing to acknowledge that Jesus took on corporeal form as well as being divine.[15] Indeed, Richard Giannone sees a very direct connection between the images on Parker's body and his encounter with God: "The more he decorates his body, the more fully he receives wonder, until, after intervals of dejection, the mystery of the divine figure stenciled on his back becomes manifest and fills him with the Spirit" (*Mystery of Love* 224). While Giannone seems to overstate the initial wonder that Parker is able to achieve from his tattoos, he accurately reveals the power of the final image of

Christ. On this level, it is important to note that "Usurpation" and "Parker's Back" are pushing in opposite directions: "Usurpation" stresses the danger of idolatry while "Parker's Back" emphasizes the importance of accepting the physical reality of Christ, a divergence that points up a central distinction between Judaism and Catholicism. What is not so clear is exactly what Parker's crying signifies. John May finds that his crying like a baby points toward Parker's new life in Christ (119). Marshall Bruce Gentry believes the beating and tears reveal "Parker's entrance into the suffering community" (81). Margaret Whitt insists that "Parker has become symbolically a crucified Christ on Calvary," since the welts from the broom appear in the Christ's face on his back (155). Although each interpretation has some merit, it also seems quite plausible that Parker is simply confused at the end: he had thought his wife would applaud his conversion, but instead she beats him. As in many O'Connor stories, the ending resists one easy interpretation. What does remain clear, though, is that in some mysterious way, the tattoo of the Byzantine Christ has assumed surprising and life-altering powers. As Preston Browning explains, "this, surely, is the subject of the story: the awakening to the awe-ful presence of the numinous (the Holy) in one who had beforehand been as insensitive as a stone" (526). Through her use of the tattoo, O'Connor shocks both Parker and the reader into confronting divine mystery, using a physical image to evoke a sense of the numinous.

"PUTTERMESSER AND XANTHIPPE" AND "THE ENDURING CHILL": NATURAL OBJECTS, SUPERNATURAL POWER

Closely related to the way that an object or image on the body has a mysterious effect on the religious sensibility of a character in "Usurpation" and "Parker's Back" is the supernatural power that seemingly natural objects take on in Ozick's "Puttermesser and Xanthippe" and O'Connor's "The Enduring Chill." These narratives, too, give a sense of verisimilitude, only to disrupt that surface calm with an astounding eruption of the divine.

Originally released as a short story, "Puttermesser and Xanthippe" was published in 1997 as one of five sections in a novel, *The Puttermesser Papers*. Ozick combined three previously published Puttermesser stories with two new ones in creating this novel, which was a finalist for the National Book Award. "Puttermesser and Xanthippe" is the second story about this unmarried lawyer and civil servant. This section begins with an apparently high degree of verisimilitude. Puttermesser is feeling "attacked on all sides,"[16] for she in short succession loses her lover (he thinks she is inattentive), her apartment (the building was damaged by arsonists), her job (she is the victim of political patronage), and her teeth (she has periodontal disease). Although these seem to be losses of Jobean proportions, the story does not much focus on their cumulative effect since Puttermesser has a new apartment and initially another—albeit more menial—job with the city. More prominent in the story is Puttermesser's concern with justice: she "loved the law and its language. She caressed its meticulousness. She thought of law as Apollo's chariot" (27). This emphasis on the law, by which Puttermesser primarily refers to civil law, certainly calls to mind the Jewish law that should be prominent in this Jew's mind. But even in her reflection on the law, her imagery that it is "Apollo's chariot" points to a tension between Judaism and the allure of pagan or secular forces, a tension that is developed throughout the story. With her emphasis on justice, she is outraged that her job, which she performs admirably, is taken from her, and so she writes letters to Mayor Malachy Mavett protesting the situation. The mayor, however, whose name is likely a pun on the Hebrew *Malach ha-Mavet*—the angel of death (Sarah Cohen 95)—neglects her letters.

It is as she is wishing for a reply from the mayor—as well as for a daughter that she fears she will never have—that she carries the Sunday *Times*, as heavy as a "dead child," to her bed.

> A naked girl lay in Puttermesser's bed. She looked dead—she was all white, bloodless. . . . Puttermesser moved to one side of the bed, then circled back around the foot to the other side. She put on her slippers; summoning reason, she continued to move around and around the bed. There was no doubt that a real body was in it. Puttermesser reached out and touched the right shoulder—a reddish powder coated her fingers. (37–38)

She attempts to make sense of this girl—perhaps she is a "junkie or prostitute" who slipped into Puttermesser's apartment (38). As Puttermesser examines the body more closely, she sees that portions of the features do not seem formed quite right; she adjusts the nose and mouth, blowing out a bit of dust. She discovers a bit of paper in the girl's mouth and finds on it a single Hebrew word. When she reads the slip, thus speaking the Name of Names, "the inert creature, as if drilled through by electricity, as if struck by some principle of instantaneous vitality, leaped straight from the bed" (40). Puttermesser watches her fingernails and eyelashes appear. Although Puttermesser orders the girl to leave the house, she writes in response that Puttermesser is her mother. She dresses in clothes that Puttermesser gives her, but refuses to wear shoes, writing: "No shoes. This is a holy place. I did not enter. I was formed. Here you spoke the Name of the Giver of Life. You blew in my nostril and encouraged my soul. You circled my clay seven times. You enveloped me with your spirit. You pronounced the Name and brought me to myself. Therefore I call you mother" (42). After some hesitation, Puttermesser accepts the girl and attempts to name her Leah. The creation refuses, insisting instead to be called Xanthippe, the name of Socrates' wife, again drawing attention in the story to the conflict between Hebrew and Greek traditions.

With this fantastic occurrence, the reader is thrust into unfamiliar territory. Is one really to believe that Puttermesser brought this creature to life? Puttermesser decides that Xanthippe is a golem, a creation reported in Jewish legends who cannot speak but is intelligent. The idea of a golem is in some measure connected to the creation of Adam (Scholem 161), since Adam, in a sense, is God's golem. Another biblical source that is cited in rabbinical literature for the creation of golems is Genesis 12.5, where Abraham and his family leave for Canaan "with the persons that they had acquired in Haran"; in this understanding, the "persons" Abraham takes along were created by him, although other rabbis dispute this interpretation (Scholem 171). Various rabbinical stories deal with this issue of creation of life.[17] One rabbinic tale tells how Rava created a man who could not speak and sent him to another rabbi; although the account does not explain how this creation occurred, it has traditionally been assumed to have involved magic, largely since it is followed in the text by a story about two rabbis who create a calf using the *Book of Creation* (Scholem 166). These rabbis' action was sanctioned by Rashi, writing in the eleventh century C.E.: "They used to combine the letters of the Name by which the universe was created; this is not to be considered forbidden magic, for the works of God were brought into being by His holy Name" (qtd. in Trachtenberg 84). Thus, the concept that one can create life largely comes from an interpretation of the *Book of Creation*, written between the third and sixth centuries C.E., which says that each of the twenty-two Hebrew letters controls a part of the universe (Scholem 167–69). As Gershom Scholem, scholar of Jewish mysticism, explains, "Though the treatise is presented as a theoretical guide to the structure of creation, it may quite conceivably have been intended also as a manual of magical practices, or at least as a statement of general principle, to be supplemented by more detailed instructions—perhaps oral—concerning the application of these principles to other things" (169). Eleazer of Worms, writing in the late twelfth and early thirteenth centuries C.E., gave the most precise directions for the creation of golems, which involved walking around the creature and reciting combinations of letters (Scholem 185). In a later tradition, the golem is created by writing the Hebrew word *emet* ("truth") on the creature's forehead (Scholem 199–201).

One story Puttermesser reads in her research about golems involves the renowned scholar Judah Loew in the sixteenth century. After making a figure from dirt, he walked around it, placed the Name in its mouth, and chanted with his followers, "And he breathed into his nostrils the breath of life; and man became a living soul"; at those words, the golem came to life and saved the Jews of Prague, who were being accused of using the bodies of Christian infants to make Passover wafers. After Prague was cleansed, Puttermesser reads, Rabbi Judah Loew "climbed a ladder (a golem grows bigger every day), reached up to the golem's forehead" and erased a letter, changing the word on his forehead from "truth" to "dead" (46). Nevertheless, while this golem had a specific purpose, Scholem points out that golems, at least initially, were created not for a practical purpose but to show the power of the Name. Because of that power, golem-making is a dangerous activity, especially for the creator who on some level rivals God (190–91).

Puttermesser sees the broken flowerpots in her house and remembers how she adjusted the golem's features; she thus realizes that she created the golem. And she decides there is nothing to be ashamed of in its creation: just as she is "no mystic, enthusiast, pneumaticist, ecstatic, kabbalist" but rather a "rationalist"

(44), so the golem-makers in the past were, "by and large, scientific realists—and, in nearly every case, serious scholars and intellectuals" (48). Within the logic of the story, then, the existence of the golem appears to slip into a Todorov's category of the marvelous: the fantastic event is explained as a supernatural happening. Yet the sense of mystery in the story is quite profound, particularly through the emphasis on the power of the Name. Only when the Name is spoken does the golem receive life, suggesting that there are indeed realities not obviously visible to the human eye.

But whether or not Puttermesser's using the power of the Name for her purposes is appropriate remains an important question throughout the story. As suggested earlier, Scholem points out that obviously someone "who creates a golem is in some sense competing with God's creation of Adam; in such an act the creative power of man enters into a relationship, whether of emulation or antagonism, with the creative power of God" (159). Moshe Idel, however, suggests that because mystical contemplation is connected to this magical act, the making of a golem may be legitimized: "What can be regularly conceived as a magical operation, can be understood not so much as an attempt to confront the divinity by the accumulation of an independent power, but an attempt to imitate Him by verifying the *modus operandi* and so testifying to the grandeur of the creator" (xxvi). And since Xanthippe was apparently not consciously planned by Puttermesser, she may be somewhat absolved for the action (Friedman 135). Yet even though the golem was created through the power of God's name, Puttermesser begins to take on the role of the ultimate creator, evaluating the features of Xanthippe and ordering her what to do (Pifer "Ozick" 98). Further, the name she had chosen for the golem, Leah, means "wild cow," possibly suggesting a connection to the golden bull in Israel's history (Kauvar *Tradition and Invention* 135). Such questions about the appropriateness of Puttermesser's action become more pronounced as the story continues.

Because Xanthippe is the result of Puttermesser's joint desire for a daughter and for a cleaner, less corrupt city, Xanthippe comes up with a PLAN to save New York City. It begins with Puttermesser as mayor, so Xanthippe toils tirelessly to get Puttermesser elected. On her campaign signs, Puttermesser has an apple tree with a serpent on it, symbolizing, she says, that she will "transform the City of New York into Paradise" (72). Yet such an image on her sign might also suggest a more negative perspective, indicating her desire for absolute knowledge (Pifer "Ozick" 102). Initially, Puttermesser is extremely successful as mayor: streets are clean and safe; the "Bureau of Venereal Disease Control has closed down"; "ex-pimps are learning computer skills" (78). Yet this paradise on earth is not to last, for Xanthippe, who has steadily been growing larger (as golems do), gets a taste of physical pleasure through a fling with Puttermesser's ex-lover, Rappoport. In her sex-crazed charge through the city, almost all of Puttermesser's carefully chosen city managers are "felled" and "depleted" (86). Crime, dirt, and corruption return to the city. Too late, Puttermesser realizes that, like Rabbi Judah Loew, she must undo her creation. Using Rappoport as a decoy, Puttermesser lures Xanthippe back to her mayoral mansion so that she can remove the power of life from her. Since golems have on their foreheads the word *emet*, to destroy them, one must remove the "e," changing the word to *met* ("dead") (Trachtenberg 85–86). With the erasure of the letter, Xanthippe returns to the elements. The ending of Puttermesser's attempt at an earthly paradise seems to suggest, as she herself says, that "[t]oo much Paradise is greed" (99). In other words, "the recovered Paradise will need to be a creation of God, not a heavenly kingdom we have ourselves invented in the image of our desires" (Krupnick 362). Humans can never claim to have full knowledge of what God wants to have accomplished. Thus, while the golem does have a place in Jewish tradition and lore of showing the power of the Name, this creation by a human simultaneously contains a tension about the appropriateness of such an action. Particularly given Ozick's concerns expressed in essays over whether the creation of literature is idolatry, the questions about creating a golem certainly have resonances with Ozick's own struggle as an artist. In what ways does human creation rival the action of the Creator?[18] The story's conclusion suggests that Puttermesser's conduct, although having some initially positive benefits for the city, was more the result of her desire to get back at the corrupt city officials than a yearning to display God's power. But Puttermesser's inability to control the supernatural force she unleashed points to the uncontrollable nature of God, to the fact that humans can never command divine power.

The story ends with a reiteration of the supernatural power of the golem. Present at the golem's destruction, Rappoport is reduced to a babbling, weakened man; he has witnessed divine power and cannot integrate it into his understanding of the universe. And even the remains of Xanthippe seem to have preternatural power: they are placed in a park and planted over with geraniums, guarded by a sign that reads, "DO NOT TOUCH OR PICK." "Yet whoever touches or picks these stems of blood-colored blossoms soon sickens with flu virus, or sore throat, or stuffed nose accompanied by nausea—or, sometimes, a particularly vicious attack of bursitis" (101). The extraordinary existence of the golem, sparked by the power of the Name, has an ongoing mysterious effect on those it touches, just as Ozick's story has a disturbing effect on the reader, pushing him or her toward the nonrational. Through the physical elements of dirt imbued with supernatural power, the story evokes a sense of the numinous, a feeling of awe and wonder.

In O'Connor's "The Enduring Chill," the supernaturally enlivened figure does not appear until the conclusion. Throughout much of the story, O'Connor pokes fun, as she often does, at a pretentious intellectual, Asbury Fox. Asbury is a failed writer, returning from New York City to his mother's home in Timberboro, believing that he is about to die. He has written his mother a long (unintentionally hilarious) Kafkaesque letter for her to read after he is dead:

> I came here [to New York] to escape the slave's atmosphere of home, . . . to find freedom, to liberate my imagination, to take it like a hawk from its cage and set it "whirling off into the widening gyre" (Yeats) and what did I find? It was incapable of flight. . . . I

have no imagination. I have no talent. I can't create. I have nothing but the desire for these things. Why didn't you kill that too? Woman, why did you pinion me? (364)

Facing his despair, he hopes that this letter will leave his mother with "an enduring chill and perhaps in time lead her to see herself as she was" (365). His mother, of course, is aware of none of these great traumas that she has "caused"; her only concern is to try and get her boy healthy. So she calls in the country doctor, Dr. Block. In scorn, Asbury insists, "What's wrong with me is way beyond Block" (359). When Asbury repeats his contempt directly to Dr. Block, the doctor responds, "Most things are beyond me. I ain't found anything yet that I thoroughly understood" (367), suggesting a sense of the mystery of existence that Asbury will not acknowledge. Nevertheless, the doctor draws blood and attempts to determine Asbury's ailment. Asbury, meanwhile, does little but lie in his bed and look at the water stains on the ceiling above him. One leak "had made a fierce bird with spread wings. It had an icicle crosswise in its beak and there were smaller icicles depending from its wings and tail" (365).

Convinced that he is on his deathbed, Asbury thinks of a scheme that both will offer him some enjoyment and should outrage his Methodist mother: he asks to see a Catholic priest. While he had been in New York, he had met a Jesuit priest at a lecture and discussion, a man whom Asbury had found to be interesting company. In the course of the discussion during which one of Asbury's friends defined salvation as "the destruction of a simple prejudice, and no one is saved," Asbury had asked Father Vogle his opinion. "'There is,' the priest said, 'the real possibility of the New Man, assisted, of course,' he added brittlely, 'by the Third Person of the Trinity'" (360). Apparently seeking to ingratiate himself with these pseudo-sophisticates, the priest declines directly to declare his message but "chooses, instead, to state his Faith in abstractions that he hopes will appeal to his urbane listeners" (Wood 122). This cultured approach is exactly what Asbury wants to hear, so he hopes that the priest he requests will be as suave, ready to discuss James Joyce with him. Father Finn who comes to see him is a far cry from the urbane Vogle: "He had a large red face, a stiff brush of gray hair and was blind in one eye, but the good eye, blue and clear, was focused sharply on Asbury. There was a grease spot on his vest" (375). Besides his unimpressive appearance, this priest does not respond to him as Asbury had hoped. When Asbury asks Father Finn's opinion of Joyce, the priest says, "I haven't met him. . . . Now. Do you say your morning and night prayers?" (375). Determining that Asbury has little religious understanding or, apparently, interest, the priest admonishes him that he needs the Holy Ghost, but the "Holy Ghost will not come until you see yourself as you are—a lazy ignorant conceited youth!" (377). Feeling the emptiness of his life the next day, Asbury becomes convinced that he is about to die; as he thinks, he had "failed his god, Art, but he had been a faithful servant and Art was sending him Death" (373). His mother has no such lofty thoughts—she simply wants to keep him alive, so she again calls Dr. Block. This time, Block arrives triumphantly: he has discovered the source of Asbury's illness, undulant fever from drinking unpasteurized milk. Mrs. Fox exults, "It'll keep coming back but it won't kill you!" (381).

This news that Asbury will have to face life rather than death is deeply disturbing to him. He glances in the mirror and sees that his eyes "looked shocked clean as if they had been prepared for some awful vision about to come down on him." He falls back on his bed and looks at the ceiling:

> The old life in him was exhausted. He awaited the coming of the new. It was then that he felt the beginning of a chill, a chill so peculiar, so light, that it was like a warm ripple across a deeper sea of cold. His breath came short. The fierce bird which through the years of his childhood and the days of his illness had been poised over his head, waiting mysteriously, appeared all at once to be in motion. Asbury blanched and the last film of illusion was torn as if by a whirlwind from his eyes. He saw that for the rest of his days, frail, racked, but enduring, he would live in the face of a purifying terror. A feeble cry, a last impossible protest escaped him. But the Holy Ghost, emblazoned in ice instead of fire, continued, implacable, to descend. (382)

The religious significance of this figure is, of course, nearly impossible to ignore. But this Spirit descending on Asbury is a startling eruption of the supernatural in a seemingly natural tale, a surprising break of verisimilitude that pushes the reader into a confrontation with mystery. Inexplicably, a mundane image, a water stain, takes on motion and, apparently, has a profound effect on the prostrate Asbury. Particularly since this descent of the Holy Ghost in the last line of the story is described by the narrator instead of through Asbury's consciousness, it cannot be dismissed as one more of Asbury's delusions. Instead, these physical water stains actually take on life, so the reader is pushed toward a sense of the numinous.

Not surprisingly, on a second look the story does provide clues that Asbury's illness should be seen as emblematic of a deeper spiritual need. His self-description, that "[h]e had always relied on himself and had never been a sniveler after the ineffable" (378), serves as his own indictment, especially when contrasted with Block's acknowledgment that much is a mystery to him. Another hint of his spiritual searching occurs when Asbury first arrives at the train station in Timberboro. Looking around himself, he "felt that he was about to witness a majestic transformation, that the flat of roofs might at any moment turn into the mounting turrets of some exotic temple for a god he didn't know" (357). Although he rejects this vision, the course of the story does indeed show him coming face-to-face with a God unknown to him. And though Father Vogle's message is cloaked in sophisticated language, Asbury's interest in what the priest has to say points toward the final vision, especially since the priest's name is German for bird, a symbol commonly used for the Holy Ghost. Father Finn's insistent questioning Asbury about the state of his soul prepares for Asbury's final vision. The priest roars at Asbury:

"How do you expect to get what you don't ask for? God does not send the Holy Ghost to those who don't ask for Him. Ask Him to send the Holy Ghost."

"The Holy Ghost?" Asbury said.

"Are you so ignorant you've never heard of the Holy Ghost?" the priest asked.

"Certainly I've heard of the Holy Ghost," Asbury said furiously, "and the Holy Ghost is the last thing I'm looking for!"

"And He may be the last thing you get," the priest said, his one fierce eye inflamed. "Do you want your soul to suffer eternal damnation? . . . The Holy Ghost will not come until you see yourself as you are—a lazy ignorant conceited youth!" (376–77)

This tongue-lashing catechism does not immediately bring about a change in Asbury, but—linked to his recognition that he is sentenced to life—the final image of the descending Holy Ghost suggests that Asbury has acknowledged his sinful state. The priest has said that the Holy Ghost will not come until Asbury asks for him. Since the final image of the story shows the Spirit coming to Asbury, the logic of the story implies that Asbury is at last ready for the grace the Holy Ghost can offer. The supernaturally infused bird's descent on Asbury symbolizes his recognition—and probable acceptance—of the grace offered by the Spirit.[19]

In both "Puttermesser and Xanthippe" and "The Enduring Chill," the authors disrupt the expected verisimilitude of the story by endowing an item or image with supernatural power. In so doing, Ozick and O'Connor force the reader to consider that a deeper reality may be at work behind the surface existence we commonly experience. This making physical of religious mystery has clear connections to the concretization of mystery in Judaism and Catholicism discussed earlier. In these two stories, though, the authors make use of a more overtly religious ritual to portray a sense of the holy than is common in many of their stories. The golem is created by invoking the Name, while the water stain is explicitly linked to the Holy Ghost. Yet the way this supernatural occurrence is structured within each narrative still reflects the divergent emphases of each religion. In Ozick's story, the supernatural creation takes place early in the tale, and the full implications of the creation do not become clear until we see how Puttermesser interacts with the golem. Thus, the supernatural action must be evaluated in light of the earthly behavior of the character, underlining the Jewish emphasis on righteous action. On the other hand, the sacramental coming of the Holy Ghost in O'Connor's story takes place in the last paragraph. The placement of this event suggests the more direct action of grace that is central to O'Connor's theology. Certainly proper action should grow out of this interaction with the Divine, but any change in Asbury must come from this action of grace in his life.

Despite these differences, each of these stories has a clear sense of divine power being evidenced through the animation of natural objects, thus using the effects of the supernatural on physical objects as doors to the holy. By breaking free from the expected verisimilitude, these surprising disruptions in the stories suggest the awe and holiness of the numinous. Rudolf Otto explains that amazing or even miraculous happenings are particularly helpful in evoking the numinous, for nothing so fully suggests "the religious consciousness of the ineffable, unutterable mystery, the 'absolute other,' as the incomprehensible, unwonted, enigmatic thing, in whatever guise it may confront us" (63). Through the incomprehensible and enigmatic presentation of inanimate objects taking on supernatural power, Ozick and O'Connor plunge the reader into a sense of the numinous.

THROWING EVERYTHING OFF BALANCE

The final group of stories to be considered are arguably the purest examples of Ozick's fantastic and O'Connor's grotesque. In them, the authors start with convincing depictions of the verisimilitude expected in stories, only to disrupt those perceptions with a physical action that cannot be explained through purely rational means. Although the specific techniques of the authors are obviously different, these stories can usefully be joined because they similarly explode the bounds of verisimilitude—and of rationality. Thus, the reader is forced into a different kind of logic, one that must take into account the mystery inherent in religious belief since the stories carry with them, to use Otto's description of the numinous, "a clear overplus of meaning" (5).

Ozick's "Levitation" starts off as the blandest of accounts: a New York husband and wife, both unimpressive people with no friends of the first rank in society, are each working on a second novel. Their most basic agreement is that they will not do the "Forbidden Thing," writing about writers, for such an approach falls into "solipsism, narcissism, tedium, lack of appeal-to-the-common-reader, who knew what other perils."[20] (Ozick, of course, is having fun with this idea, since she is herself doing the "Forbidden Thing": she is a New York author who in this story is writing about New York authors—who do not write about writing.) Lucy, a minister's daughter, wanted to marry "[o]ut of my tradition," so she became an "Ancient Hebrew" and married Feingold (3). Feingold married Lucy both "[f]or love, and also because he had always known he did not want a Jewish wife" (3). Lucy writes domestic novels, constantly rereading Jane Austen's *Emma*; Feingold writes about Jews, currently working on an historical novel about a survivor of a 1328 massacre in Spain. In the course of the story, the Feingolds decide to host a cocktail party at which they hope to break out of the rut they feel they have gotten into by attracting some first-class people such as Irving Howe, Susan Sontag, and Philip Roth. None of these luminaries, though, comes to the party, so the group is made up of the usual assortment of secondary actors, authors, and critics. The party is a failure; it "washed and turned like a sluggish tub; it lapped at all the walls of all the rooms" (9).

Yet even in this first portion of the story that seems a common description of a boring party, Ozick suggests that this surface existence is somehow less than real. During the party, the narrator describes the apartment as a triptych, with the guests as "free-standing figures in the niches of a cathedral" or "dressed up cardboard dolls" (9). Through the suggestion of a picture, figurines, and cutouts, it seems that this party is little more than illusion, a dim reflection of what is actually real. The lack of real life is underlined by the mere representations in the apartment. Someone asks, "Is that a real fireplace?" Lucy replies, "We never light it." "Do you light those candlesticks ever?" Lucy says that they do not (11), a comment that also points up their lack of following the Jewish traditions of Sabbath. Although the verisimilitude of the scene is convincing, the images suggest an illusory existence.

This presentation makes even more stark the startling action that occurs in the second part of the story. Someone suggests that they light the fire. Feingold rolls up the Sunday *Times* and lights it. He begins to speak with a friend from the seminary and suddenly realizes that he wants "to talk about God. Or, if not God, then certain historical atrocities" (11). While Feingold is pondering theological questions, the story shifts to Lucy's perspective. She is uncomfortable, wondering if she is a backslider in her conversion to Judaism, for "[s]ometimes she spoke of Jesus to the children" (12). As she gazes around the living room, Lucy realizes that everyone there is a Jew. There were Jews in the dining room, but only the kind "who went off to studio showings of *Screw on Screen* on the eve of the Day of Atonement" (12). Lucy is angry at Feingold for having "one of his spasms of fanaticism" about Jews (12), yet the people in the living room seem hungry for something of substance, for Lucy recognizes that they "were all ravenous" (13). Suddenly, the guest of the seminary friend begins to speak, urging them to think of recent history; Lucy realizes he is a refugee. "'Yesterday,' the refugee said, 'the eyes of God were shut'" (13). Rather than being attracted to this new voice, Lucy is disgusted by him and by the "terrible intensity" with which all the Jews in the room listen (14). The refugee tells of a massacre that he had witnessed. Lucy can only imagine it as "hundreds and hundred of Crucifixions . . . . Every Jew was Jesus" (14). As the refugee continues his gruesome tale, "Lucy saw the fingers of the listeners—all their fingers were stretched out" (15), apparently reaching out to grasp this man's words.

And then, the impossible happens:

> The room began to lift. It ascended. It rose like an ark on waters. Lucy said inside her mind, "This chamber of Jews." It seemed to her that the room was levitating on the little grains of the refugee's whisper. She felt herself alone at the bottom, below the floorboards, while the room floated upward, carrying Jews. Why did it not take her too? Only Jesus could take her. . . .
>
> She craned after [the room]. Wouldn't it bump into the apartment upstairs? It was like watching the underside of an elevator, all dirty and hairy, with dust-roots wagging. The black floor moved higher and higher. It was getting free of her, into loftiness, lifting Jews. (15–16)

The levitation of a room is, of course, bizarre. But Lucy's description of the rising room, with her concern that it will bump the apartment above them and her report of the appearance of the underside of the room, forces the reader into an uneasy dilemma: how to make sense of this levitating room? This hesitation, which lasts for the remainder of the story, is the fantastic centerpiece of the story. Broken from the verisimilitude of a cocktail party, the reader must attempt to assimilate this fantastic levitation to understand the story. In so doing, he or she is forced to recognize that some special, supernatural force may be at work, a power that within the context of the Jews' conversation and the remainder of the story takes on religious overtones.

After seeing this rising room, Lucy has an "illumination," presumably setting it apart from the reality of the levitating room. In her vision, she sees herself in the park with their children, waiting to see a musical program. This time, "real peasants" from Messina are coming to sing and dance. As they perform, Lucy has a new comprehension: she learns that the Madonna is only one in a line of earth mothers going back to Venus, Aphrodite, and Astarte. She understands:

> the gods are God. How terrible to have given up Jesus, a man like these, made of earth like these, with a pulse like these, God entering nature to become god! Jesus, no more miraculous than an ordinary goatherd; is a goatherd a miracle? Is a leaf? A nut, a pit, a core, a seed, a stone? Everything is a miracle! Lucy sees how she has abandoned nature, how she has lost true religion on account of the God of the Jews. (18)

In her movement away from the Jewish belief in one, formless God to a religion of nature, Lucy is making explicit her detachment from the real Jews, an idea that has been suggested throughout the story. The separation at the party between the Jews in the living room and the "atheists" (19) in the dining room points to the real differences between those who have abandoned their Jewishness and those who are passionate about being Jews. Further, since Lucy's viewpoint in the second half of the story becomes distinct from Feingold's, the story again emphasizes the differences between the pretender and the authentic, between Lucy who on a whim becomes an "Ancient Hebrew" and Feingold who seems absorbed with his Jewishness (Friedman 124). As she leaves her illumination and returns to the party, Lucy sees that the living room is almost out of sight. The story ends with the atheists in the dining room departing while "[o]verhead Feingold and the refugee are riding the living room. Their words are specks. All the Jews are in the air" (20). It seems that this final observation is from an omniscient narrator rather than from Lucy's perspective, because this closing paragraph makes no mention of Lucy and it shifts to present tense instead of the past tense used to describe Lucy's thoughts and actions. The comment, then, that *all* the Jews are levitating gives narratorial support to the sense that only those deeply committed to Judaism are actually Jews. It seems significant that this drawing together of the Jews takes place in the living room, a designation that suggests that they are together beginning to live.

And yet, exactly what draws them together seems complicated. Their emphasis on Jewish massacres throughout history and particularly on the Holocaust may suggest simply a shared horror at the atrocities in Jewish history. But they are also inspired by the refugee's passionate conclusion that "Yesterday . . . the eyes of God were shut" (13); Feingold (with the other Jews) listens with a "terrible intensity," and "[p]ity and shock" show on his face (14). Only when the Jews are drawn together by this refugee's words does the living room begin to levitate. This combination of accounts of the Holocaust with the refugee's indictment that God had closed his eyes suggests the difficulties, after the atrocities of the Holocaust, in believing in God's Covenant with the Jews. Jewish theologians have responded in differing ways to the challenge of belief after the murders of six million Jews. Richard Rubenstein's response is a radical one. He argues, "If I believed in God as the omnipotent author of the historical drama and Israel as His Chosen People, I had to accept . . . [the] conclusion that it was God's will that Hitler committed six million Jews to slaughter. I could not possibly believe in such a God nor could I believe in Israel as the chosen people of God after Auschwitz" (qtd. in Katz 146). Yet Rubenstein does not want to leave Judaism: "I do not believe that a theistic God is necessary for Jewish religious life. . . . I believe that our problem is how to speak of religion in an age of no God" (qtd. in Rubenstein and Roth 312). So even though Rubenstein rejects a biblical conception of God, he still finds it possible—even necessary—for Jews to join together: "it is precisely because human existence is tragic, ultimately hopeless, and without meaning that we treasure our religious community" (qtd. in Katz 147).

Rubenstein's position is far from the only theological response to the Holocaust. Emil Fackenheim agrees with Rubenstein that the Holocaust is a unique event, but he strongly disagrees about the message for Jews from it. He argues that while there can be no theological explanation for the Holocaust, there is a clear message from the Holocaust: unless Jews survive and believe, Hitler triumphs, and "Jews are forbidden to hand Hitler posthumous victories" (qtd. in Katz 154). Therefore, in Fackenheim's view, Jewish faith is "neither knowledge nor superstition" but the "sole possible positive answer to the fundamental question posed by existence itself," particularly after the Holocaust (215). In Eliezer Berkovits' view, though, the Holocaust is not a unique experience; rather, it fits in with the rest of Jewish history, so the question—as it is any time a Jew is killed—is how could God let it happen (Katz 165). Berkovits emphasizes the hidden nature of God, that "at times God, mysteriously and inexplicably, and without any obvious human cause such as sin, turns his face from Man" (Katz 166). He argues that for humans to have real freedom, God must be absent; but so that the meaninglessness is not complete, God also makes his presence known through history: "The continued existence of Israel despite its long record of suffering is the strongest single proof that God does exist despite His concealment" (Katz 166). In a somewhat different way, Abraham Joshua Heschel also affirms that belief is essential, especially after the Holocaust: "There can be no nature without spirit, no world without the Torah, no brotherhood without a father, no humanity without attachment to God" (491). He goes on to say, "The martyrdom of millions demands that we consecrate ourselves to the fulfillment of God's dream of salvation" (492). Of post-Holocaust theologians, few take a more positive view of the Holocaust than Ignaz Maybaum. He argues that Israel's purpose is to bring Gentiles to God and, therefore, Jews must do so in language that Gentiles—and especially Christians—will understand. Since Christians understand the language of crucifixion and sacrifice, the Holocaust, with the millions of Jewish victims, is the only way to get Christians to identify with Jews (Katz 157–59). He says, "In Auschwitz Jews suffered vicarious atonement for the sins of mankind" (qtd. in Katz 160). Thus, in a chilling statement, Maybaum insists that God says, "Hitler, My servant" since he was acting as part of God's plan (qtd. in Katz 163).

Understanding these various theological responses to the Holocaust helps to make sense of the story. For the Jews in the living room seem drawn together despite—perhaps even because—"the eyes of God were shut." While it is not clear from the story how they reconcile the Holocaust with the Covenant, their levitation together after the refugee's assertion that God had closed his eyes to Jewish suffering suggests that, at the least, they are affirming with Rubenstein the importance of commitment to community even if God cannot be trusted. It is also quite plausible to understand their response as reiterating belief in God, along with Fackenheim, Berkovits, and Heschel, in the face of the atrocities. Further, Lucy's connection of the Jewish victims with Jesus very clearly underlines Maybaum's understanding of the Holocaust. But, perhaps in a critique of his view, in the story, Lucy is not drawn to Judaism by identifying the murdered Jews with Jesus but is rather shifting to an acceptance of nature religions. Ozick's own response to the Holocaust underlines this implied critique. She suggests that we want to find redemption because redemptive acts—the Red Sea, the Resurrection—are a part of Jewish and Christian traditions. But with the Holocaust, "there was no redemption, the Red Sea did not open, nobody walked through the parting of the waters, the waters remained high and cold and deadly and closed. Nor did the tomb of salvation open to release the spirit of redemption; the tomb of salvation remained shut and sealed" ("Roundtable" 279).

By using a fantastic occurrence to push Lucy—and the reader—to recognize the distinction between the Covenant of Judaism and nature religions, Ozick draws attention to the reality that more than a nominal commitment to Judaism is required. In Feingold's earlier actions, particularly in wanting to marry out of his tradition, he, too, had seemed to be showing only slight dedication to Judaism. In fact, this marriage to Lucy combined with his fascination of Jewish massacres suggests that he is not drawn to Jewish life but is rather misusing past catastrophes (Horowitz "Pin" 148). His study of Jewish massacres also appears to be only rational inquiries without feeling any of the horror of the accounts: his novel about the slaughter is a "triumphant story" since one survivor becomes a scholar, an emphasis that seems incongruous in the face of such horror (5–6). The story seems to show that a passionate, even nonrational, commitment to the Covenant is necessary for the Jews to be a truly joined together.

Besides the specific message of the ending, the fantastic levitation of the room evokes a feeling of mystery and awe.[21] With the religious emphasis throughout the story, this sensation tends to push the reader toward the idea that there is divine power behind this Covenant. Thus, although on the surface level the levitation is unbelievable, in a deeper sense, the evocation of the holy in the second part of the story suggests that it is this part of the story that reflects reality while the earlier portion was only an illusory existence.

The action of "The Pagan Rabbi" is very different from "Levitation," but the basic structure of the stories is similar: the narrative's presentation of verisimilitude is infused with a fantastic occurrence. The first-person narrator of the tale is a former seminary student who, because of a withering faith, dropped out of seminary and married a Christian wife, whom he has since divorced. Isaac Kornfeld, on the other hand, was an apparently pious rabbi, a great scholar, who had married Sheindel, a Holocaust survivor. On one level, the action of the story is a kind of detective story: the narrator is trying to determine why, just before his thirty-sixth birthday, Isaac hanged himself from a tree by his prayer shawl (Friedman 62). Besides his curiosity, the narrator has always been attracted to Sheindel and hopes that after an appropriate period, he may be able to court her. In his effort to understand the suicide, the narrator first visits the site of Isaac's death: "The tree was almost alone in a long rough meadow, which sloped down to a bay filled with sickly clams and a bad smell. The place was called Trilham's Inlet, and I knew what the smell meant: that cold brown water covered half the city's turds."[22] He notices that the bark on the tree is rubbed at the next to lowest branch but draws no particular conclusion from the evidence he has seen.

Instead, he goes to visit Sheindel in an effort to understand the event. Since the narrator was the bookseller from whom Isaac bought his books, Sheindel immediately questions him about the kinds of books Isaac was reading. The narrator insists that he does not remember specific ones; Isaac bought a vast range of books, he says, since he was a "scholar. A rabbi. A remarkable Jew." Sheindel laughs a furious laugh and declares, "He was not" (12–13). The narrator is beginning to fear that Sheindel has become mentally unstable since the suicide. But she simply continues with her description of her husband, explaining how he invented stories for their children of mice that danced, clouds that spoke, a turtle that married a blade of grass, a pig with a soul. He insisted that the family go on picnics, every time "farther and farther into the country" (13). Then, Isaac joined a hiking club and took to writing fairy tales. One day, he burned his stories, put a notebook in his pocket, and went to the park where he began to spend the night. Sheindel became so disturbed over his love of plants that she threw away all of the ones she had in the house. Finally, since the narrator can make no sense of this collection of evidence, Sheindel gives him Isaac's notebook to read. But this notebook, too, seems only a muddle to the narrator: it is filled with a collection of Greek verses, bits of Hebrew Scripture, and English Romantic poetry. The biblical passages are primarily from Leviticus and Deuteronomy, excerpts such as, "Ye shall utterly destroy all the places of the gods, upon the high mountains, and upon the hills, and under every green tree" (16). The notebook ends, "Great Pan lives" (17). The narrator cannot understand these passages, but Ruth Rosenberg suggests that this inability occurs because he is secularized: he has "lost the rabbinic method for making inferences from conjoined passages, . . . but to the pious widow, they record her husband's growing paganism" (223). From this vantage point, the narrator's inability to understand Isaac is more a commentary on the narrator's lack of connection to Judaism than to the difficulty of Isaac's writing. Bewildered, he returns the notebook to Sheindel, convinced that she is taunting him for his impolitic curiosity about this death.

Instead of allowing him to leave, Sheindel hands him what she describes as a love letter, which the police found in Isaac's pocket. The narrator is shocked and tries to refuse it, but Sheindel insists, eventually reading it to him herself. The letter is addressed to a creature called Loveliness, and its central concern is Isaac's effort to support his idea that life exists in all things: "There is nothing that is Dead. There is no Non-life. Holy life subsists even in the stone, even in the bones of dead dogs and dead men. Hence in God's fecundating Creation there is no possibility of Idolatry" (20–21). Since Isaac is focusing on the immanence of God, he has eliminated the possibility of violating the Second Commandment against idolatry since, if God resides in nature, any worship of nature is paying homage to God, not violating a commandment (Kauvar *Tradition and Invention* 44). Isaac is particularly convinced that there are two kinds of souls, the indwelling and the free; "[w]e human ones are cursed with the indwelling" (21). In a kind of contemporary midrash, he goes so far as to determine that Moses knew of this truth, but decided not to tell it to the Israelites for fear they would disobey God by sending out only their souls while their bodies remained in Egypt (22). Interestingly, though, by focusing on such a split between body and soul, Isaac is accepting a conception that, while it is one part of Jewish thought, grew out of Greek influence on Judaism rather than on an understanding from biblical material, which posited no split between body and soul (Elior 887). The duality between body and soul became highly developed in medieval thought and especially in the mystical kabbalah, which focused on freeing the soul from the physical to reach for greater spiritual purity (Elior 890). While it is not clear that his motivation is enhanced spiritual purity, Isaac's continued searching leads him to this conclusion: "if only I could couple with one of the free souls, the strength of the connection would likely wrest my own soul from my body—seize it, as if by tongs, draw it out, so to say, to its own freedom" (28). Such an idea again has overtones of the kabbalah, since one kabbalistic text, the *Sefer ha-Bahir*, uses sexual language to speak of the creation of souls through a cosmic union (Elior 891–92). As Isaac searches for a free soul, one night he runs into a tree, and after caressing and embracing it, calls to Nature, "Come, couple with me." He reports, "Without warning I was flung to the ground. My face smashed into earth . . . . A superb ache lined my haunch. I began to weep because I was certain I had been ravished by some animal. I vomited the earth I had swallowed and believed I was defiled, as it is written: 'Neither shalt thou lie with any beast'" (29). While he waits to see what has attacked him, he realizes: "I had been fully positioned and aroused and exquisitely sated, all in half a second, in a fashion impossible to explain, in which, though I performed as with my own wife, I felt as if a preternatural rapine had been committed upon me" (29). What he finds is a young girl, with skin the color of eggplant, hands like leaves, body covered with a "spore-like material"—in short, it is a dryad from the tree who has copulated with him (30–31). Her nature is particularly good news to him since "Scripture does not forbid sodomy with the plants" (32).

Isaac is delighted when the dryad informs him that his soul has indeed become separated from his body. The dryad is saddened, though, claiming that Isaac has spoiled himself, but Isaac insists that his soul only loves her. She scorns him and points him toward his soul, walking along the road: "He is half bent over under the burden of a dusty old bag. The bag is stuffed with books" (34). And though the road is lined with beautiful flowers, the soul continues to read in his Tractates. So Isaac confronts his own soul who tells him that if he had kept his soul, it would have stayed with him to the end. "'But you expelled me, your ribs exile me from their fate, and I will walk here alone always, in my garden'—he scratched on his page—'with my precious birds'—he scratched at the letters—'and my darling trees'—he scratched at the tall side-column of commentary" (36). In his anger, Isaac shakes his soul, only to be told, "The sound of Law is more beautiful than the crickets. The smell of the Law is more radiant than the moss. The taste of the Law exceeds clear water" (36). In despair, Isaac grabs the prayer shawl off his soul, ties it to the tree, and calls to the dryad; she does not come—and here the letter ends. Even the details of Isaac's suicide reveal the theological conflict that he is unable to resolve: he hangs himself with a symbol of piety, his prayer shawl, from a emblem of his love of nature, the tree (Friedman 64).

Clearly, the story is dealing with issues of how a commitment to Judaism is compatible with a love of nature, a conflict set out in the epigraph of the story from *The Ethics of the Fathers*: "Rabbi Jacob said: 'He who is walking along and studying, but then breaks off to remark, "How lovely is that tree!" or "How beautiful is that fallow field!"—Scripture regards such a one as having hurt his own being'" (3). As Ozick herself spells out the problem in an essay, "*how can we keep ourselves from sliding off from awe at God's Creation to worship of God's Creation?*" (*Art & Ardor* 206). Even Isaac Kornfeld's name, with the biblical resonances of the first name and the suggestions of nature of the second, point to the conflict. On one level, then, the story seems to have a connection to a midrash by Rashi, in which he suggested that when the biblical Isaac went out to the field to wait for the arrival of his wife, he was praying rather than thinking erotic thoughts. On the other hand, "Ozick's midrash tells of what happens when one goes out into nature for nonliturgical purposes" (Lowin 70–71). The conflict with nature is underlined by the location of the tree where Isaac commits suicide: by the city sewage pond. Such a connection certainly undercuts the purity of nature that Isaac believes he is seeking. And while the location is far from an Eden, that it is with a tree that Isaac loses his soul certainly has resonances of the

Tree of Knowledge in Eden, suggesting that Isaac may be overreaching in his search for understanding.

Nor is it only a confrontation between Judaism and nature. As has been noted, Isaac's suggestion of animism within Judaism hints at some of the mystical or kabbalistic strains within Judaism, a strand of Jewish thought opposed to the rationalism of Sheindel (Kauvar *Tradition and Invention* 47). Thus, since Sheindel in Yiddish means "loveliness," the term Isaac uses to address the dryad, it is possible to see the two women as representing competing branches of Judaism (Rosenberg 224). In this allegorical understanding, besides the conflict between Jewish and Greek thought that he outlines in his notes, Isaac is caught between the more mainstream Judaism with its emphasis on God's transcendence and the kabbalistic strain with its focus on God's immanence.

But at least as prominent as the theme of the story is its fantastic character. The narrator is in the same position as the reader: how should he assimilate this fantastic account? He is put off by the obvious contempt in which Sheindel holds her husband. Her insistence that he is a pagan and not to be pitied seems harsh and uncaring to him. As a rationalist, he seems tempted to believe that Isaac was simply crazy. Yet the story concludes, "I remembered her earlier words and dropped three green house plants down the toilet; after a journey of some miles through conduits they straightway entered Trilham's Inlet, where they decayed amid the civic excrement" (37). This conclusion leaves the narrator—and the reader—residing in the fantastic realm: it is unclear if Isaac's actions have a rational explanation (he was crazy) or a supernatural one (the dryad actually exists). The reader is forced out of any easy solution, hesitating between rival explanations. As Todorov explains, such an indecision is inherent in the fantastic since the fantastic "implies an integration of the reader into the world of the characters; that world is defined by the reader's own ambiguous perception of the events narrated" (31). While this dilemma is never finally solved, that this rationalistic narrator, this child of the Enlightenment, has been moved to get rid of his plants seems to validate the disconcerting supernatural quality that is present in Isaac Kornfeld's account. The narrator's response suggests that he has felt a brush of the numinous, and his action of flushing his houseplants evokes a similar feeling of dread and awe in the reader. Rational explanations are inadequate in the face of these nonrational actions. This overplus of meaning in the story suggests that the mystery of belief must be taken seriously, that one must choose between God and nature.

In O'Connor's stories "Greenleaf" and "A Good Man Is Hard to Find," she, too, uses bizarre events, which carry religious overtones, to surprise the reader and point him or her toward mystery. The events themselves—a goring and a shooting—are certainly not an established religious ritual, but in some way that transcends complete understanding, the incidents take on sacramental meaning for the characters as well as for the reader. Showing the mysterious action of grace, O'Connor uses these grotesque events to elicit a sense of the numinous.

Although on one level "Greenleaf" is a story about the struggle by Mrs. May to protect her property and her cows from a stray bull, from the opening paragraph the bull seems to have added significance. The bull appears outside Mrs. May's window, "like some patient god come down to woo her," wearing a hedge-wreath on his horns (311). Convinced that the bull will mate with her cows and thus ruin her breeding schedule, Mrs. May becomes obsessed with getting him off her land, particularly when she learns that he is owned by the sons of her hired man, Mr. Greenleaf. Mrs. May is annoyed by the way these boys have succeeded with their dairy farm after they had "managed to get wounded" in the war and now receive government pensions (318). Their success is especially galling because Mrs. May's adult sons, who are, she believes, from much better society than the Greenleafs, are failures who still live at home. And Mrs. May finds Mrs. Greenleaf a disgrace: "Instead of making a garden or washing their clothes, her preoccupation was what she called 'prayer healing'" (315). Each day she would cut out any newspaper stories about accidents, criminal acts, or other tragedies and bury them in a hole in the woods. She "fell on the ground over them and mumbled and groaned for an hour or so moving her huge arms back and forth under her and out again and finally just lying down flat and, Mrs. May suspected, going to sleep in the dirt" (316). The first time Mrs. May encounters this prayer healing, she hears a loud agonized voice shouting, "Jesus! Jesus!" Mrs. May is shocked: "The sound was so piercing that she felt as if some violent force had broken out of the ground and was charging toward her. Her second thought was more reasonable: somebody had been hurt on the place and would sue her for everything she had" (316).

This "more reasonable" explanation accurately reflects Mrs. May's highest values. She thinks of everything in material terms, with all parts of her land being her private property, as she reveals when she complains to Mr. Greenleaf that his boys are not remembering all the good things she had done for them: "If I recall, they wore *my* boys' old clothes and played with *my* boys' old toys and hunted with *my* boys' old guns. They swam in *my* pond and shot *my* birds and fished in *my* stream" (328, emphasis added). Materialist that she is, she winces at Mrs. Greenleaf's repeated shouting of the name Jesus: "She thought the word, Jesus, should be kept inside the church building like other words inside the bedroom. She was a good Christian woman with a large respect for religion, though she did not, of course, believe any of it was true" (316). In this wonderfully comic-satiric line, Mrs. May's lack of commitment is shown in stark contrast to Mrs. Greenleaf's shriek, "Oh Jesus, stab me in the heart" (317).

So after repeatedly trying—and failing—to convince the Greenleaf boys that they must remove their bull from her land, Mrs. May decides that the only option is to kill it. She orders Mr. Greenleaf to get his gun and drives him to the pasture to shoot the bull. Mrs. May is pleased with her resolution, and she mentions gaily to Mr. Greenleaf in the car, "Spring is here!" (330). The bull escapes into the woods, so Mrs. May orders Mr. Greenleaf in after it. As she waits, she reflects that she has lived a good life: "Before any kind of judgement seat, she would be able to say: I've worked, I have not wallowed" (332). In contrast, she believes that Mrs. Greenleaf has done nothing during her life; she remembers that she once mentioned to Mr. Greenleaf that his wife had let her religion warp her: "Everything in moderation, you know" (332). Tired of waiting for Mr. Greenleaf, she begins to honk the car horn. After a bit, she sees that the bull has come out of the woods and is heading for her, seeming "overjoyed" to see her:

> She remained perfectly still, not in fright, but in a freezing disbelief. She stared at the violent black streak bounding toward her as if she had no sense of distance, as if she could not decide at once what his intention was, and the bull had buried his head in her lap, like a wild tormented lover, before her expression changed. One of his horns sank until it pierced her heart and the other curved around her side and held her in an unbreakable grip. She continued to stare straight ahead but the entire scene in front of her had changed—the tree line was a dark wound in a world that was nothing but sky—and she had the look of a person whose sight has been suddenly restored but finds the light unbearable. (333)

Mr. Greenleaf runs toward her and shoots the bull. While Mrs. May does not hear the shots, "she felt the quake in the huge body as it sank, pulling her forward on its head, so that she seemed, when Mr. Greenleaf reached her, to be bent over whispering some last discovery into the animal's ear" (334).

The imagery surrounding this vicious, shocking death has clear resonances with the scene of Mrs. Greenleaf's prayer healing, with the violent force coming at her and the horn piercing her heart. Further, the descriptions of Mrs. May's first look of "freezing disbelief," of the trees looking like a wound (calling to mind Christ's wounds) leading to her new vision of the scene in front of her, and finally of her apparent whisper of a "last discovery" to the bull suggest that something of religious significance has happened here. But how can a gruesome goring death by a bull be a religious experience? To make sense of this ending, the reader must step outside of a strictly rational approach to the story and accept that a different kind of logic is at work here. In the grotesque world of O'Connor's tale, the physical piercing of the heart is in some bizarre way connected with Mrs. May's spiritual understanding. This linkage, which does not make rational sense, endows the story with a feeling of religious mystery, a sensation that a deeper reality is at work than simply the surface conflict between a woman and a bull.

As already briefly noted, the imagery of the story very much supports the added layer of meaning. The bull's identification as a suitor suggests the role of Christ as the bridegroom of the Church (Rev. 19.7), a role underlined by the bull's having a "prickly crown" (312). While the bull also has classical overtones, especially to the story of Jove and Europa, the primary focus seems to be on the Christian connotations; as Nancy Gidden says, "Classical myth, it seems, has been employed in the service of Christian conversion" (202). Additionally, the Greenleafs, despite all their unlikable characteristics, seem marked as agents of grace. Mr. Greenleaf's face is shaped like a "rough chalice" (314), but the

Greenleafs' connection to grace is most prominently made by Mrs. Greenleaf's prayer healing. Although it seems distorted and excessive, her total commitment to belief is set in contrast to Mrs. May's careful disbelief.[23] Further, in what Mrs. May means to be an insult, she thinks that the Greenleafs live "like the lilies of the field," not worrying about their existence. But Jesus' teaching, to which this line alludes, holds up the lilies as a positive example of the way people should have faith rather than worrying about their future (Matt. 6.28). The Greenleafs' religiously significant role is also suggested when Mrs. May earlier in the story goes to the Greenleaf home to tell them about the bull; she is quickly surrounded by six silent children, so "[s]he felt as if she were on trial for her life, facing a jury of Greenleafs" (324), a comment that connects the Greenleafs to the judgment she will shortly face at her death. And, of course, the Greenleaf name suggests the new life possible through Christ, as is underlined by Mrs. May's comment that spring is here.

Given all the clues, it seems clear the conclusion does have religious significance. Whether or not Mrs. May receives the grace offered by the bull, though, is the subject of critical controversy. Steven Ryan believes that although Mrs. May's eyes are open, "her damnation is suggested (although certainly not confirmed) when she 'finds the light unbearable'" (48). Likewise, A.R. Coulthard asserts, "If God brings Mrs. May into the fold, He does so by main force and apparently without her consent" (92). On the other hand, Lorine Getz suggests that Mrs. May had sought to reassert control over her farm by killing the bull, but instead the bull kills her. Therefore, "She is forced to see that she is not ultimately in control of her destiny, and that in wrongly valuing her material goods and warding off the divine lover, she has chosen a merely natural goal which grace must ultimately reverse" (63). Whether or not Mrs. May accepts the grace that God—through the bull—offers is not finally certain from the story, although the last, whispered discovery suggests such a conversion. What is certain is that Mrs. May is forced beyond the moderation she advocates to realize that material existence is not the only—or highest—goal.

O'Connor has used the grotesque goring to push the story toward a higher level of signification, toward the numinous. Rudolf Otto argues that there is an element of belief in God and the divine which we can rationally understand, but there is also beyond "this sphere of clarity and lucidity . . . a hidden depth, inaccessible to our conceptual thought"—the numinous (58). In a manner that parallels Otto's conception, the religious content in "Greenleaf" is on one level understandable, as we examine the Christian imagery. But on another more profound level, the action of grace that occurs when the bull gores Mrs. Greenleaf is beyond human reason. As such, O'Connor is less concerned with what exactly happens to Mrs. May and more preoccupied with what occurs in the reader. For this stabbing of the heart is designed to change the reader as well, aiming for "an emotion that cuts deep enough to plant a new attitude or resolution in the unbelieving reader's heart" (Giannone *Hermit Novelist* 201). The sense evoked when

Mrs. May's heart is pierced cannot be explained, only experienced as O'Connor uses this violent death to push the reader to encounter the numinous.

"A Good Man Is Hard to Find" is for obvious reasons one of O'Connor's most commonly anthologized stories since it so well illustrates her use of the comically grotesque method—not to mention that it is a compelling story. In it, as in "Greenleaf," O'Connor uses a shockingly violent conclusion to jar her characters and her readers to a confrontation with God's grace. The early part of the story focuses on a Georgia family—made up of a taciturn father, a mother with a face "as broad and innocent as a cabbage," a baby and two bratty children, and a pretentious grandmother—leaving for a vacation trip to Florida (117). Critics often point to this caricature of a family to illustrate O'Connor's grotesque. But while this method is one element of O'Connor's style, the opening of the story still maintains a plausible enough level of verisimilitude that it does not prepare the reader for the startling conclusion.

This early section of the story establishes the grandmother's manipulative approach, as she tries to frighten the family with tales of an escaped convict, The Misfit. Her elitist attitude becomes clear, too, since the grandmother is dressed properly for the trip in a navy blue hat and dress; "[i]n case of an accident, anyone seeing her dead on the highway would know at once that she was a lady" (118). Her social snobbishness is made clear when, driving past a naked black boy, she exclaims, "Oh look at the cute little pickaninny! . . . If I could paint, I'd paint that picture" (119). The family stops for lunch at The Tower, run by fat Red Sammy Butts, for sandwiches. The grandmother feels that she can connect with Red Sammy, that he is a good man. They reminisce together about the way that a good man is hard to find these days, what with everything "getting terrible" (122). This linkage between the grandmother and Red Sammy exposes her pseudo-gentility, for he is the "personification of the red-necked South" (Renner 126), not the gentleman the grandmother assumes. As they are driving, the grandmother remembers that an old plantation she once had visited is close by and manages to convince her son, Bailey, to stop. Before they can get to the plantation (which, it turns out, is in Tennessee instead of Georgia), the grandmother inadvertently releases her smuggled cat, which leaps on Bailey and causes an accident.

With no one too seriously injured, the family waits after the accident for help. Soon, a car does arrive and the occupants get out. Suddenly the grandmother exclaims, "You're The Misfit!" "'Yes'm,' the man said, smiling slightly as if he were pleased in spite of himself to be known, 'but it would have been better for all of you, lady, if you hadn't of reckernized me'" (127). With this introduction, the story takes a bizarre twist. For this murderous killer maintains perfect manners, apologizing to the ladies for not wearing a shirt and soothing the grandmother when Bailey swears at her for identifying The Misfit. Beside herself with fear, the grandmother begins saying anything that comes to mind, hoping in this way to save herself. She says, "You wouldn't shoot a lady, would you?" "I would hate to have to," the Misfit responds (127). She insists, "I know you're a good man" (128). First, the Misfit say, "I pre-chate that, lady," but a bit later he acknowledges, "Nome, I ain't a good man" (128). As they continue their conversation, The Misfit calmly and politely invites the various members of the family into the woods, where his henchmen shoot them. In terror, the grandmother attempts to get The Misfit to change his life, encouraging him to settle down in a comfortable life and to pray. Though he acknowledges that "somebody is always after you" (129), suggesting the "Hound of Heaven" image of God's pursuing sinners, he asserts that he will not pray because "I don't want no hep" (130). The Misfit reveals that he does not remember being bad, but one time he got sent to the penitentiary: "I forgot what I done, lady. I set there and set there, trying to remember what it was I done and I ain't recalled it to this day" (130). Showing that he is a kind of literalist in his belief in documentation (Bellamy 105), The Misfit insists that he was not mistakenly put in prison because "[t]hey had the papers on me" (130). "No lady," he declares, "I found out the crime don't matter. You can do one thing or you can do another, kill a man or take a tire off his car, because sooner or later you're going to forget what it was you done and just be punished for it" (130–31). Therefore, The Misfit has decided to sign all his crimes.

By this time, all the rest of the members of the family have been murdered. The grandmother can think of nothing to say: "Finally she found herself saying, 'Jesus, Jesus,' meaning Jesus will help you, but the way she was saying it, it sounded as if she might be cursing" (131). The Misfit draws a parallel between himself and Jesus, because neither of them seems to have a crime to fit his punishment:

> "Jesus was the only One that ever raised the dead," The Misfit continued, "and He shouldn't have done it. He thown everything off balance. If He did what He said, then it's nothing for you to do but thow away everything and follow Him, and if He didn't, then it's nothing for you to do but enjoy the few minutes you got left the best way you can—by killing somebody or burning down his house or doing some other meanness to him. No pleasure but meanness," he said and his voice had become almost a snarl. (132)[24]

Not knowing what she is saying, the grandmother denies Christ, suggesting, "Maybe He didn't raise the dead."

> "I wasn't there so I can't say He didn't," The Misfit said. "I wisht I had of been there," he said, hitting the ground with his fist. "It ain't right I wasn't there because if I had of been there I would of known. Listen lady," he said in a high voice, "if I had of been there I would of known and I wouldn't be like I am now." His voice seemed about to crack and the grandmother's head cleared for an instant. She saw the man's face twisted close to her own as if he were going to cry and she murmured, "Why you're one of my babies. You're one of my own children!" She reached out and touched him on the shoulder. The Misfit sprang back as if a snake had bitten him and shot her three times through the chest. (132)

Given that the murder takes place in the midst of the conversation between The Misfit and the grandmother, this murder seems in some way connected to their discussion of Jesus' resurrection. Yet, as with the goring by the bull in "Greenleaf," one can make no logical sense how a murder is religiously significant. Once again, O'Connor's grotesque approach throws the reader off stride, forcing him or her toward something more than psychological realism to explain the ending. While it is always somewhat dangerous to follow an author's comments on her story, O'Connor seems on the mark when she says, "in this story, you should be on the lookout for such things as the action of grace in the Grandmother's soul, and not for the dead bodies" (*Mystery* 113).

This ending, though, has been interpreted in many different ways, from extremely bleak to singularly affirmative. Josephine Hendin believes, "That a pet, a cat, leaping at random for no great reason, should cause the destruction of an entire family expresses the randomness, the pointlessness of the murders" (150–51). Likewise, Stephen Bandy insists that the grandmother merely in desperation appeals to her "only remaining . . . weapon: motherhood" when she reaches out to The Misfit (3). Bandy finds that the story's "message is profoundly pessimistic and in fact subversive to the doctrines of grace and charity, despite heroic efforts to disguise the fact" (1). Yet what makes the story so intriguing is that even though the murders are on the surface random and senseless, they seem, on a deeper level, to have meaning. The grandmother throughout the story has been shown to be living on the surfaces, focusing on the importance of her appearance as a Christian lady, but she has never seemed to internalize any of her beliefs. Her inane babble is in many ways parallel to the chatter of the monkey chained to the tree at Red Sammy's restaurant. It is only when she is thrust out of her comfortable life that she is forced to recognize that she is, on a most basic level, no better than even a murderer. After her mindless chatter, her reaching out to The Misfit and claiming him as her own son shows a true self-appraisal that indicates an openness to grace. In some mysterious way, as The Misfit realizes, "She would of been a good woman if it had been somebody there to shoot her every minute of her life" (133)—somebody to force her beyond her smug surface existence. Even the symbolic positioning of her legs indicates a change: while she had earlier slumped to the ground with her legs twisted under her, at death we see her with her legs crossed, suggesting a change from disorder to harmony of the cross (Bellamy 108). The description of the sky, too, indicates that something mysterious is happening: just before the grandmother is shot, there is "not a cloud in the sky nor any sun" (131). Except for an eclipse, such a description resists natural explanations. Instead, it calls to mind the supernatural darkness that happens at the time of Christ's crucifixion, suggesting—as the bizarre phenomena surrounding the crucifixion do—that an otherworldly event is taking place.

It thus seems too simplistic to say the murderers embody evil, as Abigail Hamblen asserts (296); they are evil, yes, but The Misfit also in some bizarre way acts as an agent of grace for the grandmother, much as the unlikable Mary Grace functions for Mrs. Turpin in "Revelation." Yet it may be giving too much credit to The Misfit to say that "[d]estruction is his answer to the false happiness of paralyzed worlds that individuals and groups have created to shield themselves from any kind of change" (Spivey *Flannery O'Connor* 124)—The Misfit, as he says, is merely having fun as he knows how. What seems to happen is that in some manner beyond human reasoning, the evil that the Misfit intends becomes a means of grace for the grandmother. Facing her death, her surface veneer is shattered, leaving room for a deeper transformation to take place.

As if that were not enough for a story, what is even more astonishing is that the conclusion suggests that the grandmother may have also acted to bring grace to The Misfit. When he begins to talk to the grandmother, he is just planning to while away a bit of time in conversation, but the discussion gets out of his control (Gentry 37). The Misfit is a supreme rationalist who insists he is agnostic about Jesus since he could not independently verify the events of his life. Yet, unlike the grandmother, who mouths platitudes about following Christ, The Misfit realizes the implications of Jesus' life: if he did rise from the dead, he must be followed. Just as in "The Pagan Rabbi" Sheindel sees a clear distinction between Judaism and nature religions, The Misfit realizes that Jesus forces an either/or decision. But since he cannot prove Jesus' existence, he has chosen for evil—"meanness," as he says. The grandmother seems to have had an effect on him, however, for after he has shot her, one of his partners, Bobby Lee, says, "Some fun!" In a significant change from his earlier assessment that the only pleasure comes from meanness, The Misfit say, "Shut up, Bobby Lee. It's no real pleasure in life" (133).[25] While it is not clear that he has received into himself the offered grace, The Misfit, too, has been knocked off of his calm acceptance of life without Jesus. In her reaching out to him, the grandmother has also acted as a vehicle of grace. Kathleen Ochshorn, though, sees the grandmother as too limited to be an agent of grace since she is self-centered. Ochshorn asserts that The Misfit finds it "repulsive" to think that he is her child. "With good reason, The Misfit is unwilling to be adopted by this grandmother" (115–16). But it is precisely the surprise of the grandmother's change from her narrowness to her reaching out to another sinner that points to the mysterious quality of this ending. In a shocking manner, the physicality of the grandmother's touch and the Misfit's shooting both take on a sacramental quality as they confer grace on the recipient, giving this story a feeling of the numinous.

In differing ways, both Ozick and O'Connor see themselves as writing for an audience that is likely not particularly aware of or attracted to their perspective. Discussing the story "Usurpation (Other People's Stories)," Ozick acknowledges her non-Jewish audience's difficulty in understanding her viewpoint: "I had written 'Usurpation' in the language of a civilization that cannot imagine its thesis" (Preface to *Bloodshed* 10). Ozick's point seems to hold for more than this one story; her fiction seeks to get at religious issues that are not readily available to her readers. Writing from a Catholic perspective, O'Connor, too, laments, "Making grace believable to the contemporary reader is the almost insurmountable problem of the novelist who writes from the standpoint of Christian orthodoxy" (*Presence of Grace* 16). Since they recognize the difficulty of making apparent their religious concerns to their audience, both Ozick and O'Connor use in their stories techniques that jar their readers into an understanding that may be foreign to them. Rather than giving structure to mystery by showing their characters on a quest as Malamud and Percy do, Ozick and O'Connor parallel the operation of *mitzvot* and sacraments by having specific images and actions opening up to a sense of the holy. Through the shock of these fantastic and grotesque stories, the reader is forced beyond psychological or sociological interpretations to realize that something wholly other is at work in these stories. To cite again Robert Detweiler's words, these authors' fiction seems finally to resist a complete explication but rather needs a "contemplative fellowship" (34) to enter into the stories as they evoke a sense of the numinous.

In an interview, Ozick agrees that metaphor can "convey a leap of faith," and adds, "That is why it is so dangerous," particularly in fiction, "which is a lie that tells that truth" (Ozick with Rainwater and Scheick 263). Her sense of the power of fiction is a prime reason, no doubt, that she fears the potential idolatry in creating literature, but Ozick's comment also points toward her sense that something more than can be rationally explained is at work in fiction. Similarly, in a letter, O'Connor writes that fiction is embedded in mystery and "is not answerable to any of our formulas. It does't rest finally in a statable kind of solution. It ought to throw you back on the living God" (*Habit* 516). In their separate ways, both Ozick and O'Connor are expressing their sense that fiction with a religious intent must encompass a wider view than merely a rationally understandable explanation. Their fantastic and grotesque fiction portrays the mystery of belief by forcing the reader to see reality through a different, nonrational logic—to recognize that religious mystery is at the heart of existence.

NOTES

1. "An Interview with Cynthia Ozick," with Elaine M. Kauvar, *Contemporary Literature* 26 (1985), page 400.

2. *Mystery and Manners*, Ed. Sally and Robert Fitzgerald, New York: Farrar, Straus and Giroux, 1969, page 153.

3. Percy, who is effusive in his praise of both O'Connor and her stories, nevertheless feels that O'Connor may have overstated the religious impact of her fiction: "She sees her fiction in much more univocal, theological terms than I would see it. I think it works without that rather simple theological reading, and I think it had *better* work without that, or otherwise, if you have to share that feeling of grace with her to understand her fiction, I think she's in trouble" (*Conversations with Walker Percy* 233). In evaluating her own writing, Ozick makes a similar point as Percy makes about O'Connor as she emphasizes that the message cannot overwhelm the story. She acknowledges that "The Pagan Rabbi" and "Usurpation" are "representative of certain ideas; but I think of them as parables rather than as allegories. In an allegory, the story stands for an idea, and the idea can be stated entirely apart from the story; in a parable, story and idea are so inextricably fused that they cannot be torn free from each other" (Ozick with Rainwater and Scheick 262–63).

4. Alfred Hornung argues that Ozick, along with Philip Roth, has found a middle ground of using some postmodern techniques but also modifying then: "Both Roth and Ozick have clearly recognized the dangerous tendencies implicit in playful textual games of postmodernism. In their transgression of this postmodern fiction they have created a form of writing that uses postmodern techniques but is also conscious of the effects of language in the real world" (249).

5. She says, for instance, that in *The Violent Bear It Away*, she is concerned with Old Tarwater's relationship with God, not with his denomination: "I'm not interested in the sects as sects; I'm concerned with the religious individual, the backwoods prophet. Old Tarwater is the hero of *The Violent Bear It Away*, and I'm right behind him 100 per cent" (*Conversations with Flannery O'Connor* 83).

6. The similar techniques and religious impulses that O'Connor and Ozick share in their stories have led other critics to link them—either to point out problems in their approach or to praise them. Harold Bloom insists, "Devotional short stories are as dubious as devotional poems, despite say Flannery O'Connor's weird self-deception that her superbly brutal 'A Good Man Is Hard to Find' was a Catholic narrative, or Ozick's equally strange conviction that the savage and sublime 'Envy; or Yiddish in America' somehow might become a contribution 'Toward a New Yiddish,' toward a survival that Ozick wistfully but wrongly identifies with Jewish liturgy" (Bloom *Cynthia Ozick* 5). Joseph Epstein also finds difficulties in the two authors' stories: "Cynthia Ozick's most Jewish stories remind me in fact of the Catholic stories of Flannery O'Connor—both seem to me ambitious, impressive, yet finally, somehow, static" (68). More positive is Sarah Cohen's assertion: "both writers, often theological in their orientation, ridicule fallen-away characters, desecraters of the faith: O'Connor with her penchant for writing about freaks at odds with the theological . . . and Ozick's mockery of emotional and spiritual grotesques because they are far from being fully realized individuals" (5).

7. See Ozick's conversation with Joshua O. Haberman, page 159.

8. Ozick's admiration of Malamud's fantastic writing is made particularly clear in a series of letters she wrote to him after her reading of his manuscript of *God's Grace*. Addressing him as "Maestro," Ozick lauds Malamud's novel in a February 1, 1982 letter: "One half-second ago I came to page 205 of GOD'S GRACE. An a astonishment, . . also an anguish. I am in grief. I have been weeping with these losses you have hacked into my ribs. This is one of your most powerful inventions; perhaps the most stunning of all" (II:1).

9. Ozick also occasionally uses fantastic elements in stories that seem not to have religious overtones. For instance, in *The Shawl*, Ozick uses the fantastic to get at the unspeakable horror of the Holocaust. The shawl takes on magical qualities, even conjuring up for Rosa her child who was killed in a concentration camp. Ozick transformed this story into a play, originally called *Blue Light* and performed in Sag Harbor, New York, and gave the drama a new focus: a man tries to convince the main character, Rosa, that her Holocaust memories are a fraud. As Ozick explains, "My new play is about a new phenomenon, called Holocaust denial. . . . The play is about the devil and his seductions. It is pessimistic. The devil, though he is ultimately confronted by passionate opposition, nevertheless walks out and goes freely into the world, where the devil can always be found, peddling his wares and snatching souls" (qtd. in Klingenstein "Cynthia Ozick" 258). Renamed *The Shawl*, the play opened in New York City in the spring of 1996.

10. Vera Emuna Kielsky does not see such a clear role of mystery in these fantastic tales. She finds that Ozick's "nightmare images of Greek and Jewish mythology and history have no autonomous function; they serve only to emphasize the danger of deception and self-deception in the lives of her characters, to illustrate the seductive power of the imagination—idolatry—of the freedom to change one's life" (18). While the fantastic features may have such a role, such an easy explanation seems to domesticate a bit too easily the disruptive force of Ozick's fantastic tales.

11. Not all of O'Connor's readers are convinced that her grotesques lead to the holy. In a famous article, "Flannery O'Connor's Devil," John Hawkes insists that "a good many readers would mistake Flannery O'Connor's belief in the Holy for its opposite" (94). Andre Bleikasten also finds the demonic a strong force in O'Connor's writing, and, given her portrayal of humans, he further asserts, "one may wonder whether her Catholicism was not, to some extent, an alibi for misanthropy" (142). More recent critics have used a variety of approaches to allow them better to approach O'Connor's vision. David Danow examines the non-verbal elements—gestures and expressions—in O'Connor's stories, wondering, "What might we learn if our focus remains concentrated on the moments in dialogue of *communicative* silence?" (119). Ruthann Knechel Johansen understands O'Connor's anagogical impact by linking O'Connor's disturbing stories with archetypal "tricksters" from earlier literature. Using a different approach, Joanne Halleran McMullen uses a linguistic and reader-response criticism to explore why readers often miss O'Connor's intended sense of mystery.

12. *Bloodshed and Three Novellas*, page 134. Future references to this story are to this edition and are cited within the text.

13. This comment is particularly telling given that Ozick was threatened with a lawsuit over her use of factual material in another piece of fiction. See the interview with Penny Kaganoff for Ozick's discussion of this threat of a suit.

14. *The Complete Stories*, Flannery O'Connor, page 512–13. Future references to O'Connor's stories are to this collection and are cited in the text.

15. John Desmond, though, argues that Parker's tattoo was an idolatrous confusion of the image with God. In his view, Sarah Ruth's beating of Parker was simply a loving attempt on her part to bring his wayward spirit into line (77–78).

16. *The Puttermesser Papers*, page 23. Future references to this story are to this edition and are cited within the text.

17. For many years, Gershom Scholem stood alone as the great scholar of Jewish mysticism, yet in the last few years Moshe Idel's work has challenged aspects of Scholem's study. Specifically on the subject of golems, Idel's *Golem: Jewish Magical and Mystical Traditions on the Artificial Anthropoid* contests Scholem's conception of a single, unitary idea and origin of the golem. Instead, Idel sees the Jews' interactions with the various pagan cultures they encountered as having a significant influence on their understanding of golems. Thus, the idea of golems was shaped by "different syntheses between ancient Jewish magical traditions and alien types of thought" (xxii). In part because of these influences, Idel finds more divergences among Jewish traditions from varying geographical areas than does Scholem. Idel is also hesitant to accept a solely "progressive" view of the evolution of golems, since he finds that "later strata of Kabbalistic literature may contain also older elements or structures, not so visible in the earlier bodies of literature" (xxiii). Nevertheless, I have largely followed Scholem's explanation of golems in my study, primarily because it is Scholem's work that Puttermesser (and

Ozick) apparently knew, since Puttermesser has "Dr. Gershom Scholem's bountiful essay 'The Idea of the Golem' virtually by heart" (48).

18. Indeed, in a speech at the Jewish Museum in New York, Ozick identifies Xanthippe as a "metaphor for art" (qtd. in Klingenstein "Cynthia Ozick" 256).

19. John Desmond plausibly argues that the story shows Asbury coming to a true recognition of himself, but what he then "*choose[s]* to do with that new insight is left open by O'Connor" (85). The ending does leave this question without a certain answer, but drawing together Father Finn's assertions that the Holy Ghost will not come to someone who does not ask for it with the final image of the descending Spirit suggests that Asbury has made a new commitment.

20. *Levitation: Five Fictions*, page 4. Future references to this story are to this collection and are cited in the text.

21. Not surprisingly, this fantastic ending to the story has been variously interpreted. In what must be the most commonly quoted critical assessment of the story, Joseph Epstein acknowledges that Ozick no doubt has a purpose in showing Jews in the air, but he insists, "I may sound more like a landlord than a critic here, but I react to this story by asking, 'Madam, what is that living room doing on the ceiling? Madam, I implore you, get those Jews down, please!'" He adds, "I prefer my Jews grounded" (67). Sarah Cohen is more certain about the ending, finding it ironic since the Jews in the living room are determining their identity solely through the Holocaust: "For Ozick, such an identity is suspect because it is based only on the dire persecution of the Jews divorced from the meaningful practices of being Jewish. . . . Their levitation is, therefore, another flight from this world" (71).

22. *The Pagan Rabbi and Other Stories*, page 4. Future references to this story are to this collection and are cited in the text.

23. Steven Ryan, though, inexplicably identifies the woods and the Greenleafs with the devil: "Mrs. Greenleaf's faith healing is a vulgar transformation of Christianity into devil worship" (42).

24. I here follow O'Connor's original spelling of The Misfit's dialect, "thow" and "thown," instead of the standardized form in *The Complete Stories*.

25. Rather than seeing The Misfit as changing, Giannone believes that his comment that there is no pleasure in life reflects The Misfit's own sinfulness: "The killer's inability to find delight in the world results from his desires being out of line with the rights of others and the will of God. Such maladjustment of his will, not his being a social outcast, gives the gravest meaning to his name, The Misfit" (*Hermit Novelist* 106).

5

Conclusion

In C.S. Lewis' fantastic allegory *The Lion, the Witch, and the Wardrobe*, Mr.and Mrs. Beaver are preparing to take the children, who have stepped through a wardrobe into a strangely different world of talking animals, to meet Aslan, the Christ-figure. The children have some questions for the Beavers concerning their upcoming visit:

> "Is—is he a man?" asked Lucy.
>
> "Aslan a man!" said Mr. Beaver sternly. "Certainly not. I tell you he is the king of the wood and the son of the great Emperor-Beyond-the-Sea. Don't you know who is the King of Beasts? Aslan is a lion—*the* Lion, the great Lion."
>
> "Ooh!" said Susan, "I'd thought he was a man. Is he—quite safe? I shall feel rather nervous about meeting a lion."
>
> "That you will, dearie, and make no mistake," said Mrs. Beaver. "If there's anyone who can appear before Aslan without their knees knocking, they're either braver than most or else just silly."
>
> "Then he isn't safe?" said Lucy.
>
> "Safe?" said Mr. Beaver. "Don't you hear what Mrs. Beaver tells you? Who said anything about safe? 'Course he isn't safe. But he's good. He's the King, I tell you." (64)

Through this allegory, Lewis suggests something of the mystery of the Divine—the sense that the power of this lion can only in part be rationally understood, that there is something both aweful and fearful about this beast. In their own manners, the narratives of Bernard Malamud, Walker Percy, Cynthia Ozick, and Flannery O'Connor also convey something of this religious mystery. As one reads their fiction, the seemingly ordinary world of characters and experiences begins to take on a deeper significance, to operate on an anagogical level. Malamud's and Percy's novels tend to show a gradual movement of the protagonist toward a nonrational commitment. Ozick's and O'Connor's stories usually contain a sudden eruption of the supernatural. But whatever the technique, the fiction of these four authors contains an "overplus of meaning" that pushes toward religious mystery.

For a variety of reasons, though, understanding such an anagogical level is not always easy. Malamud, for instance, insists that any message has to be presented without "preachment," so it seems quite plausible that for him and others who share that concern, any spiritual movement may not appear in the fiction as overtly religious. Percy speaks of the "used-up" quality of religious words, so his fiction, too, will likely diverge from traditionally religious modes of expression. Both Ozick and O'Connor make use of techniques—the fantastic and the grotesque—that are outside the realm of what we often experience in a story, so their method in itself resists easy interpretation. On top of these difficulties with the specific texts is the overarching challenge of representing what goes beyond the rational. Rudolf Otto's observation about communicating the numinous seems to have validity for the general category of religious mystery: "The consciousness of a 'wholly other' evades precise formulation in words, and we have to employ symbolic phrases which seem sometimes sheer paradox . . . . it is non-rational, as is the beauty of a musical composition, which no less eludes complete conceptual analysis" (59). Religious mystery in these writers' fiction, therefore, will likely not be presented in straightforward expository prose.

It is helpful, then, to realize that these four authors seem to follow the pattern of their religions in giving form to mystery. Although there are significant differences between the two practices—since *mitzvot* involves sanctifying the ordinary while sacraments remain specifically religious rituals—both following *mitzvot* and partaking of the sacraments offer believers a concrete way to encounter God. This understanding provides an important aid in discovering how mystery functions in these authors' fiction. In ways both large and small, the novels and stories give form to mystery through established structures and tangible actions. Generally, both the Jewish and Catholic authors seem to use a combination of everyday events that suggest an added significance as well as actions that have a more specifically religious connection. At times, though, the differences between the two religious practices become clear. For instance, in Ozick's "Puttermesser and Xanthippe," the fantastic creation of the golem occurs fairly early in the story, with the bulk of the narrative given over to presenting Puttermesser's actions after the creation. Such a formation suggests the emphasis of *mitzvot* on righteous living. On the other hand, O'Connor's "The Enduring Chill"—and, indeed, most of O'Connor's stories—shows the action of grace at the end of the story, indicating a sacramental, saving act. Norma Rosen suggests that this infusion of grace just before death indicates a "tip of the ice-berg" view of the Christian life: "afterlife—or whatever it is that follows the moment of enlightenment-in-death" is what is important, and she argues that this conception is not shared by Jews (37). Yet O'Connor also combines the everyday with the holy, since it is often an ordinary, seemingly unholy action that she invests with sacramental power.

Malamud's and Percy's use of the quest form is, in itself, a kind of mirroring of the pattern that Judaism and Catholicism have established, since the quest, too, offers a way to approach mystery. In using such a defined form, which is laden with religious overtones, Malamud and Percy have given their readers a handle through which they can grasp the nonrational movements of the protagonists. Throughout these quests, too, specific actions and images seem to take on religious significance, hinting at mystery. Thus, when Yakov Bok in *The Fixer* agrees to claim as his son a boy he has not fathered, we can see that something has changed within Yakov. Or when Frank Alpine in *The Assistant* acknowledges the stench of garbage in his own bed, we can recognize with him the odor of his sinfulness. Similarly, as Will Barrett in *The Second Coming* watches the orderlies care for a frightened old woman, we can sense with him the early stirrings of grace in his life. Or when Binx Bolling, the cool and detached protagonist of *The Moviegoer*, kisses his new fiancée Kate's bloody thumb, we get a hint of the sacramental action that is occurring within his life. In none of these instances is the character's nonrational alteration spelled out, but through these physical actions, the readers can get a hint of mystery.

Such a making physical of mystery is central to the fiction of Ozick and O'Connor. For in these stories, the structure of the fiction revolves around a fantastic or grotesque action or image that seems to embody mystery. In Ozick's tales these fantastic images of a magical crown, created golem, levitating room, or tree dryad force the reader out of the usual verisimilitude of fiction. Yet these bizarre occurrences are also linked to the here and now, whether through the realities of political corruption or the physicality of flushing a houseplant. O'Connor, too, shows startling images of a tattooed Christ, enlivened water stain, bull goring, or vicious shooting that are also thrust onto seemingly ordinary situations. As these various outlandish incidents push the reader beyond usual explanations, the religious symbolism within the text urges the reader toward the anagogical level. The way these stories combine actions beyond the rational with religious significance points toward religious mystery and, often in Ozick's and O'Connor's fiction, toward the numinous sense of fear and awe.

As these brief recapitulations suggest, this study has primarily sought to emphasize what draws these religions and writers together instead of what separates them. It seems intriguing—and instructive in this time of too widespread religious intolerance—that even though there is much that separates these two religions, fiction from each tradition shows a similar approach to mystery, whether through Malamud's and Percy's quests or Ozick's fantastic and O'Connor's grotesque. Finding such a commonality within these two pairings of authors seems an important basis for understanding how the nonrational aspect of belief is represented in contemporary Jewish and Catholic fiction. Indeed, recognizing these patterns for suggesting mystery may prove useful for understanding fiction by other writers within these religious traditions—and, perhaps, even serve as a point of connection for believers from the two religions.

Even though my work seeks to link together the fiction of these authors, as suggested in the Introduction and hinted at throughout the book, there are also important different traditions that the authors draw upon, particularly regarding their narrative themes or patterns. For the Jewish writers, certainly the narratives from the Hebrew Bible and rabbinical sources provide an important backdrop. For instance, in *The Assistant*, Frank Alpine converts to Judaism shortly after Passover, a reference to the Jewish commemoration of their salvation in Egypt; placing Frank's change in the context of Passover brings with it immediate resonances of the saving acts of God throughout Jewish history. In "The Pagan Rabbi," Ozick clearly draws on rabbinical writings, both for the content as well as for the form, since the story is a kind of contemporary midrash. Stories outside the rabbinical tradition also form part of the context for these writers, especially for Ozick; her use of fantasy and magic seems very closely allied to Jewish legends.[1]

Through specific items, too, Malamud and Ozick are able to suggest and extend Jewish traditions. The phylacteries and prayer shawl in *The Fixer* and "The Pagan Rabbi" or the golem in "Puttermesser and Xanthippe" are examples of the way that by mentioning an item from their Jewish heritage, Malamud and Ozick are able to call to mind the narratives and stories behind the item. But these examples also show how contemporary authors complicate those traditions, for Yakov Bok breaks open a phylactery and Isaac Kornfeld hangs himself with his prayer shawl; the authors thus add a new and problematic level to the understanding of these ritual items.

A final way that the Jewish writers draw on a shared heritage is by making reference to nonbiblical historical events. Particularly in the twentieth century, the outrage of the Holocaust has been at the forefront of Jewish writers' minds and narratives. Thus, in *The Fixer*, Malamud makes use of various events from Jewish history, including the Beiliss case as well as the Holocaust in his depiction of the inhumanity toward Yakov Bok. "Levitation," too, points out atrocities toward Jews throughout the centuries before also dwelling on the Holocaust and the theological problems it raises. Even in "The Pagan Rabbi," where the Holocaust is not the central focus, that event is brought to memory since Sheindel is a survivor. As these several examples suggest, Jewish narratives draw on a range of established patterns and themes as the writers seek to communicate religious understanding.

For the Catholic writers, the biblical narratives—particularly the New Testament—provide important paradigms. Central to the Catholic understanding is the story of Christ's redemption through his death and resurrection. Therefore, showing the movement of grace that Catholics hold comes from that event is certainly a dominant pattern. That theme is very significant in both Percy's and O'Connor's work, but Percy tends to develop a long movement toward an acceptance of Christ's grace—as he shows in Binx Bolling's journey in *The Moviegoer*—while O'Connor tends toward a sudden, shocking eruption of grace—such as Mrs. May's being violently gored in "Greenleaf." Since showing the eventual acceptance of grace is a prominent theme, it is hardly surprising that these writers—and particularly O'Connor—draw on the common Catholic concept that it is often the obvious sinners who are closer to the Church than the satisfied saints. In "Parker's Back," for example, it seems to be the irreligious Parker rather than the fundamentalist Sarah Ruth who receives grace. Or if the self-satisfied grandmother in "A Good Man Is Hard to Find" or Mrs. May in "Greenleaf" do encounter God, they do so only after their smug exterior has been stripped away. Besides the specific biblical narratives, Catholic writers also draw on the Church traditions that have grown up around these stories. This tradition is especially important in *The Moviegoer*, where Binx Bolling experiences grace on Ash Wednesday, the first day of Lent. Percy is able to draw on this tradition of contrition and repentance in the period before Easter as he suggests Binx's conversion.

Thus, both Jewish and Catholic writers draw on the narrative traditions and patterns that are part of their religious heritage. These distinctions are never completely neat and easy, though, especially for Malamud. Even though he is a Jewish writer, he makes prominent use of the quest myth with its Christian overtones. Further, in *The Assistant*, Malamud very clearly draws on the life and teaching of St. Francis, again showing a blending of religious traditions. And many critics question if the redemptive suffering in Malamud's novels is not more closely allied to Christian tropes than to Jewish tradition. Although a detailed examination of these issues of Jewish and Catholic narratives is outside the scope of the present study, clearly such patterns do play a role in how the authors within each religious tradition present mystery.

But the central focus of this study has been to search for commonalities across the religious boundaries, to examine the similar ways that Malamud and Percy as well as Ozick and O'Connor represent mystery. Such a focus is important because a religious understanding is central to an adequate reading of this fiction, and the nonrational is a part of both Judaism and Catholicism. Whether showing a movement toward mystery or serving to evoke it, the fiction by these four authors demonstrates an interaction with the nonrational element of belief, an element that readers need to sense if they are to enter into this religious fiction.

NOTE

1. Malamud's stories also show an affinity with Jewish legends of angels and talking animals. I have not included Malamud's stories in my study since I was focusing on his use of the quest form. Yet interestingly, even though his stories do show a connection to Jewish literary traditions, Malamud suggests that he has been primarily influenced by American literature: "as a writer, I've been influenced by Hawthorne, James, Mark Twain, Hemingway, more than I have been by Sholem Aleichem and I.L. Peretz, whom I read with pleasure" (*Talking Horse* 20).

Works Cited

Agus, Jacob B. "Medieval Jewish Philosophy." *Contemporary Jewish Religious Thought: Original Essays on Critical Concepts, Movements, and Beliefs*. Ed. Arthur A. Cohen and Paul Mendes-Flohr. New York: Macmillan, 1987. 573–79.

Ahokas, Pirjo. *Forging a New Self: The Adamic Protagonist and the Emergence of a Jewish-American Author as Revealed through the Novels of Bernard Malamud*. Turku: Turun Yliopisto, 1991.

Allison, Henry R. *Benedict de Spinoza: An Introduction*. New Haven: Yale UP, 1987.

Alter, Iska. "The Good Man's Dilemma: *The Natural*, *The Assistant*, and American Materialism." *Critical Essays on Bernard Malamud*. Ed. Joel Salzberg. Boston: G.K. Hall, 1987.

Alter, Robert. "Jewishness as Metaphor." *Bernard Malamud and the Critics*. Ed. Leslie A Field and Joyce W. Field. New York: New York UP, 1970. 29–42.

Appel, Gersion. *A Philosophy of Mitzvot*. New York: Ktav, 1975.

Aquinas, Thomas. *Faith, Reason, and Theology*. Trans. Armand Aurer. Medieval Sources in Translation 32. Toronto: Pontifical Institute of Medieval Studies, 1987.

———. *Summa Theologiae*. Ed. David Bourke. Westminster: Blackfriars, 1975.

———. *On the Truth of the Catholic Faith: Summa Contra Gentiles*. Trans. Charles O'Neil. Vol. 4. Garden City, NY: Image, 1957.

Ariel, David S. *What Do Jews Believe? The Spiritual Foundations of Judaism*. New York: Schocken, 1995.

Auerbach, Erich. *Mimesis: The Representation of Reality in Western Literature*. Trans. Willard Trask. Princeton: Princeton UP, 1953.

Baeck, Leo. "Romantic Religion." *Judaism and Christianity*. Trans. Walter Kaufmann. Philadelphia: Jewish Publication Society, 1958. 189–292.

Bahti, Timothy. "Ambiguity and Indeterminacy: The Juncture." *Comparative Literature* 38 (1986): 209–23.

Bandy, Stephen. "'One of my babies': The Misfit and the Grandmother." *Studies in Short Fiction* 33.1 (Winter 1996): 107–17. Proquest. 28 June 2000. Printout 1–8.

Baumbach, Jonathan. *The Landscape of Nightmare: Studies in the Contemporary American Novel*. New York: New York UP, 1965.

Bellamy, Michael O. "Everything Off Balance: Protestant Election in Flannery O'Connor's 'A Good Man Is Hard to Find.'" "*A Good Man Is Hard to Find.*" Ed. Frederick Asals. Women Writers: Texts and Contexts. New Brunswick: Rutgers UP, 1993. 103–11.

Bettenson, Henry, ed. and trans. *The Early Christian Fathers: A Selection from the Writings of the Fathers from St. Clement of Rome to St. Athanasius.* New York: Oxford UP, 1956.

———, ed. and trans. *The Later Christian Fathers: A Selection from the Writings of the Fathers from St. Cyril of Jerusalem to St. Leo the Great.* New York: Oxford UP, 1970.

The Bible. New Revised Standard Version.

Bleikasten, Andre. "The Heresy of Flannery O'Connor." *Critical Essays on Flannery O'Connor.* Ed. Melvin J. Friedman and Beverly Lyons Clark. Boston: G.K. Hall, 1985. 138–58.

Bloom, Harold. Introduction. *Cynthia Ozick.* Ed. Harold Bloom. Modern Critical Views. New York: Chelsea House, 1986. 1–7.

———. Introduction. *Walker Percy.* Ed. Harold Bloom. Modern Critical Views. New York: Chelsea House, 1986. 1–7.

Borowitz, Eugene B. *Choices in Modern Jewish Thought.* New York: Behrman, 1983.

———. "Reason." *Contemporary Jewish Religious Thought: Original Essays on Critical Concepts, Movements, and Beliefs.* Ed. Arthur A. Cohen and Paul Mendes-Flohr. New York: Macmillan, 1987. 749–54.

Bourke, David. Introduction. *Summa Theologiae.* By Thomas Aquinas. Vol. 56. Westminster: Blackfriars, 1975.

Boyarin, Daniel. *Intertextuality and the Reading of Midrash.* Indiana Studies in Biblical Lit. Bloomington: Indiana UP, 1990.

Brooks, Roger. *The Spirit of the Ten Commandments: Shattering the Myth of Rabbinic Legalism.* New York: Harper and Row, 1990.

Brown, Ashley. "Walker Percy: The Novelist and Moralist." *Walker Percy: Novelist and Philosopher.* Ed. Jan Nordby Gretlund and Karl-Heinz Westarp. Jackson: UP of Mississippi, 1991. 169–76.

Browning, Preston Jr. "'Parker's Back': Flannery O'Connor's Iconography of Salvation by Profanity." *Studies in Short Fiction* 6 (1969): 525–35.

Buber, Martin. *Two Types of Faith.* Trans. Norman P. Goldhawk. London: Routledge, 1951.

Bugge, John. "Arthurian Myth Devalued in Walker Percy's *Lancelot.*" *The Arthurian Tradition: Essays in Convergence.* Ed. Mary Flowers Braswell and John Bugge. Tuscaloosa, AL: U of Alabama P, 1988. 175–87.

Burstein, Janet Handler. "Cynthia Ozick and the Transgressions of Art." *American Literature* 59 (1987): 85–101.

Buxbaum, Yitzhak. *Storytelling and Spirituality in Judaism.* Northvale, NJ: Jason Aronson, 1994.

Campbell, Joseph. *The Hero with a Thousand Faces.* The Bollingen Series 17. New York: Pantheon Books, 1949.

Capek, Milic. *The Philosophical Impact of Contemporary Physics.* Princeton: D. Van Nostrand Co, 1961.

Caputo, John. "A Commentary: Deconstruction in a Nutshell." *Deconstruction in a Nutshell: A Conversation with Jacques Derrida.* Ed. John Caputo. New York: Fordham UP, 1997. 29–202.

———. *The Prayers and Tears of Jacques Derrida: Religion without Religion.* Indiana Ser. in the Philosophy of Religion. Bloomington: Indiana UP, 1997.

Catechism of the Catholic Church. Washington DC: United States Catholic Conference, 2000.

Chavel, Charles B. Foreword and Appendices. *The Commandments*. By Maimonides. 2 vols. London: The Soncino P, 1967.

Ciuba, Gary M. *Walker Percy: Books of Revelation*. Athens: U of Georgia P, 1991.

Cohen, Sandy. *Bernard Malamud and the Trial by Love*. Melville Studies in American Culture 1. Amsterdam: Rodopi N. U., 1974.

Cohen, Sarah Blacher. *Cynthia Ozick's Comic Art: From Levity to Liturgy*. Jewish Literature and Culture Series. Bloomington: Indiana UP, 1994.

Cohon, Samuel S. *Essays in Jewish Theology*. Cincinnati: Hebrew Union College P, 1987.

Connes, Gregory. *The Ethics of Indeterminacy in the Novels of William Gaddis*. Gainesville: UP of Florida, 1994.

Cottingham, John. *The Rationalists*. A History of Western Philosophy 4. New York: Oxford UP, 1988.

Coulthard, A.R. "Flannery O'Connor's Deadly Conversions." *Flannery O'Connor Bulletin* 13 (1984): 87–98.

"The Council of Trent." *The Encyclopedia of American Religions: Religious Creeds*. Ed. J. Gordon Melton with James Sauer. Vol. 2. Detroit: Gale, 1994.

Criswell, Jeanne Salladé. "Cynthia Ozick and Grace Paley: Diverse Visions in Jewish and Women's Literature." *Since Flannery O'Connor: Essays on the Contemporary American Short Story*. Ed. Loren Logsdon and Charles W. Mayer. Mocomb, IL: Yeast Printing, 1987. 93–100.

Cronin, Gloria. "Redemption for the Twice Fallen: Walker Percy's *Second Coming*." *Literature and Belief* 1 (1981): 113–22.

Culler, Jonathan. *On Deconstruction: Theory and Criticism after Structuralism*. Ithaca, NY: Cornell UP, 1982.

Danow, David K. *Models of Narrative: Theory and Practice*. New York: St. Martin's, 1997.

Dante Alighieri. *Literary Criticism of Dante Alighieri*. Trans. and ed. Robert S. Haller. Lincoln: U of Nebraska P, 1973.

Davies, P.C.W., and J.R. Brown. *The Ghost in the Atom: A Discussion of the Mysteries of Quantum Physics*. Cambridge: Cambridge UP, 1986.

Davis, Stephen T. *Faith, Skepticism, and Evidence: An Essay in Religious Epistemology*. Lewisburg, PA: Bucknell UP, 1978.

Derrida, Jacques. "The Villanova Roundtable: A Conversation with Jacques Derrida." *Deconstruction in a Nutshell: A Conversation with Jacques Derrida*. Ed. John Caputo. New York: Fordham UP, 1997. 3–28.

Desmond, John F. *Risen Sons: Flannery O'Connor's Vision of History*. Athens: U of Georgia P, 1987.

Detweiler, Robert. *Breaking the Fall: Religious Readings of Contemporary Fiction*. Cambridge: Harper, 1989.

Dowie, William J. "*Lancelot* and the Search for Sin." *The Art of Walker Percy: Stratagems for Being*. Ed. Panthea Reid Broughton. Baton Rouge: Louisiana State UP, 1979. 245–59.

Edwards, Bruce L., Jr. "Flannery O'Connor: Defamiliarizing the Mystery of Godliness." *Literature and Belief* 4 (1984): 69–78.

Elior, Rachel. "Soul." *Contemporary Jewish Religious Thought: Original Essays on Critical Concepts, Movements, and Beliefs*. Ed. Arthur A. Cohen and Paul Mendes-Flohr. New York: Macmillan, 1987. 887–96.

Elliott, Emory. "Gesture and Style in *The Moviegoer.*" *Walker Percy's Feminine Characters.* Ed. Lewis Lawson and Elzbieta Oleksy. Troy, NY: Whitston Publishing Co., 1995. 34–49.

Elon, Menachem. *Jewish Law: History, Sources, Principles.* Vol. 1. Trans. Bernard Auerbach and Melvin J. Sykes. Philadelphia: Jewish Publication Society, 1994.

Epstein, Joseph. "Cynthia Ozick, Jewish Writer." *Commentary* 77.3 (March 1984): 64–69.

Fackenheim, Emil L. "An Outline of a Modern Jewish Theology." *Faith and Reason: Essays in Judaism.* Ed. Robert Gordis and Ruth B. Waxman. New York: Ktav, 1973. 211–20.

Feeley, Kathleen. *Flannery O'Connor: Voice of the Peacock.* New Brunswick: Rutgers UP, 1972.

Fewell, Danna Nolan, ed. *Reading Between Texts: Intertextuality and the Hebrew Bible.* Louisville: Westminster/John Knox P, 1992.

Fisch, Harold. "Biblical Archetypes in *The Fixer.*" *Studies in American Jewish Literature* 7 (1988): 162–76.

Fitzgerald, Sally. "Sources and Resources: The Catholic Imagination of Flannery O'Connor." *Logos* 1.1 (Spring 1997): 78–95.

Fletcher, John, and Malcolm Bradbury. "The Introverted Novel." *Modernism: 1890–1930.* Ed. Malcolm Bradbury and James McFarlane. Atlantic Highlands, NJ: Humanities P, 1978. 394–415.

Foster, Richard J., and James Bryan Smith, eds. *Devotional Classics.* New York: HarperSanFrancisco, 1993.

Fowler, Doreen A. "Answers and Ambiguity in Percy's *The Second Coming.*" *Critique* 23.2 (Winter 1981–82): 13–23.

Fox, Marvin. "Kierkegaard and Rabbinic Judaism." *Faith and Reason: Essays in Judaism.* Ed. Robert Gordis and Ruth Waxman. New York: Ktav, 1973. 115–23.

Frankel, Zecharias. "On Changes in Judaism." *The Jew in the Modern World: A Documentary History.* Ed. Paul R. Mendes-Flohr and Jehuda Reinharz. New York: Oxford UP, 1980. 173–76.

Fraser, Theodore P. *The Modern Catholic Novel in Europe.* New York: Twayne, 1994.

Friedman, Lawrence S. *Understanding Cynthia Ozick.* Understanding Contemporary American Literature. Columbia: U of South Carolina P, 1991.

Furman, Andrew. "Did Malamud's Jewish Vision Wane?" *Modern Jewish Studies* 10.4 (1997): 34–46.

Futrell, Ann Mace. *The Signs of Christianity in the Work of Walker Percy.* San Francisco: Catholic Scholars P, 1994.

Ganoczy, Alexandre. *An Introduction to Catholic Sacramental Theology.* Trans. William Thomas. New York: Paulist P, 1984.

Gellner, Ernest. *Postmodernism, Reason, and Religion.* New York: Routledge, 1992.

Gentry, Marshall Bruce. *Flannery O'Connor's Religion of the Grotesque.* Jackson: UP of Mississippi, 1986.

Getz, Lorine M. *Nature and Grace in Flannery O'Connor's Fiction.* Studies in Art and Religious Interpretation 2. New York: Edwin Mellen P, 1982.

Giannone, Richard. *Flannery O'Connor and the Mystery of Love.* New York: Fordham UP, 1989.

———. *Flannery O'Connor, Hermit Novelist.* Urbana: U of Illinois P, 2000.

Gibbs, Nancy. "The Message of Miracles." *Time* 10 Apr. 1995: 65–73.

Gidden, Nancy Ann. "Classical Agents of Christian Grace in Flannery O'Connor's 'Greenleaf.'" *Studies in Short Fiction* 23 (1986): 201–2.

Gitenstein, R. Barbara. "The Temptation of Apollo and the Loss of Yiddish in Cynthia Ozick's Fiction." *Studies in American Jewish Literature* 3 (1983): 194–201.

Gitlin, Todd. "Hip-Deep in Post-modernism." *New York Times Book Review* 6 Nov. 1988: 1+.

Goldenberg, Robert. "Law and Spirit in Talmudic Religion." *Jewish Spirituality: From the Bible Through the Middle Ages*. Ed. Arthur Green. World Spirituality: An Encyclopedic History of the Religious Quest 13. New York: Crossroad, 1987. 232–53.

Goodman, L.E. "Rational Law/Ritual Law." *A People Apart: Chosenness and Ritual in Jewish Philosophical Thought*. Ed. Daniel H. Frank. SUNY Ser. in Jewish Philosophy. Albany: State U of New York P, 1993. 109–200.

Gordis, Robert. *The Dynamics of Judaism: A Study in Jewish Law*. Bloomington: Indiana UP, 1990.

Greenberg, Irving. "Cloud of Smoke, Pillar of Fire: Judaism, Christianity, and Modernity after the Holocaust." *Auschwitz: Beginning of a New Era? Reflections on the Holocaust*. Ed. Eva Fleischner. New York: Ktav, 1974. 7–55.

Gunn, Giles. *The Interpretation of Otherness: Literature, Religion, and the American Imagination*. New York: Oxford UP, 1979.

Guttmann, Allen. *The Jewish Writer in America: Assimilation and the Crisis of Identity*. New York: Oxford UP, 1971.

Haberman, Joshua O. "Righteousness." *Contemporary Jewish Religious Thought: Original Essays on Critical Concepts, Movements, and Beliefs*. Ed. Arthur A. Cohen and Paul Mendes-Flohr. New York: Macmillan, 1987. 833–39.

Hamblen, Abigail Ann. "Flannery O'Connor's Study of Innocence and Evil." *The University Review* 34 (1968): 295–97.

Handelman, Susan A. *The Slayers of Moses: The Emergence of Rabbinic Interpretation in Modern Literary Theory*. SUNY Ser. on Modern Jewish Literature and Culture. Albany: State U of New York P, 1982.

Handy, W.J. "The Malamud Hero: A Quest for Existence." *The Fiction of Bernard Malamud*. Ed. Richard Astro and Jackson J. Benson. American Authors Ser. Corvallis: Oregon State UP, 1977. 65–86.

Harap, Louis. *In the Mainstream: The Jewish Presence in Twentieth-Century American Literature, 1950s-1980s*. Contributions in Ethnic Studies 19. New York: Greenwood P, 1987.

Hardy, John Edward. *The Fiction of Walker Percy*. Urbana: U of Illinois P, 1987.

Hartman, Geoffrey H. *Criticism in the Wilderness: The Study of Literature Today*. New York: Yale UP, 1980.

———. "Imagination." *Contemporary Jewish Religious Thought: Original Essays on Critical Concepts, Movements, and Beliefs*. Ed. Arthur A. Cohen and Paul Mendes-Flohr. New York: Macmillan, 1987. 451–72.

———. "The State of the Art of Criticism." *The Future of Literary Theory*. Ed. Ralph Cohen. New York: Routledge, 1989. 86–101.

Hassan, Ihab. "Desire and Dissent in the Postmodern Age." *Kenyon Review* ns 5.1 (1983): 1–18.

Hawkes, John. "Flannery O'Connor's Devil." *Critical Essays on Flannery O'Connor*. Ed. Melvin J. Friedman and Beverly Lyon Clark. Boston: G.K. Hall, 1985. 92–100.

Hawkins, Peter S. *The Language of Grace: Flannery O'Connor, Walker Percy, and Iris Murdoch*. Cambridge, MA: Cowley Publications, 1983.

Hays, Peter L. "The Complex Pattern of Redemption in *The Assistant*." *Centennial Review* 13 (1969): 200–14.

Helterman, Jeffrey. *Understanding Bernard Malamud*. Understanding Contemporary American Literature. Columbia: U of South Carolina P, 1985.

Hendin, Josephine. *The World of Flannery O'Connor*. Bloomington: Indiana UP, 1970.

Herrera, R.A. Introduction. *Mystics of the Book: Themes, Topics, and Typologies*. Ed. R.A. Herrera. New York: Lang, 1993.

Hershinow, Sheldon J. *Bernard Malamud*. New York: Frederick Ungar, 1980.

Heschel, Abraham Joshua. "The Meaning of this Hour." *Out of the Whirlwind: A Reader of Holocaust Literature*. Ed. Albert H. Friedlander. Garden City, NY: Doubleday, 1968. 488–92.

Hirsch, David H. "Jewish Identity and Jewish Suffering in Bellow, Malamud, and Philip Roth." *Saul Bellow Journal* 8.2 (Summer 1989): 47–58.

Hobson, Linda Whitney. *Understanding Walker Percy*. Understanding Contemporary American Literature. Columbia: U of South Carolina P, 1988.

Horne, Lewis B. "Yakov Agonistes." *Research Studies* 37 (1969): 320–6.

Hornung, Alfred. "The Transgression of Postmodern Fiction: Philip Roth and Cynthia Ozick." *Affirmation and Negation in Contemporary American Culture*. Ed. Gerhard Hoffmann and Alfred Hornung. Heidelberg: Carl Winter Universitätsverlag, 1994. 229–49.

Horowitz, Sarah R. "The 'Pin with which to Stick Yourself': The Holocaust in Jewish American Women's Writing." *Daughters of Valor: Contemporary Jewish American Women Writers*. Ed. Jay Halio and Ben Siegel. Newark: U of Delaware P, 1997. 141–59.

———. *Voicing the Void: Muteness and Memory in Holocaust Fiction*. SUNY Ser. in Modern Jewish Literature and Culture. Albany: State U of New York P, 1997.

Hutcheon, Linda. *A Poetics of Postmodernism: History, Theory, Fiction*. New York: Routledge, 1988.

Hyman, Stanley Edgar. "Moviegoing and Other Intimacies." *Critical Essays on Walker Percy*. Ed. J. Donald Crowley and Sue Mitchell Crowley. Boston: G.K. Hall, 1989. 35–38.

Idel, Moshe. *Golem: Jewish Magical and Mystical Traditions on the Artificial Anthropoid*. SUNY Ser. in Judaica: Hermeneutics, Mysticism, and Religion. Albany: State U of New York P, 1990.

Jacobs, Louis. *God, Torah, Israel: Traditionalism Without Fundamentalism*. Cincinnati: Hebrew Union College P, 1990.

Johansen, Ruthan Knechel. *The Narrative Secret of Flannery O'Connor: The Trickster as Interpreter*. Tuscaloosa: U of Alabama P, 1994.

John Paul II. *On the Relationship between Faith and Reason*. Washington, DC: United States Catholic Conference, 1998.

Katz, Steven T. *Post-Holocaust Dialogues: Critical Studies in Modern Jewish Thought*. New York: New York UP, 1983.

Kauvar, Elaine M. *Cynthia Ozick's Fiction: Tradition and Invention*. Jewish Literature and Culture Ser. Bloomington: Indiana UP, 1993.

Kayser, Wolfgang. *The Grotesque in Art and Literature*. Trans. Ulrich Weisstein. New York: McGraw-Hill, 1963.

Kazin, Alfred. "The Pilgrimage of Walker Percy." *Critical Essays on Walker Percy*. Ed. J. Donald Crowley and Sue Mitchell Crowley. Boston: G.K. Hall, 1989. 93–103.

Kegan, Robert. *The Sweeter Welcome: Voices for a Vision of Affirmation: Bellow, Malamud, and Martin Buber*. Needham Heights, MA: Humanitas P, 1976.

Kielsky, Vera Emuna. *Inevitable Exiles: Cynthia Ozick's View of the Precariousness of Jewish Existence in a Gentile Society*. Twentieth Century American Jewish Writers 2. New York: Peter Lang, 1989.

Klingenstein, Suzanne. "Cynthia Ozick." *Contemporary Jewish-American Novelists*. Ed. Joel Shatzky and Michael Taub. Westport, CT: Greenwood P, 1997. 252–63.

———. "'In Life I Am Not Free': The Writer Cynthia Ozick and her Jewish Obligations." *Daughters of Valor: Contemporary Jewish American Women Writers*. Ed. Jay Halio and Ben Siegel. Newark: U of Delaware P, 1997. 48–79.

Knopp, Josephine Zadovsky. *The Trial of Judaism in Contemporary Jewish Writing*. Urbana: U of Illinois P, 1975.

Kobre, Michael. "The Teller and the Tale: Walker Percy's *Lancelot* as Metafiction." *Critique* 41.1 (Fall 1999): 71–78. Proquest. 28 June 2000. Printout 1–6.

Kort, Wesley. *Story, Text, and Scripture: Literary Interests in Biblical Narrative*. University Park: Pennsylvania State UP, 1988.

Kremer, S. Lillian. *Witness through the Imagination: Jewish American Holocaust Literature*. Detroit: Wayne State UP, 1989.

Krupnick, Mark. "Cynthia Ozick as the Jewish T.S. Eliot." *Soundings* 74 (1991): 351–68.

Lasher, Lawrence M. Introduction. *Conversations with Bernard Malamud*. Ed. Lawrence M. Lasher. Jackson: UP of Mississippi, 1991. ix–xx.

Lawson, Lewis A. "Walker Percy's Indirect Communications." *Texas Studies in Literature and Language* 11 (1969): 869–900.

Leeming, David Adams. "Quests." *The Encyclopedia of Religion*. New York: Macmillan, 1987.

Leibowitz, Yeshayahu. "Commandments." *Contemporary Jewish Religious Thought: Original Essays on Critical Concepts, Movements, and Beliefs*. Ed. Arthur A. Cohen and Paul Mendes-Flohr. New York: Macmillan, 1987. 67–80.

Lewis, C. S. *The Lion, the Witch, and the Wardrobe*. New York: Macmillan, 1950.

Lidston, Robert C. "Malamud's *The Natural*: An Arthurian Quest in the Big Leagues." *West Virginia University Philological Papers* 27 (1981): 75–81.

Lister, Paul A. "Sir Walker and Sir Lancelot." *The Arthurian Myth of Quest and Magic*. Ed. William E. Tanner. Dallas: Caxton's Modern Arts Press, 1993. 77–89.

Lopes Cardozo, Nathan T. *Between Silence and Speech: Essays on Jewish Thought*. Northvale, NJ: Jason Aronson, 1995.

Lowin, Joseph. *Cynthia Ozick*. Twayne's United States Authors Ser. 545. Boston: Twayne, 1988.

Lundin, Robert. *The Culture of Interpretation: Christian Faith and the Postmodern World*. Grand Rapids: Eerdmans, 1993.

Luschei, Martin. *The Sovereign Wayfarer: Walker Percy's Diagnosis of the Malaise*. Southern Literary Studies. Baton Rouge: Louisiana State UP, 1972.

Lyotard, Jean-François. *The Postmodern Condition: A Report on Knowledge*. Trans. Geoff Bennington and Brian Massumi. Theory and History of Literature 10. Minneapolis: U of Minnesota P, 1984.

MacGregor, Geddes. "Doubt and Belief." *The Encyclopedia of Religion*. New York: Macmillan, 1987.

Magaw, Malcolm O. "Certitude Be Not Proud: Percy's View of Will Barrett's Extended Stay in Ambivalence." *The Southern Quarterly* 25.2 (Winter 1987): 76–88.

Maimonides, Moses. *The Commandments*. Ed. and trans. Charles B. Chavel. 2 vols. London: The Soncino P, 1967.

———. *The Guide for the Perplexed*. Trans. M. Friedlander. 2nd ed. New York: Dover, 1956.

Malamud, Bernard. *The Assistant*. New York: Farrar, Straus and Cudahy, 1957.

———. The Bernard Malamud Papers. Library of Congress, Washington, DC.

———. *Conversations with Bernard Malamud*. Ed. Lawrence. M. Lasher. Jackson: UP of Mississippi, 1991.

———. *The Fixer*. New York: Farrar, Straus and Giroux, 1966.

———. *The Natural*. New York: Farrar, Straus and Giroux, 1952.

———. "Reflections of a Writer: Long Work, Short Life." *New York Times Book Review*. 20 Mar. 1988: 15+.

———. *Talking Horse*. Ed. Alan Cheuse and Nicholas Delbanco. New York: Columbia UP, 1996.

———. "The Writer's Task." *Writing in America*. Ed. John Fischer and Robert B. Silvers. New Brunswick: Rutgers UP, 1960. 173.

Martos, Joseph. *Doors to the Sacred: A Historical Introduction to Sacraments in the Catholic Church*. Garden City, NY: Doubleday, 1981.

Matarasso, P.M., trans. *The Quest of the Holy Grail*. London: Penguin, 1969.

May, John R. *The Pruning Word: The Parables of Flannery O'Connor*. Notre Dame: U of Notre Dame P, 1976.

McHale, Brian. *Constructing Postmodernism*. New York: Routledge, 1992.

———. *Postmodernist Fiction*. New York: Methuen, 1987.

McMullen, Joanne Halleran. *Writing against God: Language as Message in the Literature of Flannery O'Connor*. Macon, GA: Mercer UP, 1996.

Muller, Gilbert H. *Nightmares and Visions: Flannery O'Connor and the Catholic Grotesque*. Athens: U of Georgia P, 1972.

Nathanson, Stephen. *The Ideal of Rationality: A Defense, within Reason*. Chicago: Open Court, 1994.

Neusner, Jacob. *The Way of Torah: An Introduction to Judaism*. The Religious Life of Man. Belmont, CA: Dickenson Publishing, 1970.

Nilsen, Helge Normann. "Malamud's *The Assistant*: A Return to Jewishness? A Note on the Text." *International Fiction Review* 15 (1988): 44–47.

Nisly, Paul W. "Wart Hogs from Hell: The Demonic and the Holy in Flannery O'Connor's Fiction." *Ball State University Forum* 22.3 (Summer 1981): 45–50.

Oates, Joyce Carol. "*Lancelot*." *Walker Percy*. Ed. Harold Bloom. Modern Critical Views. New York: Chelsea House, 1986. 63–67.

O'Brien, Conor Cruise. *Maria Cross: Imaginative Patterns in a Group of Modern Catholic Writers*. Fresno: Academy Guild P, 1963.

Ochshorn, Kathleen G. "A Cloak of Time: Contradictions in 'A Good Man Is Hard to Find.'" *Studies in American Fiction* 18.1 (1990): 113–17.

O'Connor, Flannery. *The Complete Stories*. New York: Farrar, Straus and Giroux, 1989.

———. *Conversations with Flannery O'Connor*. Ed. Rosemary M. Magee. Jackson: UP of Mississippi, 1987.

———. *The Habit of Being*. Ed. Sally Fitzgerald. New York: Farrar, Straus and Giroux, 1979.

———. *Mystery and Manners*. Ed. Sally and Robert Fitzgerald. New York: Farrar, Straus and Giroux, 1969.

———. *The Presence of Grace and Other Book Reviews*. Comp. Leo J. Zuber. Ed. Carter W. Martin. Athens: U of Georgia P, 1983.

Orvell, Miles. *Flannery O'Connor: An Introduction*. Jackson: UP of Mississippi, 1991.

Ostriker, Alicia Suskin. *The Nakedness of the Fathers: Biblical Visions and Revisions*. New Brunswick: Rutgers UP, 1994.

Ottenberg, Eve. "The Rich Visions of Cynthia Ozick." *New York Times Magazine* 10 Apr. 1983: 47+.

Otto, Rudolf. *The Idea of the Holy*. Trans. John W. Harvey. New York: Oxford UP, 1950.

Ozick, Cynthia. *Art & Ardor: Essays*. New York: Alfred A. Knopf, 1983.

———. "The Art of Fiction XCV: Cynthia Ozick." With Tom Teicholz. *The Paris Review* 29.102 (1987): 155–90.

———. *Bloodshed and Three Novellas*. New York: Alfred A. Knopf, 1976.

———. *Fame & Folly: Essays*. New York: Alfred A. Knopf, 1996.

———. "Imagination Unbound: An Interview with Cynthia Ozick." With Mario Materassi. *Salmagundi* 94–5 (Spring–Summer 1992): 85–113.
———. "An Interview with Cynthia Ozick." With Catherine Rainwater and William J. Scheick. *Texas Studies in Literature and Language* 25 (1983): 254–65.
———. "An Interview with Cynthia Ozick." With Elaine M. Kauvar. *Contemporary Literature* 26 (1985): 375–401.
———. "An Interview with Cynthia Ozick." With Elaine M. Kauvar. *Contemporary Literature* 34 (1993): 358–94.
———. Interview. With Joshua O. Haberman. *The God I Believe In*. New York: Macmillan, 1994. 153–73.
———. *Levitation: Five Fictions*. New York: Alfred A. Knopf, 1982.
———. *Metaphor & Memory: Essays*. New York: Vintage, 1991.
———. *The Pagan Rabbi and Other Stories*. New York: Penguin, 1983.
———. Preface. *Bloodshed and Three Novellas*. New York: Alfred A. Knopf, 1976. 3–12.
———. *The Puttermesser Papers: A Novel*. New York: Vintage, 1997.
———. "PW Interviews Cynthia Ozick." With Penny Kaganoff. *Publishers Weekly* 27 Mar. 1987: 33–34.
———. *Quarrel & Quandary: Essays*. New York: Alfred A. Knopf, 2000.
———. "Roundtable Discussion." *Writing and the Holocaust*. Ed. Berel Lang. New York: Holmes and Meier, 1998. 277–84.
———. "Trust the Teller." With Edward Grossman. *Jerusalem Post Magazine* 19 Sept. 1986: 6–7.
Percy, Walker. *Conversations with Walker Percy*. Ed. Lewis A. Lawson and Victor A. Kramer. Jackson: UP of Mississippi, 1985.
———. *Lancelot*. New York: Farrar, Straus and Giroux, 1977.
———. *The Message in the Bottle: How Queer Man Is, How Queer Language Is, and What One Has to Do with the Other*. New York: Farrar, Straus and Giroux, 1975.
———. *More Conversations with Walker Percy*. Ed. Lewis A. Lawson and Victor A. Kramer. Jackson: UP of Mississippi, 1993.
———. *The Moviegoer*. New York: Alfred A. Knopf, 1962.
———. *The Second Coming*. New York: Farrar, Straus, and Giroux, 1980.
———. *Signposts in a Strange Land*. Ed. Patrick Samway. New York: Farrar, Straus and Giroux, 1991.
Pifer, Ellen. "Cynthia Ozick: Invention and Orthodoxy." *Contemporary American Women Writers*. Ed. Catherine Rainwater and William J. Scheick. Lexington: UP of Kentucky, 1985. 88–116.
———. "Malamud's Unnatural *The Natural*." *Studies in American Jewish Literature* 7 (1988): 138–52.
Pinsker, Sanford. "Bernard Malamud's Ironic Heroes." *Bernard Malamud: A Collection of Critical Essays*. Ed. Leslie Field and Joyce W. Field. Englewood Cliffs: Prentice-Hall, 1975. 45–71.
Plotnitsky, Arkady. *Complementarity: Anti-Epistemology after Bohr and Derrida*. Durham: Duke UP, 1994.
Potok, Chaim. *The Promise*. New York: Fawcett Crest, 1969.
Presley, Delma Eugene. "The Moral Function of Distortion in Southern Grotesque." *South Atlantic Bulletin* 37.2 (1972): 37–46.
Prochaska, Bernadette. *The Myth of the Fall and Walker Percy's Last Gentleman*. American University Studies 32. New York: Lang, 1992.
Quinlan, Kieran. *Walker Percy: The Last Catholic Novelist*. Baton Rouge: Louisiana State UP, 1996.

Ragen, Brian Abel. *A Wreck on the Road to Damascus: Innocence, Guilt, and Conversion in Flannery O'Connor.* Chicago: Loyola UP, 1989.

Raiger, Michael. "'Large and Startling Figures': The Grotesque and the Sublime in the Short Stories of Flannery O'Connor." *Seeing into the Life of Things: Essays on Literature and Religious Experience.* Ed. John L. Mahoney. New York: Fordham UP, 1998. 242–270.

Reed, Walter L. *Dialogues of the Word: The Bible as Literature According to Bakhtin.* New York: Oxford UP, 1993.

Renner, Stanley. "Secular Meaning in 'A Good Man Is Hard to Find.'" *College Literature* 9 (1982): 123–32.

Richman, Sidney. *Bernard Malamud.* Twayne's United States Authors Ser. 109. Boston: Twayne, 1966.

———. "Malamud's Quarrel with God." *Critical Essays on Bernard Malamud.* Ed. Joel Salzberg. Boston: G.K. Hall, 1987. 203–21.

Rosen, Norma. *Accidents of Influence: Writing as a Woman and a Jew in America.* SUNY Ser. in Modern Jewish Literature and Culture. Albany: State U of New York P, 1992.

Rosenberg, Ruth. "The Ghost Story as Aggada: Cynthia Ozick's 'The Pagan Rabbi' and Sheindel's Scar." *Haunting the House of Fiction: Feminist Perspectives on Ghost Stories by American Women.* Ed. Lynette Carpenter and Wendy K. Kolmar. Knoxville: U of Tennessee P, 1991. 215–28.

Roth, Philip. "[From Imagining Jews]." *Critical Essays on Bernard Malamud.* Ed. Joel Salzberg. Boston: G.K. Hall, 1987. 98–108.

Rovit, Earl H. "Bernard Malamud and the Jewish Literary Tradition." *Critique* 3 (Winter 1960): 3–10.

Rubenstein, Richard L., and John K. Roth. *Approaching Auschwitz: The Holocaust and Its Legacy.* Atlanta: John Knox P, 1987.

Ruotolo, Lucio P. "Yakov Bok." *Critical Essays on Bernard Malamud.* Ed. Joel Salzberg. Boston: G.K. Hall, 1987. 125–39.

Russell, Bertrand. *Religion and Science.* Home University Library of Modern Knowledge 150. New York: Holt, 1935.

Ryan, Steven T. "The Three Realms of O'Connor's 'Greenleaf.'" *Christianity and Literature* 29.1 (1979): 39–51.

Safer, Elaine B. "The Allusive Mode, the Absurd, and Black Humor in Bernard Malamud's *God's Grace.*" *Studies in American Humor* 7 ns (1989): 104–117.

Salzberg, Joel. Introduction. *Critical Essays on Bernard Malamud.* Ed. Joel Salzberg. Boston: G.K. Hall, 1987. 1–22.

Samway, Patrick. "Grappling with the Philosophy and Theology of Walker Percy." *Biography and Source Studies* 4 (1998): 15–30.

———. *Walker Percy: A Life.* New York: Farrar, Straus and Giroux, 1997.

Sant, Arvindra. "Surrealism and the Struggle for Identity in *The Fixer.*" *Studies in American Jewish Literature* 7 (1988): 177–88.

Scholem, Gershom G. "The Idea of the Golem." *On the Kabbalah and Its Symbolism.* Trans. Ralph Manheim. New York: Schocken Books, 1965. 158–204.

Schwartz, Howard. Introduction. *Gabriel's Palace: Jewish Mystical Tales.* New York: Oxford UP, 1993. 3–38.

———. Introduction. *Lilith's Cave: Jewish Tales of the Supernatural.* New York: Harper and Row, 1988. 1–21.

Scott, Nathan A., Jr. "Faith and Art in a World Awry." *The Climate of Faith in Modern Literature.* Ed. Scott. New York: Seabury Press, 1964. 3–18.

Seidel, Ethan. Telephone interview. 3 July 1996.

Seltzer, Robert M. "Enlightenment." *Contemporary Jewish Religious Thought: Original Essays on Critical Concepts, Movements, and Beliefs*. Ed. Arthur A. Cohen and Paul Mendes-Flohr. New York: Macmillan, 1987. 171–75.

Sheridan, Eugene R. Introduction. *Jefferson's Extracts from the Gospels*. Ed. Dickinson W. Adams. The Papers of Thomas Jefferson, Second Ser. Princeton: Princeton UP, 1983.

Shloss, Carol. *Flannery O'Connor's Dark Comedies: The Limits of Inference*. Southern Literary Studies. Baton Rouge: Louisiana State UP, 1980.

Spivey, Ted R. *Flannery O'Connor: The Woman, the Thinker, the Visionary*. Macon, GA: Mercer UP, 1995.

———. "Religion and the Reintegration of Man in Flannery O'Connor and Walker Percy." *The Poetry of Community: Essays on the Southern Sensibility of History and Literature*. Ed. Lewis P. Simpson. Spectrum: Monograph Ser. in the Arts and Sciences. Atlanta: Georgia State U, 1972. 67–79.

Stern, Daniel. "Aggadah." *Contemporary Jewish Religious Thought: Original Essays on Critical Concepts, Movements, and Beliefs*. Ed. Arthur A. Cohen and Paul Mendes-Flohr. New York: Macmillan, 1987. 7–12.

———. "Midrash and Indeterminacy." *Critical Inquiry* 15.1 (1988): 132-61.

Strandberg, Victor. *Greek Mind/Jewish Soul: The Conflicted Art of Cynthia Ozick*. The Wisconsin Project on American Writers. Madison: U of Wisconsin P, 1994.

Strehle, Susan. *Fiction in a Quantum Universe*. Chapel Hill: U of North Carolina P, 1992.

TANAKH: A New Translation of the Holy Scriptures. Philadelphia: The Jewish Publication Society, 1985.

Taylor, Dennis. "The Need for a Religious Literary Criticism." *Seeing into the Life of Things: Essays on Literature and Religious Experience*. Ed. John L. Mahoney. New York: Fordham UP, 1998. 3–30.

Todorov, Tzvetan. *The Fantastic: A Structural Approach to a Literary Genre*. Trans. Richard Howard. Cleveland: P of Case Western Reserve U, 1973.

Tolson, Jay. *Pilgrim in the Ruins: A Life of Walker Percy*. Chapel Hill: U of North Carolina P, 1992.

Torrance, Robert M. *The Spiritual Quest: Transcendence in Myth, Religion, and Science*. Berkeley: U of California P, 1994.

Trachtenberg, Joshua. *Jewish Magic and Superstition*. New York: Atheneum, 1970.

Van Cleave, Jim. "Versions of Percy." *The Southern Review* 6 (1970): 990–1010.

von Hugel, Friedrich. *The Mystical Element of Religion as Studied in Saint Catherine of Genoa and Her Friends*. Vol. 1. New York: Dutton, 1927.

Walden, Daniel. "Malamud and His Universal Heroes." *Studies in American Jewish Literature* 7 (1988): 153–61.

Wasserman, Earl R. "*The Natural*: Malamud's World Ceres." *Bernard Malamud and the Critics*. Ed. Leslie A. Field and Joyce W. Field. New York: New York UP, 1970. 45–65.

Whitt, Margaret Earley. *Understanding Flannery O'Connor*. Understanding Contemporary American Literature. Columbia: U of South Carolina P, 1995.

Willis, Lawrence M. *The Jewish Novel in the Ancient World*. Myth and Poetics. Ithaca: Cornell UP, 1995.

Wirth-Nesher, Hana. "From Newark to Prague: Roth's Place in the American Jewish Literary Tradition." *What Is Jewish Literature?* Ed. Hana Wirth-Nesher. Philadelphia: Jewish Publication Society, 1994. 216–29.

Wolfe, Gregory. "'Ever Ancient, Ever New': The Catholic Writer in the Modern World." *The Catholic Writer*. Ed. Ralph McInerny. San Francisco: Ignatius P, 1991. 13–30.

Wood, Ralph C. *The Comedy of Redemption: Christian Faith and Comic Vision in Four American Novelists*. Notre Dame: U of Notre Dame P, 1988.

Index

About the Author

L. LAMAR NISLY is Associate Professor of English at Bluffton College. He has published in such journals as *Studies in American Jewish Literature* and *Journal for Peace and Justice Studies*.

CPSIA information can be obtained
at www.ICGtesting.com
Printed in the USA
BVHW071108201118
533061BV00035B/40/P